by
Chris
Shaffer

The Definitive Guide to

fishing

in Southern California

Book Design and Production by Timeless Communications, Tarzana, Ca.

Books Distributed by Shafdog Publications

Send all questions and comments to Shafdog Publications:

23548 Calabasas Rd., Suite 202
Calabasas, Ca. 91302
818-224-2145
cshaffer@fishingcalifornia.net

All Photos Taken by Chris Shaffer except:

P.23 Blake Lezak, P.26, 206 (Top) Brett Ross, P.44 Gary Seely, P. 68, (Bottom), 233, 244, 245 Provided by Taylor Tackle, P.72, 75, 76, 80 Provided by Erik's Guide Service, P. 91 Tom Bomar, P. 139. 140. 195. 196 Provided by Santa Ana River Lakes, P.140,144 Provided by Laguna Niguel Lake, P.183 Provided by Oak Tree Village, P.189,190 Provided by Guy Williams, P.192 Provided by Anglers Lake, P.201,210, 211, 212, 213 Provided by Lake Cuyamaca, P. 220, 221, 226, 227 Nicole Shaffer, P. 261. 264. 275 Tony Abel, P. 267, 270, 271 Provided by Castaway Guide Service

Dedication

When it comes to life unexpected obstacles are thrown our way each day,

But when you have a grandfather like I do there's no reason to fear going astray.

No matter how big or small it may be, there was no obstacle that could keep his love away from me.

When times are hard and smiles are rare, grandpa Phil is always there.

I've rarely had to struggle or be scared to see the light of day, not when I know grandpa's just a phone call away.

If more people had a grandfather like me, this world would surely be a lot less worry free.

Now that I'm grown up I've learned that my success has not been an accident, it can be attributed to the love and care that my grandpa has given me.

Thanks for being the best grandfather anyone could ever have. This book is dedicated to my grandpa, Phil Schwartzberg.

INTRODUCTION

It was about 85 degrees. The pine trees above were motionless and the humidity was unbearable, somewhere between 90 and 95 percent. I was sitting on top of a beaver dam, admiring nature.

A few mallards were swimming across the small beaver pond, along a dammed portion of Hale Creek. A loon could be heard in the distance. Two deer were drinking their daily supply of water near the creek inlet and the water looked like glass. There wasn't a ripple. It was so quiet I could hear every bullfrog croak.

It was roughly an hour before sunset and all the swimmers, ATV riders and hikers had gone home for the day. Only trout and bullhead fishermen remained. I had run about a mile on a dirt path through a dense wooded forest to watch the usual anglers work the evening bite.

This was a regular routine for me. School ended nearly two weeks ago and my parents sent me across the country to my aunt and uncle's house to get away from the big city life. I'd visited the same small creek in the woods behind the house each evening observing everything from casting to reeling, watching fish rise to the surface in search of scrumptious little flies and the beavers repairing leaks in their dam.

I was jealous and eager to be part of the action. And my wishes were about to come true. Tomorrow was going to be my first fishing adventure.

The ensuing night was a long one. I'd been preparing for my trip the entire day, mowing the lawn and making sure it was wet enough to entice the nightcrawlers to come out of the soil. I was planning on catching my own bait.

I spent the last hour before nightfall watching the lawn, waiting for my first nightcrawler to creep out of the moist soil. Doesn't sound like California? Well, it's not. I was in upstate New York close to the Adirondack Mountains, in a small town called Johnstown, about 15 miles from the Great Scaganada Reservoir – home to some of the largest northern pike in the world.

I was only seven years old at the time, but stories of anglers landing large northerns bigger than I had me eager to go fishing. I didn't even eat dinner that night. I was too busy with my head out the back window, a flashlight in one hand and a pair of old, muddy tennis shoes in the other, ready to dash outside the instant the sun sunk below the horizon.

It was already 9 p.m., but in summer the sun didn't set till later. I was so exhausted my eyes had trouble staying open that last hour before sunset. But once darkness was close, I was suddenly wide-awake, determined to catch bait on that hot, muggy, cloudy night.

As soon as the lightening bugs gave the signal that it was dark enough, I raced out the back door, turned on my flashlight and began searching for the biggest nightcrawler I could find. With my back hunched over and the flashlight's beam searching from my right hand, my left hand was open to nab the worm. Seconds later I saw my first worm and dashed to grab it and put it safely in the pale.

"Yah, Got it!" I said to my Uncle Alan who was watching through the porch window with a big smile on his face.

I raised my hand to show him my prize. Wait! There was nothing there but grass and dirt.

"See, it's not as easy as you thought," he said. "You have to be quicker and stop shining the light on the worms. Light scares them and sends them back underground."

I took his advice and came away with two-dozen crawlers that night, but I wasn't allowed to come back in the house until my cousin, David, came outside and hosed all the dirt, mud and grass off me.

It rained all through the night, but before the sun rose David and I set out to go fishing. Although the thunderstorms had passed by the time we got to Scagandaga, rain continued to fall all morning.

I usually hated waking up early in the morning, but this morning I was delighted because we were going to go fishing.

We drove the car over muddy lawns, down to the water and walked in full rain gear to the aluminum boat chained to a tree near the shoreline. I got in and David pushed us off.

My cousin didn't say much that morning. He was obviously ticked I woke him up so early, but a smile never left my face. I was having the time of my life. Sitting on a wood seat full of splinters with my feet splashing around in the four inches of water in the bottom of our boat, I admired the birds flying overhead as David rowed us into a shallow cove on the west end of the lake.

We finally anchored and David let me begin fishing. Oops, there was a problem. All the worms I caught last night died. I left them in the trunk of the car and they got so hot and humid, they looked melted. Even worse was the smell. My uncle's car never recovered.

David had me fish with a dead worm. He thought maybe a bullhead would come pick it up. He fished with a minnow, looking to catch something bigger.

When the pole first touched my hands, I was like a mama holding her new baby for the first time. I wouldn't let go of it. One hand had a firm grip on the rod, and one finger from the other hand touched the line so I could feel the fish nibbling on my bait.

The two of us had been fishing for more than three hours, and my dead worm had yet to entice anything. All of a sudden, David's bobber, which was located about 30 yards behind our boat near a bunch of submerged trees and weeds, disappeared. I looked carefully for the red and white bobber to make sure it didn't just drift away, before saying anything to David.

There was no sign of it. Nothing! I was positive that bobber had been pulled under water. I wasted no time.

"Daavve, hurry, hurry, you got something," I said, jumping up and down, screaming from the bow of our boat.

The instant he grabbed his pole, the line began peeling off the reel. Then came the grand finale. The fish jumped nearly three feet out of the water and spit out the hook. It was about 50 yards away, so I couldn't make out what type of fish it was, but David knew it was a northern pike.

"Damn, missed it. See kid, I told you there are big northerns in here. That one was probably bigger than you Chris," he said. "Well, we'll get 'em next time. Let's call it a day."

That was fine with me. I wanted to get home and call my dad back in California to tell him what had happened. Heck, I wanted to call everybody, all my friends and family, and I did. I still haven't asked my aunt how much that day's phone bill was, but I can guess she wasn't pleased when she got it.

Neither of us caught any fish that day, but I wasn't disappointed. I was hooked... hooked on what has shaped my life ever since: fishing.

Ever since that first experience, fishing has been my passion. Whether driving at 3 a.m. on a dark, snow covered road to ice fish Lake Sabrina during the Eastern Sierra Trout Opener in late April; hiking 10 miles through mosquito infested trails to catch my first golden trout in Sequoia National Park;

or fishing the Salton Sea for corvina under 110 degree temperatures when the air is so dry your throat feels like sandpaper – I've spent my entire life fishing and teaching it to others.

I can remember the satisfaction I felt when I worked as a fishing instructor at Sierra Day Camp during my teenage years. While most of my friends spent the summer tearing tickets at movie theatres, flipping burgers and taking orders or just watching TV, I was fishing with kids.

Most of the kids had never been fishing before and I decided to show them how exciting it could be. The proceeding summers they'd only stocked 100 catfish under a pound, but I conned the camp director into approving my order for 25 largemouth bass from one to five pounds, 200 pounds of catfish to six pounds, 200 pounds of carp to 10 pounds and 100 small bluegill. They were all put into a pond that averaged three feet deep, was 25 feet long and 15 feet wide. I called it the best fishery in the state and quickly earned the name "Chris Fishing."

The pond was so murky from the fish swimming around and stirring the mud on the bottom that you could never see the fish, but the second bait hit the water, no matter what kind it was, the kids had a fish. My first day, a six-year-old girl got pulled in the lake by a 10 pound carp. Later that day, "the runaway pole" was hooked by another kid. "Chris Fishing I caught a pole," he said. When I told him to reel it in, he gave me a broad smile and showed me the girl's 10 pound carp. Putting smiles on youngsters' faces made me feel special and was one of the reasons I was prompted to write this book.

Catching fish has always been rewarding for me, giving me a high sense of self-worth. But even more valuable is sharing those secrets with others, especially children, who are tremendously curious about fishing.

"Can the fish hear me?" one kid asked during orientation at the day camp. "Do they have names?" "What is the fish thinking when he sees a hook?" "Are you sure there are fish in here?"

I've heard all the questions in the world, and sometimes they can even get annoying. But all the annoyances disappear the instant a child catches his or her first fish.

"I got one, I one got one. Chris Fishing I got one. Can I keep it?"

Fishing is about brightening people lives and turning a bad day into good. It's an alternative activity to keep kids from crime and drugs and a way to show others where they can go to escape fast food restaurants, smog, traffic and shopping malls and experience the wild outdoors. So, I've taken it upon myself to show others how to be more successful, making fishing a more enjoyable experience for everyone.

However, this book is not just for fisherman, but also for hikers, backpackers and nature lovers. It's for all outdoor enthusiasts. Not only does it show you how and where to fish, it also describes the surrounding pine forests, dry deserts, chaparral covered foothills and cool coastal mountains that you see when you go fishing. It also teaches you where to sight deer, bald eagles, bobcats, raccoons and other wildlife that live near various bodies of water. For those who prefer to make it a day trip, it also lists nearby attractions, including waterfalls, hiking trails, tourist spots and more.

As you may have, I've spent my life reading other fishing guides in attempt to catch more fish and discover new places. However, I've wanted to read about more than just what type of fish are present and how many were stocked. I've wanted to know what the area looks like, what I needed to do to catch fish at a particular place and what else there is to do close by if I wanted to make a day trip out of it or bring the family along. I've looked for information that tells me if a particular stream gets crowded on the weekends; if it's safe to bring the kids; where I can find wild trout as opposed to stockers; how much

money it's going to cost to fish; and if I should plan on catching a lot of fish or if fishing is going to be slow. These are all questions this book answers.

It tells you about catching rainbow trout in Arroyo Seco Creek, near Pasadena, in the morning and then taking a short hike to Switzer Falls without having to move your car. It describes rafting, swimming, fishing and cliff jumping all in the same pool at the Santa Ynez River, about a 20-minute drive from Santa Barbara. What about the chance of catching a record large-mouth bass and catfish from San Vicente Reservoir near San Diego or fishing for large stripers in the morning, trout mid-day, taking a cruise for lunch and then gambling the afternoon away? It happens daily at the Colorado River and this book shows you how to do it.

What makes this book so valuable is that I, the author, have personally spent time at each individual lake, river or stream in order to provide the most accurate and up-to-date information. Only by using this book can you learn how to snorkel to locate fish, where to

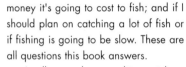

hike to less-fished waters, what times of the year are best to visit and where to fish when it rains.

This book aims at making fishing fun, exciting and interesting through real life stories and adventures, in addition to describing the area as if you were there yourself. It brings fishing to life.

Over the past three years, I've dedicated my life to talking with the pros, park rangers, Department of Fish and Game biologists, game wardens, fishing guides, oldtimers and locals, in order to uncover the secrets, pin-point the hot-spots and the best fishing holes, and put them in a simple format, easy for you, the reader, to follow.

I feel fortunate to be able to write such a complete book on fishing. Being asked to share my secrets and tips with fellow fishermen is an honor for me. By using this book, you will be able to catch more fish, more frequently and spend less time doing so.

With Southern California becoming increasingly populated, more and more people are searching for a quick getaway from all the chaos. Fishing has been the most logical answer. Fishing is a cost-free way to enjoy the outdoors with friends. In writing this book, my goal has been to bring my old memories back to life, and to open the window to new opportunities for you by opening your eyes to new places and methods of fishing, so you can create your own memories.

Although much of it has gone unnoticed, Southern California is one of the most diverse regions in the United States. Imagine fishing in a float tube with snowflakes drifting down from above and trout breaking water beside you at Arrowbear Lake; or basking in the desert sun as you look to catch corvina in the Salton Sea; or standing in the middle of the swift East Fork of the San Gabriel River with a pair of waders working a fly rod vigorously just after a spring hatch; or snorkeling Sespe River in search of the prized steelhead. It all happens here daily and this book will show you where to go to experience it.

This book has been a pleasure to compile. I hope you enjoy it as much as I enjoyed writing it.

Chris Shaffer
Author

TABLE OF **CONTENTS**

How to use this book

This book has been carefully designed to make finding your ideal fishing spot easy. First, it helps you to figure out how to plan the proper destination to fit your particular tastes and life-style, and to provide you, your family and friends with the most enjoyable fishing experience possible.

When you flip the pages to the graph located after this section, you'll see a listing of all the fishing spots written about in this book, along with eight categories to help you choose your destination. These categories ("easy access," "camping," "good for kids," "backpacking option," "family friendly," "beginners welcome," "hard-core fishermen" and "scenery") provide an overview of what each fishing spot has to offer. By cross-indexing your requirements and desires, you'll be able to quickly locate those few fishing holes that you might want to visit.

For those who want to choose their desired fishing location by geography, the book has been broken into 17 geographical regions, all located in Southern California. After selecting your desired region, go to the map preceding the section about that particular region. It will list all of the lakes, rivers and streams in that area. Then, it's as simple as choosing your ideal fishing spot and flipping to the corresponding page to learn more about it.

If you already know which body of water you want to fish, open to the table of contents and turn to the page with your favorite fishing hole.

Once you've chosen a location, the rest is easy. Each article is written and structured in a user-friendly format that provides you with quick, fun and easy reading.

The book is set up with 10 different categories containing all the information you could ever want to know about each lake, river or stream. The structure is as follows.....

Name of fishing hole
Rating
Species present
Fish Stocked
Facilities
Contact Information
Directions
Lake Information
Tips For Making the Trip
Nearby Attractions

The ratings are based upon a comparison of all fishing spots in California, not just in Southern California. A "ten" is the best possible score and "one" is the worst. A "one" means there are no fish present at all and a "ten" qualifies it as one of the top 20 fisheries in the state.

All of the ratings are based on ideal weather and fishing conditions. Remember, fishing conditions can change in an instant: skies can darken, bites can shut off, fish can die when water becomes too warm or cold, or due to a lack of oxygen.

The ratings are based on a number of factors, including, but not limited to, cleanliness, scenery, catch rates, the amount of fish in the body of water and the overall outdoor experience.

Species:

Just below the rating is a list of all the species of catchable fish inhabiting the waters. Species include: rainbow, brown and brook trout; channel, flathead, blue and white catfish; largemouth, smallmouth, striped and hybrid bass; green and red ear sunfish; carp; bluegill; crappie; black and brown bullhead; goldfish; sturgeon; corvina; tilapia; sargo; and croaker. Non-game fish such as shad and minnows are not listed, but may be present.

Stocks:

Both trout and catfish are stocked in most Southern California lakes, rivers and streams. Stocking numbers are provided in pounds, which usually differs greatly from the actual number of fish planted. For example, in most places in Southern California, the California Department of Fish and Game stocks trout that are one-third of a pound; for every pound, three fish are stocked. To find the actual number of fish stocked in any particular place, consult the "Lake Information" section of its write-up.

Stocking information totals are from 1999. Each year the amount of fish stocked can change. Places can be added to, or deleted from the stocking list. Also, poor water quality, low water levels and high water levels can affect the number of fish planted. Check the "Lake Information" section for the times of the year that plants take place.

Trout are planted by any of seven different companies and/or agencies, including the CA DFG, Mt. Lassen Trout Farms, Whitewater Trout Farm, the US Fish and Wildlife Service, Calaveras Trout Farm and companies that truck in fish from Utah and Idaho.

Fish stocked by the CA DFG come from either the Fillmore Fish Hatchery in Ventura County or the Mojave River Fish Hatchery located in Victorville in San Bernardino County. The fish that come from the CA DFG, Whitewater, US FWS, as well as the fish that are shipped from Utah and Idaho, are all rainbow trout. In addition to rainbows, Calaveras plants brown and brook trout, and Mt. Lassen plants a new breed of trout called the "lightening trout."

As for catfish, the CA DFG does stock them but they don't raise them. They are mostly purchased from breeders in the Imperial and Coachella Valley's, and a few are raised in the Bakersfield area. The number of pounds of catfish planted is listed, however a total number of fish is not tallied. Almost all catfish planted are channel cats, but every few years some San Diego area lakes plant blue cats. The catfish generally range from one to three pounds, but trophy size fish up to 60 pounds are stocked.

Facilities:

Listed in the "Facilities" section are the services provided at the various lakes and streams. Services in the surrounding communities are not discussed in that section, however they are sometimes mentioned elsewhere. Services listed are as follows: Fish Cleaning Stations, Ranger Stations, Restrooms, Launch Ramps, Gas, General Stores, Campgrounds, RV Hookups, Snack Bars, Restaurants, Boats, Canoes, Kayaks, Paddleboat and Sailboat Rentals, Lodging, Picnic Areas, Recreation Areas, Fishing Piers, Playgrounds, Horseshoe Pits, Visitor Centers, Boat Tours, Marinas and Bait & Tackle Shops.

Contact Information:

The "Contact" section is dedicated to providing phone numbers to help you plan your trip. This section includes numbers to check on the latest weather and fishing conditions, and to find lodging, tourist information and the best fishing guides at your destination.

All of the fishing guides written about in this book have been thoroughly checked to ensure they are qualified, well mannered, certified, courteous, knowledgeable, fair and will provide you with an enjoyable fishing experience.

Directions:

To make accessing some of these remote locations easy, all of the directions tell you how to get to your desired destination from a major city. If four-wheel drive is required, or if the roads are poorly maintained, that information will also be discussed in this section.

Lake Information:

The "Lake Information" section can be found in the body of each write-up. It tells you everything you need to know about fishing your favorite lake, river or stream. It includes information about how to catch the fish, where to find the fish and which baits and lures are best to use. In addition, the surrounding area and its wildlife are often described. In an attempt to help bring these exciting destinations to life, I sometimes tell about interesting and humorous personal experiences.

Tips For Making the Trip:

One of the most helpful sections is called "If You Plan to Make the Trip." This covers the "plan ahead" stage where you are warned of obstacles and/or hazards you might want to prepare for prior to visiting these various destinations. For example, in the winter some destinations may require chains; fishing and day-use fees may be charged; some streams dry-up by summer; and roads to certain locations are often closed by heavy rains or torrential flows. Other questions that might arise are also answered. Is night fishing allowed? Is this destination sometimes closed to fishing? Are there special regulations? Are only electric boat motors allowed? Where can you buy supplies? Do you need to keep an eye out for rattlesnakes? All this and more is covered in this section.

Nearby Attractions:

Perhaps you want to spend a whole day at your destination instead of just a few hours, and you want to bring the family along. No problem. Listed in the "Also Nearby" section are ideas for places to take your family, including amusement parks, other fishing sites, waterfalls, hiking trails, historic sites, shopping and more.

Location	Easy Access	Camping	Good for Kids	Backpacking Option	Family Friendly	Beginners Welcome	Hardcore Fisherman	Great Scenery
ANTELOPE VALLEY/LEEWARD SIDE OF THE SAN GABRIEL MOUNTAINS								
Apollo Park Lake	X		X			X		
Aqueduct	X						X	
Big Rock Creek	X	X	X	X	X	X		X
Hesperia Lake	X	X	X			X		
Jackson Lake	X	X	X		X	X		X
Jess Ranch Lakes	X	X	X					
Littlerock Creek								
Littlerock Reservoir	X	X	X			X		
Mojave Narrows Lake	X	X	X			X		
COLORADO RIVER DISTRICT								
Colorado River	X	X					X	
Lake Havasu	X	X					X	
IMPERIAL VALLEY								
Alamo River							X	
All-American Canal							X	
Finney Lake	X	X					X	
Ramer Lake	X						X	
Wiest Lake	X	X	X			X		
LOS ANGELES/ORANGE COUNTY METRO AREAS								
Anaheim Lake	X		X			X		
Centennial Park Lake	X		X			X		
Echo Park Lake	X		X			X		
Irvine Lake	X		X			X	X	
Laguna Niguel Lake	X		X			X	X	
Puddingstone Res.	X		X			X	X	
Santa Fe Reservoir	X		X			X		
San Juan Creek	X	X						
Santa Ana River Lakes	X		X			X		
LOS ANGELES COUNTY (WEST) AND VENTURA COUNTY (EAST)								
Balboa Park Lake	X		X			X		
Century Lake	X		X		X	X		
Hansen Dam Lake	X		X			X		
Hansen Ponds			X		X			
Malibu Creek	X		X			X		
Rancho Simi Lake	X		X			X		
Troutdale	X		X			X		
PALOMAR/JULIAN AREA								
Doane Pond	X	X	X		X	X		X
Lake Cuyamaca	X	X	X		X	X	X	X
Lake Henshaw	X	X				X	X	
Lake Wolhford	X	X	X			X	X	
San Luis Rey River	X		X			X		
Sutherland Reservoir	X						X	
Sweetwater River	X	X	X			X		
SALTON SEA								
Salton Sea	X	X	X			X	X	
Wister Unit	X						X	

Location	Easy Access	Camping	Good for Kids	Backpacking Option	Family Friendly	Beginners Welcome	Hardcore Fisherman	Great Scenery
RIVERSIDE COUNTY								
Anglers Lake	X	X	X			X		
Corona Lake	X	X	X			X	X	
Diamond Valley Res.								
Fisherman's Retreat	X	X	X			X		
Lake Cahuilla	X	X	X			X		
Lake Elsinore	X	X	X			X		
Lake Perris	X	X	X			X	X	
Lake Skinner	X	X	X			X	X	
Oak Tree Village	X		X		X	X	X	
Reflection Lake	X	X	X			X		
Whitewater Trout Farm	X		X			X		
Yucapia Park Lake	X	X	X			X		
SAN BERNARDINO MOUNTAINS								
Alpine Trout Lake	X		X			X		X
Arrowbear Lake	X		X			X		X
Bear Creek				X			X	X
Big Bear Lake	X	X	X	X		X		X
Cleghorn Creek	X		X			X		
Deep Creek	X			X			X	X
Green Valley Lake	X	X	X		X	X		X
Holcomb Creek	X		X	X		X		X
Jenks Lake	X		X		X	X		X
Lake Arrowhead			X		X			X
Lake Gregory	X	X	X		X		X	X
Mill Creek	X		X			X		
Miller Canyon Creek	X	X				X		
Santa Ana River	X	X	X	X		X	X	X
Silverwood Lake	X	X	X			X	X	
SAN DIEGO COUNTY (EAST)								
Barrett Lake	X					X	X	
Lake Morena	X	X	X			X	X	
Loveland Reservoir	X					X	X	
Twin Lakes	X	X	X			X		
SAN DIEGO COUNTY URBAN WATERS								
Chollas Reservoir	X		X			X		
El Capitan Reservoir	X						X	
Lake Dixon	X	X	X			X	X	
Lake Hodges	X						X	
Lake Jennings	X	X	X			X	X	
Lake Miramar	X		X			X	X	
Lake Murray	X		X			X	X	
Lake Poway	X	X	X			X		
Lindo Lake	X					X		
Lower Otay	X						X	
San Vicente	X		X			X	X	
Santee Lakes	X	X	X			X	X	
Upper Otay	X					X	X	
SAN GABRIEL MOUNTAINS (EAST)								
Cucamonga Creek	X		X	X		X		
Cucamonga/Gusti Lake	X		X			X		
Glen Helen Park Lake	X	X	X					
Green Mountain Ranch	X		X		X	X		

Location	Easy Access	Camping	Good for Kids	Backpacking Option	Family Friendly	Beginners Welcome	Hardcore Fisherman	G... Sc...
Lytle Creek	X	X	X			X		
Mt. Baldy Trout Pools	X		X			X		
SAN GABRIEL MOUNTAINS (WEST)								
Arroyo Seco Creek	X		X	X	X	X		X
Crystal Lake	X	X	X	X	X	X		X
Lower Big Tujunga Crk	X		X			X		
Santa Anita Creek	X		X		X	X		X
San Garbiel Reservoir							X	
San Gabriel River (E)	X	X	X			X	X	
San Gabriel River (N)	X		X			X		X
San Gabriel River (W)	X		X	X	X	X	X	X
San Dimas Reservoir	X		X			X		
Upper Big Tujunga Crk .	X	X	X	X		X	X	X
SAN JACINTO MOUNTAINS								
Fuller Mill Creek	X		X		X	X		X
Fulmor Lake	X		X		X	X		X
Hemet Lake	X	X	X		X	X	X	X
N. F. San Jacinto Riv.	X	X	X			X		X
Strawberry Creek	X		X			X		X
SANTA BARBARA MOUNTAINS								
Davy Brown Creek	X	X	X	X		X		
Lake Cachuma	X	X	X			X	X	
Lion Canyon Creek	X	X	X			X		
Manzana Creek	X	X	X	X		X		
Santa Ynez River	X	X	X			X		
SANTA CLARITA VALLEY/TEJON/TEHACHAPI								
Brite Valley Reservoir	X	X	X			X		
Bouquet Canyon Crk	X	X	X			X		
Castaic Lagoon	X	X	X			X	X	
Castaic Lake	X	X	X			X	X	
Elizabeth Lake	X	X	X			X	X	
Frazier Lake	X	X	X			X		
Indian Hill Ranch	X	X	X			X		
Lake Hughes	X	X	X			X		
Lake Piru	X	X	X	X		X	X	
Piru Creek	X		X	X		X	X	
Pyramid Lake	X					X	X	
Quail Lake	X					X		
Tait Trout Farms	X	X	X			X	X	
Tejon Ranch Lakes	X					X	X	
VENTURA COUNTY MOUNTAINS								
Lake Casitas	X	X				X	X	
Matilija Creek	X	X				X	X	
N.F. Ventura River	X					X	X	
Reyes Creek	X	X	X	X		X		
Rose Valley Lakes	X	X	X	X		X		
Santa Paula Creek	X	X	X	X	X	X	X	X
Sespe River	X	X		X	X	X	X	X

REGION 1
Santa Barbara Mountains

Santa Ynez River
Lake Cachuma
Lion Canyon Creek
Davy Brown Creek
Manzana Creek

SANTA YNEZ **RIVER**

Set at 1,500 feet in Los Padres National Forest, the river has something for everyone, including fishing, camping, hiking, cliff jumping, rafting, swimming and bird watching.

Rating: 7

Species: Largemouth Bass, Bluegill, Channel Catfish and Rainbow Trout

Stocked with 4,200 pounds of rainbow trout.

Facilities: Campgrounds, Swimming Areas, Picnic Areas and Restrooms

Santa Ynez River

Need Information? Contact:
Los Padres National Forest (805) 967-3481, Paradise Store (805) 967-3254

Directions: From the 101 Freeway in Santa Barbara, exit Highway 154 and drive northeast for 11 miles (over San Marcos Pass) to Paradise Road. Turn east and continue approximately six miles to the Los Prietos Ranger Station. The river is stocked from the ranger station to the road's end, three miles from Gibraltor Reservoir at Red Rock Camp.

The Santa Ynez River is the most popular recreation spot in Santa Barbara County. Set at 1,500 feet in Los Padres National Forest, the river has something for everyone, including fishing, camping, hiking, cliff jumping, rafting, swimming and bird watching.

The Santa Ynez River offers the longest stretch of access of any free-flowing river in Southern California. Unlike most "rivers" in this part of the state, the Santa Ynez looks like a river. In some places it's as wide as 50-feet and as deep as 30-feet, and is impassable without a high-clearance vehicle because of high water levels during winter and spring runoff. At times Paradise Road is closed to vehicular traffic during the winter due to high water levels. Most of the river's shoreline is composed of rock and sand. Besides rocks there isn't much structure on the bottom, leaving fishing lines free of snags.

Despite the fact that the California Department of Fish and Game stocks about 12,000 fish in the eight to 10-inch-class from February to May, there still aren't enough fish to go around. As a matter of fact, this river is so heavily fished that many of the planters are gone within a few days of a stock.

The Santa Ynez River tends to dry up by early summer.

The Santa Ynez is an easy river to access and to fish. The road parallels the river and there are large parking areas at all of the good fishing spots, beginning right behind the ranger station and continuing all the way to Red

Rock Camp. Although fish are stocked throughout the river, the easiest places to catch them are in the larger pools. Tossing Panther Martins, Thomas Buoyants or using salmon eggs, Power Bait and nightcrawlers should catch fish.

During the warmer months, try to fish the river in the morning or evening. Midday can get crowded with people swimming, rafting and playing loud radios, all of which puts the fish out of feeding mode. Once summer comes, you can also catch small bass, bluegill and catfish in the river. The catfish and bluegill love worms, and the bass will hit small Rapalas and nightcrawlers.

The Santa Ynez River in March of 2000, near the Falls Day Use Area.

The river is also the best known cliff jumping area in Southern California, with the popular spots being Red Rock and the Falls. The daredevils come from all over, but the majority are students and alumni of the University of California, Santa Barbara and Santa Barbara City College. The "jumps" or "dives," depending on how crazy you are, range from 10 to more than 100 feet, and although the Forest Service strongly discourages diving, it's not illegal. If you're going to jump, please check to see how deep it is before you do. People have died here before.

If you plan to make the trip, supplies are available at the Paradise Store and in Santa Barbara. A Forest Service Adventure Pass is required to park in the Los Padres National Forest.

Also nearby are Lake Cachuma, Davy Brown Creek, Lion Canyon Creek, Manzana Creek and the San Rafael Wilderness.

SANTA YNEZ RIVER

LAKE CACHUMA

Located in the rolling foothills above Santa Barbara, this 3,000-acre reservoir is close enough to Los Angeles that you could make a day-trip out of it, but it feels like you are light years away.

Rating: 9

Species: Channel Catfish, Rainbow Trout, Red Ear Sunfish, Bluegill, Largemouth Bass, Smallmouth Bass
and Carp

Stocked with 80,000 pounds of
rainbow trout.

Facilities: General Store, Campgrounds, Bait & Tackle, Snack Bar, Full-Service Marina, Boat Rental, Boat Tours, Playgrounds, Swimming Pool, Gas, Fish Cleaning Stations, Restrooms, Showers, Nature Center and Laundry Facilities

Need Information? Contact: Lake Cachuma (805) 686-5054 or (805) 686-5055, Marina (805) 688-4040, Boat Tours (805) 686-5050

Directions: From the 101 Freeway in Santa Barbara, exit Highway 154 and drive northeast for 18 miles to the lake's entrance on your right.

With great weather and year-round fishing, Lake Cachuma is a superb destination to take the family. Located in the rolling foothills above Santa Barbara, this 3,000-acre reservoir is close enough to Los Angeles that you could make a day-trip out of it, but it feels like you are light years away. With no water-skiing allowed, the lake stays quiet and peaceful and offers something for everyone. For those who don't enjoy fishing, boating or camping, there are relaxing wildlife and bird watching boat tours that leave out of the marina every few hours.

Jenni Perez enjoys an afternoon of fishing at Lake Cachuma.

Acorn woodpeckers are abundant at Lake Cachuma.

Lake Cachuma is one of the region's best year-round trout fisheries. It's stocked by both the California Department of Fish and Game and Calaveras Trout Farms. The CA DFG plants 44,220 trout from eight to 12 inches, with Calaveras stocking about 35,000 trout ranging from one to 12 pounds. Catching trout is easy from November through April. In November and December the trout hang out in Cachuma and Santa Cruz Bays and in the Narrows, and can be caught with Power Bait and nightcrawlers. In January, your best bet is to troll along the back side of Arrowhead Island, and also from Santa Cruz Point to Arrowhead Island. February through April you can troll anywhere around the lake, but the easiest way to catch fish is by anchoring adjacent to the buoy line near Tunnel Area. There is a big drop-off around where the trout congregate. Using Power Bait, salmon eggs and nightcrawlers should do the trick.

During the summer when the trout move into deeper water, you need either down-riggers or leadcore line to catch them. From summer to early fall, troll the dam area, from Santa Cruz Point to the mouth of Cachuma Bay, or down the lake's main channel. Trolling black and gray Rapalas, orange broken-back Rapalas, white Phoebes and Needlefish should entice the fish to bite.

The lake record is a 14 pounder, but each week many big rainbows are taken year-round.

Largemouth bass fishing is best from April to June. The fish are located everywhere, but to catch the most bass concentrate your efforts on the east end of the lake using top-water lures like buzzbaits. Or, you might want to try poppers in the Narrows, on the back side of Arrowhead Island and off Santa Cruz Points. White spinnerbaits are your best bet later in the day. Most of the largemouths run three to five pounds, but the lake record was a 16 pounder caught in the late Eighties.

The smallmouth bite is best in May and June, usually right after the largemouths spawn. For best results with smallmouth bass, use crawdads, crankbaits and small spinnerbaits along the north shore near the cliffs.

There is also a population of big red ear sunfish. They grow up to three pounds and can be caught on nightcrawlers along the buoy line near the Tunnel Area and along drop-offs.

If you are near Arrowhead Island, keep an eye out for deer. In winter and spring they sometimes swim across the lake to the island. We saw five deer on the island and they were gone the next day. I guess we missed their swim!

If you plan to make the trip, supplies are available at the lake. There are day-use and boat launch fees.

Also nearby are the Santa Ynez River, Davy Brown Creek, Manzana Creek, Lion Canyon Creek and the San Raphael Wilderness.

LION CANYON **CREEK**

Even better than the fishing, is the scenic drive on your way to the creek.

Rating: 5

Species: Rainbow Trout

Stocked with 300 pounds of rainbow trout.

Facilities: Campgrounds

A yellow-billed magpie rests on a sign post along Happy Valley Road.

Need Information? Contact: Los Padres National Forest (805) 925-9538

Directions: From Santa Barbara, drive north on the 101 Freeway to Highway 154. Drive northeast on highway for 18 miles to Cachuma Lake. Continue past the lake for 4.5 miles to Armour Ranch Road. Turn right and continue 1.3 miles to Happy Valley Road. Turn east and follow the winding road for 11.4 miles to Cachuma Campground.

Of the three streams that are stocked in the foothills above Lake Cachuma, the smallest, Lion Canyon Creek, is the first you come to. It ceases to exist about one-fourth of a mile above Cachuma Campground where Lion Canyon Creek merges with, and becomes, Cachuma Creek.

Even better than the fishing, is the scenic drive on your way to the creek. In the spring, a drive that should take about a half-hour from Lake Cachuma can take well over an hour because of stopping to look at the beautiful scenery. Once you turn off Highway 150, you can spot acorn woodpeckers and yellow-billed magpie. The acorn woodpeckers have a white throat and belly, black wings and a red crown. Look for them in the oak trees along the roadside. The yellow-billed magpie has a black head and neck, patches of its belly and shoulders are white, and its wings and tail are a purplish green.

As you begin to climb the foothills, you'll drive through ranches covered with green grasslands, and see cows and horses roaming freely. After passing the ranches, California poppies begin to sprout up all over the hillsides. You can also feast your eyes on wildflowers such as mock orange, alkali chalice, scarlet mon-

How can you go wrong with sights like this! True love in the fields along side Happy Valley Road.

Lion Canyon Creek in April of 2001

keyflower and toton. Don't forget to bring your camera, you're going to need it.

When you're done admiring the scenery, you might want to try to get in a little fishing. Just be aware, the window of opportunity is short. Stocks typically take place from February to April when water flows are sufficient. However, with little to no pressure, fishing the small pools with Power Bait or salmon eggs can be productive for weeks after a stock. The fish are planted in two places. Most are tossed in at Cachuma Campground, but a bucketful is also poured in on the north side of the road where Lion Canyon and Cachuma Creek come together.

If you are prone to allergies, you might want to keep your distance from Lion Canyon Creek. Pollen counts are high in the spring and the place is thick with gnats and flies, which can take a bite out of your fun. An added plus for me (although you might not think of it that way), are the bobcats. They're back on the rise in the region. I was lucky enough to catch sight of one on my way home from the creek. The small bobcats might look friendly,

California poppies bloom in the spring on the hillsides near Lion Canyon Creek

but they're not always. It's best to keep your distance.

If you plan to make the trip, supplies are available at Lake Cachuma. A Forest Service Adventure Pass is required to park in the Los Padres National Forest.

Also nearby are Manzana Creek, Davy Brown Creek, Lake Cachuma and the Santa Ynez River.

LION CANYON CREEK

DAVY BROWN **CREEK**

I use a small treble hook, with either Power Bait or salmon eggs, throw my bait on the top of the falls and let the stream take it into the pool. It makes the bait look natural and the trout can't resist.

Rating: 6

Species: Rainbow Trout

Stocked with 1,200 pounds of rainbow trout.

Facilities: Campgrounds and Restrooms

Need Information? Contact: Los Padres National Forest (805) 925-9538

Davy Brown Creek

Directions: From Santa Barbara, drive north on the 101 Freeway to Highway 154. Take Highway 154 northeast for 18 miles to Cachuma Lake. Continue past the lake for 4.5 miles to Armour Ranch Road. Turn right and drive 1.3 miles to Happy Valley Road. Follow the road for approximately 14 miles to Cachuma Saddle Station. Continue 3.8 miles past Cachuma Saddle Station to Davy Brown Campground.

Davy Brown Creek is a small stream above Santa Barbara in the Los Padres National Forest, with a lot of history behind it. Davy Brown was an interesting man whom some say lived to be 100. Born in Europe around 1800, Brown took part in the War of 1812; worked as a slave trader bringing slaves to the US from Africa; fought in the Texas-Mexican War; worked as a Texas Ranger; hunted in Northern California; participated in the California Gold Rush; and, more relevant to the topic at hand, built a cabin in the 1880's along what is now referred to as Davy Brown Creek. Did he accomplish enough in his life? I'd say so. Sounds to me like he experienced as much during his travels as 15 of us would in our lifetimes today.

The only disappointing thing about the Brown saga is that his cabin burned down in the 1920's, but his legend lives on in Davy Brown Campground. The campground is a

A purple lupinus.

quiet, but popular destination, especially for Santa Barbara County residents. Running alongside the campground, Davy Brown Creek provides decent fishing after a stock. The stream is stocked from late winter through spring, as long as water levels are sufficient to sustain fish. The California Department of Fish and Game stocks 3,480 rainbow trout, the same as nearby Manzana Creek.

The small waterfalls at the southend of the campground hold many rainbow trout.

Fishing this creek can be relaxing. With heavy cover from trees, it stays cool, especially when compared to the surrounding arid, desert terrain. Trout are planted from the small waterfalls at the south end of the campground to the extreme north end. My favorite place to catch them in the pools below the small waterfalls. I use a small treble hook, with either Power Bait or salmon eggs, throw my bait on the top of the falls and let the stream take it into the pool. It makes the bait look natural and the trout can't resist. Fishing the rest of the campground is as easy as it gets. The fish are all stacked up in pools. You can see them and they can see you, but they still bite. Sounds like the ideal fishing experience, right?

If you plan to make the trip, supplies are available at Lake Cachuma and in Santa Barbara. A Forest Service Adventure Pass is required to park in the Los Padres National Forest.

Also nearby are Manzana Creek, the Manzana Wilderness, Lion Canyon Creek and Lake Cachuma.

DAVY BROWN CREEK

MANZANA **CREEK**

Over the years, recreationists from Santa Barbara and Ventura Counties have used Manzana Creek as their place to beat the crowds. Now, so many people come here that it has become overcrowded.

Rating: 6

Species: Rainbow Trout

Stocked with 1,000 pounds of rainbow trout.

Facilities: Campgrounds and Restrooms

Need Information? Contact: Los Padres National Forest (805) 925-9538

Manzana Creek

Directions: From Santa Barbara, drive north on the 101 Freeway to Highway 154. Take Highway 154 northeast for 18 miles to Cachuma Lake. Continue past the lake for 4.5 miles to Armour Ranch Road. Turn right and drive 1.3 miles to Happy Valley Road. Follow the winding road for about 14 miles to Cachuma Saddle Station. Continue 5.6 miles past Cachuma Saddle Station to Nira Campground, it's 1.8 miles past Davy Brown Campground.

After spending a successful day catching trout among the crowds at Lake Cachuma, I wanted to give my friends a different taste of fishing. I pulled out my topo map and looked for the most remote trout stream in the region. Finding blue markings (which indicate a stream) was difficult, but I came up with Manzana Creek, about 42 miles from Santa Barbara.

As we drove up the foothills towards the stream, we went through some pretty remote areas. In fact, we didn't see a building or any sign of civilization, with the exception of an abandoned ranger station, for the 45-minute drive from the ranches near Lake Cachuma all the way to the creek. I proudly told my friends, "This place is out in the boonies. There's not going to be a single, soul but us out here."

I felt like a moron when were got to the creek. "What the hell are all these people doing here?" I said. It looked like the damn swap meet. There were so many cars we had to park in overflow parking. I was stunned and my friends heckled me the rest of

Wildflowers flourish along the shoreline of Manzana Creek.

the day. "Good job, nature boy," said my friend Travis Kikugawa. "I hate to break this to you, but to me remote means that there aren't any people around. This place looks like a Burger King at lunch. Let's get out of here."

Why were these people here? The answer was quite simple; they were in search of the same thing I was, a remote mountain stream without crowds where they could escape city life. Over the years, recreationists from Santa Barbara and Ventura Counties have used Manzana Creek as their place to beat the crowds. Now, so many people come here that it has become overcrowded. Some use the creek as a way into the San Raphael Wilderness, others use it as a campground, but most are day-users trying to catch a few stocked trout.

Many anglers are disappointed when they don't catch any fish. The California Department of Fish and Game does stock the stream from late winter through spring, but with all the pressure the creek receives, catch rates remain low. Fish that are planted during the week are often taken by weekday fisherman. That leaves nothing for those arriving on Saturday morning expecting to bring home dinner. The stream is stocked from the Davy Brown Creek inlet to Nira Campground. It's a shame the CA DFG only stocks 3,020 rainbows each year, because the stream is capable of holding many more.

Manzana Creek in the Los Padres National Forest.

With a rocky bottom and well-established rock pools, Manzana creek is almost an exact replica of Sespe River, near Ojai. Located at about 1,800 feet in the Los Padres National Forest, Manzana creek is situated in a dry mountain area and has brushy shorelines. Your biggest concern when coming here should be the snakes. This is prime rattlesnake territory and although they are usually scared away by humans, it would be best to keep an eye out. For wildflower fanatics, mock orange flourishes here. Knowing what these wildflowers look like is important because if you can't find a fishing spot, you may be stuck looking at the flowers until one opens up.

If you plan to make the trip, supplies are available in Santa Ynez and at Cachuma Lake. A Forest Service Adventure Pass is required to park in the Los Padres National Forest.

Also nearby are the San Raphael Wilderness, Davy Brown Creek, Lion Canyon Creek, Cachuma Lake and the Santa Ynez River.

MANZANA CREEK

REGION 2

Ventura County Mountains

CALIFORNIA

Lake Casitas
North Fork Ventura River
Matilija Creek
Sespe River
Reyes Creek
Rose Valley Lakes
Santa Paula Creek

LAKE CASITAS

Lake Casitas is a great bass lake... one of the worlds best.

Rating: 10

Species: Rainbow Trout, Largemouth Bass, Bluegill, Crappie, Redear, and Channel Catfish

Stocked with 50,000 pounds of rainbow trout.

Facilities: Marina, Picnic Areas, Campgrounds, Restrooms, Boat Rentals, Boat Launch, Playgrounds, Café, Bait & Tackle Shop, Boat Storage, Fish Cleaning Station, Showers and RV Hookups

Amy Mitrany shows off a four-pound largemouth bass caught and released on a shad.

Need Information? Contact: Lake Casitas (805) 649-2233, Campground Reservations (805) 649-1122, Fishing Guide Marc Mitrany (805) 572-6230, Boat Rentals (805) 649-2043, Park Store (805) 649-1202

Directions: From the 101 Freeway in Carpinteria, exit Highway 150 and continue 18 miles east to the lake. The lake can also be reached from Ojai via Highway 150 west or Highway 33.

Years ago, when I first developed a love for fishing, Lake Casitas, located about twenty minutes from Ventura or a half-hour's drive from Santa Barbara, was one of my first destinations. My friends and I got up before the crack of dawn, as we were told fishermen are suppose to, and headed to the lake. When we arrived, we got all excited by the huge pictures of recently caught bass in the bait and tackle shop. Then, the man at

Lake Casitas is one of the state's best bass lakes.

the boat dock talked us into renting a boat he never should have rented to beginners.

In our first hour out on the lake, we had ticked-off about 10 fishermen driving by them at high speeds. But that wasn't the worst part. While we were trolling 5-mph for trout with bass lures (because at the time we didn't know better), my friend decided to try to make a sharp turn around one of the points off the island, and all of our lures got stuck in trees half-submerged in the water. My lures were lost, and because the guy at the store sold me lures that were $8 each, I had no money left to buy new ones. That concluded my first fishing experience at Lake Casitas.

Now that I have fished there more, I know that Lake Casitas is a great bass lake... one of the worlds best. As a matter of fact, locals think of Casitas as the lake that will kick out the next world record bass. However, most of this hype has never reached most Southern Californians. Lake Casitas has never come close to the hype nearby Lake Castiac got in the early Nineties when Bob Crupi caught a 22-pound bass that was just shy of the world record. But consider this, Casitas' lake record is not far off at 21.3 pounds. It was a bass caught in 1980, but larger fish are known to be swimming the lake. Bass in excess of 15 pounds are caught here on a regular basis.

Fishing Guide Marc Mitrany poses with a six- pound largemouth bass.

The reason that bass thrive in the lake is because there is an abundance of shad, crawdads and stocked rainbow trout for them to eat. The secret to fishing the lake is using live shad, but it's not as easy as it sounds. You have to catch the shad yourself because they don't sell them anywhere nearby. Most of the fishermen catch them using long poles attached with thin nets made with fishing line. The best way to spot shad is to look for birds in the water near the shoreline, and then quietly move your boat in and trap them. If you don't know the lake well, the process of finding shad can take a couple of hours.

Because Lake Casitas is a huge, 2,500-acre reservoir with hundreds of coves to fish, the easiest and most enjoyable way to catch fish your first time out is to plan a trip with a fishing guide. Marc Mitrany is one of the lake's best fishermen and can teach you how to fish the lake at a cost much less than other guides on the lake.

Whether you fish with a guide or not, you'll want to use small hooks and light line, preferably six to eight-pound test. Due to the clear water and the amount of pressure this lake receives, the bass will spot anything bigger. Concentrate your efforts in the coves around the island, along drop-offs and up the various arms. Make sure you bring along nightcrawlers and crawdads, just in case you can't catch shad in the shallows. If you

LAKE CASITAS

don't have a boat, your best bet is tossing live crawdads off the rocks. Each year the bass fishing slows down for about a week in late May or early June, when lake management uses chemicals to kill off the weeds on the lake's shoreline, so plan your trip around this annual event.

Chris Crawley and a two-pound bass caught and released on a white spinnerbait.

Aside from bass, the lake also provides a decent trout fishery and kicks out a good number of catfish over 20 pounds. The lake receives more than 58,000 trout from the California Department of Fish and Game (many of which are a pound or more) and a bonus of 16,000 pounds of larger fish from Calaveras Trout Farms. Casitas imported fish from Idaho in 1999, Mt. Lassen Trout Farm in 2000, however, Calaveras' bid was lower in 2001 so they earned the right to feed Casitas' bass.

The only time trout fishing from shore is productive is two to three days following a stock. At this time, anglers fish near the marina or boat launches where the trout are planted. Unless you have a downrigger or leadcore line, or can come immediately after a stock, I wouldn't bother trout fishing here. Most of the fish head for deep water within a few days after they're stocked. By deep, I mean very deep, anywhere from 100 to 200 feet. If you choose, you can target a ton of large holdovers in the lake.

Catfish to 40 pounds and crappie more than three pounds have also been recorded. Red ear can be caught on the north shore and near creek inlets, while catfish are taken on pieces of cut mackerel on the north end of the lake. As you can see, there is a wide array of opportunities for anglers. Another plus – water-skiing is not permitted.

If you plan to make the trip, supplies are available at the lake. There is a day-use and boat launch fee.

Also nearby are s the North Fork Ventura River, Matilija Creek.

Lake Casitas has been blessed with great scenery in addition to exceptional fishing.

NORTH FORK VENTURA **RIVER**

The river provides a beautiful trip for the nearby residents of Ventura County, but if you live far away there probably aren't enough fish here to warrant the trip.

Rating: 2

Species: Rainbow Trout

Stocks: None

Facilities: None

Need Information?
Contact: Los Padres National Forest (805) 646-4348

Directions: From the 101 in Ventura, exit Highway 33 and drive approximately 20 miles north through Ojai to Matilija Canyon Road. The river parallels Highway 33 from Matilija Canyon Road to Wheeler Gorge Campgrounds.

The North Fork of the Ventura River used to be a good seasonal fishing creek when the California Department of Fish and Game stocked about 7,000 trout here. These trout ranged from the seven to nine inches and were stocked each spring when water levels were sufficient. But in 1998 those stocks, along with most other streams in the region, were forced to cease. The plants were stopped in an effort to save the steelhead, placed on the endangered species list in October of 1997.

If you want to try fishing here, there are a few small wild trout left in the stream. Treat it like a hit-and-miss kind of place. If you don't catch anything after a few casts move on and try the next pool. The creek provides easy access for a three-mile stretch along Route 33, from the point where it crosses under the highway to Wheeler Gorge Campground.

The river, located in the Los Padres National Forest, is also known as the North Fork of Matilija Creek and provides a beautiful trip for the nearby residents of Ventura County, but if you live far away there probably aren't enough fish here to warrant the trip.

If you plan to make trip, supplies are available in Ojai. A Forest Service Adventure Pass is required to park in the Los Padres National Forest.

Also nearby are Lake Casitas, Matilija Creek, Sespe River and Rose Valley Lakes.

NORTH FORK VENTURA **RIVER**

MATILIJA CREEK

If fishing for the eight to nine inch stockers, concentrate on the area just past the dam where the creek can be easily accessed from the road.

Rating: 5

Species: Rainbow Trout

Stocked with 1,000 pounds of rainbow trout.

Facilities: None

Need Information?
Contact: Los Padres National Forest (805) 646-4348

Directions: From the 101 Freeway in Ventura, turn north on Highway 33 and drive 14 miles to Ojai. In Ojai, turn left, staying on Highway 33, and continue approximately five miles to Matilija Road. Turn west and drive 4.9 miles to a locked gate and parking area.

The stretch of Matilija Creek roughly three miles up stream of Matilija Reservoir.

Like all the other rivers and streams in Southern California, Matilija Creek in Ventura County, was hit hard by the El Nino of the latter-Nineties. For years, Matilija Creek was stocked each February through April, but from 1998 through 2000 those plants were put on hold because the road that lead to the creek was damaged by severe El Nino storms. The road has recently been repaired and it re-opened in October of 2000, allowing the California Department of Fish and Game to continue stocking the creek.

Located at 1,500 feet in the Los Padres National Forest, Matilija Creek is one of only

The Matilija Wilderness

two streams in Ventura County (Reyes Creek is the other) still stocked with rainbow trout. But that could all change soon. There is talk of destroying Matilija Dam, which is just below where the creek is planted. If that happens the creek will no longer be stocked. The lake is not good for fishing. It's always filled with trees, branches and trash that have floated down the creek. The dam no longer serves a purpose and is completely silted up. It's not a good fishing spot.

Local environmentalist groups are backing the destruction of the dam to restore steelhead runs. By destroying the dam, trout stockings would also cease because of a fear that the stocked trout could interbreed with the steelhead, a member of the endangered species list. If the dam were destroyed, the steelhead could get to Matilija Creek by swimming up the North Fork of the Ventura River, which Matilija Creek ultimately empties into. Matilija Creek joins with the North Fork of Matilija Creek, which becomes the North Fork of the Ventura River, just below the turnoff on Highway 33 to Matilija Road.

If fishing for the eight to nine inch stockers, concentrate on the areas where the creek can be easily accessed from the road. Be sure to stay off private property. Power Bait is your best bet. However, if water levels are high enough, you may be able to get away with using lures.

For those interested in backpacking, the Matilija Wilderness is close by, offering a remote area to get away from civilization without having to hike too far.

If you plan to make the trip, supplies are available in Ojai. A Forest Service Adventure Pass is required to park in the Los Padres National Forest.

Also nearby are the North Fork Ventura River, Sespe River, Reyes Creek, Rose Valley Lakes, Rose Valley Falls, Lake Casitas and the Matilija Wilderness.

SESPE **RIVER**

Most of Sespe River's former visitors can no longer enjoy its unique beauty because the walk is too demanding.

Rating: 10

Species: Rainbow Trout, Green Sunfish, Bluegill, Largemouth Bass and Brown Bullhead

Stocks: None

Facilities: Picnic Areas and Restrooms

Need Information?
Contact: Los Padres National Forest (805) 646-4348

Directions: From the 101 Freeway in Ventura, drive north on Highway 33 (past Ojai and Wheeler Gorge) for twenty-eight miles to the Rose Valley Lakes turnoff. Turn right and continue past the Ojai

One of Sespe's many large pools.

Gun Club to a locked gated near the turnoff for Middle Lion Campground.

Sespe River has it all, endangered species, hiking, hot springs, fishing, backpacking, camping, snorkeling, wildlife viewing, swimming, cliff jumping, rock climbing and waterfalls. Nowhere else in Southern California can you discover the diversity that Sespe offers, including the chance to see some rare forms of wildlife, like the southwestern pond turtle and California horned toad. There are also wildflowers, deer, bears, coyotes, and if you hike far enough, the California condor can be seen soaring above. That's the

The California horned toad, which is found along Sespe River.

upside. The downside? You have to be willing to work to get to these natural attractions.

Sespe River used to be the most popular trout fishing spot for fly-fishermen in all of Ventura County, but it's no longer easily accessible to those anglers. For that reason, many have chosen to pass on Sespe's pleasures, but those who've decided to put up with the inconveniences say the fishing has never been better.

For decades, Sespe River was stocked each winter and spring with more than 9,000 rainbow trout. But in 1997 Sespe River took a hit many anglers still haven't recovered from. After the steelhead was placed on the endangered species list, Sespe River was listed as one of many coastal streams that was to be protected in order to try to save the steelhead from extinction. Then came the real hurt. The United States Fish & Wildlife Service and local environmentalist groups ordered the California Department of Fish and Game to stop stocking rainbow trout in the river.

Anglers were confused and angry. "How could a steelhead get all the way up here?" they thought. Well, they can and they do.

It's true that the lower portion of the river that flows into the Pacific Ocean after joining the Santa Clara River, is dry most of the year. However, during high water after rainstorms the steelhead are able to swim up the river near to its confluence with Alder Creek. And they can remain there for a few years before heading back to the ocean. For that reason, biologists became concerned that if one of the stocked fish were to swim downstream during high water, it might interbreed with the native steelhead. Then we'd have a hybrid steelhead, and that's a conservationist's nightmare. Although chances are you'll never see a steelhead, the US Forest Service said they do exist and have been seen in the river.

Losing the trout plants was bad enough, but what was to come next was even harder for anglers to digest. There was another endangered species discovered, the Southwestern Arroyo Toad. This one was found near Lion Camp where the trout plants used to take place. To protect the toad and encourage it to breed, US FWS forced the Forest Service to take action, this time by closing the road that leads to Lion Campground to all but foot traffic and horses.

It wasn't just fishermen who felt the effects of the closing of Lion Campground. For campers and hikers, it took away one of the few popular, remote campsites in the Los Padres National Forest. The campground was closed and the area was deemed for day-use only. Doesn't sound that bad? You should try it. Walking from the locked gate near the Ojai Gun Club down to the river may only be two miles, but it is hot and dry, and there's no water anywhere to be found. It's all uphill on the way back, under a harsh sun with no shade. Most of Sespe River's former visitors can no longer enjoy its unique beauty because the walk is just too demanding.

On July 27 of 2000, Sespe devotees finally had a reason to celebrate when the Forest Service

Many deep holes make Sespe River a favorite spot to take a dip.

SESPE RIVER

An angler casts for rainbow trout in one of the larger pools near Lion campground.

was allowed to open Middle Lion Campground because studies showed there were no toads found there. Keep in mind, however, that the walk to Lion may now only be a mile, but it's just as brutal if not quite as long. There was talk of opening Beaver Campground, located just above Lion Camp, but as of now it will remain closed.

So, if you want to enjoy Sespe, you either make a day-trip out of it or do what most outdoor enthusiasts have decided to do – make it a fun backpacking trip. Remember, although Lion Campground is only open to day-use, you can camp further downstream.

Sespe is a river of drastic changes. It can be a torrent after winter storms and free flowing in spring, but by late June it turns into a trickle. That's not a totally bad thing for anglers, because Sespe is known for its deep, emerald pools that hold water year-round despite the river drying up. These pools are as long as 100 yards and as deep as 30 feet. The fish get stacked up in the pools when the river dries, and then fishing is incredible.

This section, located in the Sespe Wilderness and created in 1992, is home to many wild rainbow trout, largemouth bass, bluegill, green sunfish and brown bullhead. Trout fishing is only good in the early morning and late evening on small spinners and flies, but the bluegill, sunfish, bass and bullhead bite stays hot all day. Surprisingly, there are rainbows up to 18 inches, and the further you hike, the more

Sespe River about two miles downstream of lion campground.

you'll catch. There aren't many bass, bluegill and sunfish, but the bullhead over-populate the river.

Catching bullhead is as easy as knowing how to cast. First you need to find a pool. Then tie on a small bait hook, put on a mealworm, red worm, a small piece of a night-crawler or catfish bait, and fly-line it out into the pool. I count to 10, set the hook and catch a fish every time. My buddies and I each have caught more than 50 fish in a day. We always seem to run out of bait, but one of us is generally willing to sacrifice our lunch so we can keep fishing. I've used hot dogs, turkey, bread and chunks of tuna. They'll eat anything. It can be a little frustrating, though, because the fish range anywhere from a few inches to a few pounds.

A popular backpacking area in the Sespe Wilderness. Snorkeling anyone?

The most memorable thing I've ever done was feed bluegill. The water is so clear and calm that a friend and I will bring our masks and snorkels, and swim around look-ing for turtles and fish. Last time I visited, we encountered a school of tame bluegill. We kept swimming by them and the courageous little guys never got spooked. I went over to my bag, grabbed a few crappie nibbles and some worms, put on my mask, dove down and stuck out my hand. The bluegill came over and ate right off my fingers. In the spring and early summer I've seen schools of more than 1,000 three-to-five-inch catfish swim-ming in most of the pools. Next time I'll go back with an underwater video camera.

If you're planning to backpack, start at the locked gate and walk down to Lion Campground. At the eastern most end of the camp you'll cross the river and begin heading uphill away from the stream for about 10 minutes. Then you'll drop down and cross a feeder stream. (They might be dry depending on the season.) After about a 20-30 minute walk, begin to look on your right for a side trail that is marked by a few

Brett Ross & Gary Seely cool off in one of Sespe's many sandstone pools.

railroad ties in the ground. At that point, if you look up on the mountain to your right you should see a few pines trees about half way up.

This is the trail to Sespe's first large fishing and swimming pool. It's also a popular cliff jumping spot. Yes, cliff jumping. The jumps or dives range from 10 to 20 feet into a sandy-bottomed pool. If you're going to jump, remember to check the pool first. There is one rock below that you especially have to watch out for. This area gets a lot day-use visitation by local high school kids, so you might want to pass it by. There are plenty more pools to come. The next good one is after you cross the boundary into Sespe Wilderness.

You cross one stream and then head uphill through an old, rusted gate before gradually drifting downhill through an area surrounded by brush on both sides. Start looking to your right and you'll see a huge, emerald-green pool along a sandy beach. From here on, there are great campsites and swimming holes all along the river. Other popular destinations include Willett Hot Springs, Sespe Hot Springs, Devils Gateway and the confluence with Alder Creek. The best trip would be to start at Lion Camp and finish in Fillmore. It's a 38-mile trek, but you get to see everything.

Another popular activity along the river is frogging. There are a lot of giant bullfrogs, but with so many activities to do, many people don't get around to it.

If you plan to make the trip, supplies are available in Ojai. A Forest Service Adventure Pass is required to park in the Los Padres National Forest. Keep an eye out for rattlesnakes; the riverbed is loaded with them. Call ahead for updated road conditions. The study of the SW Arroyo Toad is an ongoing process and any new developments could either force the closures or openings of roads in the area. Beginning at the Alder Creek confluence, only artificial lures with barbless hooks may be used. No fish may be taken from the Saturday before Memorial Day through December 31.

Also nearby are Rose Valley Lakes, Rose Valley Falls, the Ojai Gun Club, Piedra Blanca, Reyes Creek, North Fork Ventura Creek, Lake Casitas and Matilija Creek.

Dare devils cliff dive into Sespe's deeper pools.

REYES **CREEK**

So, if you have the patience to make the drive, you can plan on using a lot of Power Bait and catching a lot of fish.

Rating: 5

Species: Rainbow Trout

Stocked with 1,600 pounds of rainbow trout

Facilities: Campgrounds

Need Information? Contact: Los Padres National Forest (805) 646-4348

Reyes Creek upstream of Reyes campground.

Directions: From Highway 150 in Ojai turn north on Highway 33 and drive 38 miles to the Ozena Guard Station. Turn east on Lockwood Rd. and drive 3.5 miles to Forest Service Road 7N11. Turn south and continue to the campground.

If you like long drives, low waters levels and little pressure, you've found your place. The majority of Ventura and Santa Barbara County anglers overlook Reyes Creek, a small trickle of water in a remote area of the Los Padres National Forest. In 1998, when trout plants were stopped to protect native steelhead runs at Sespe River, North Fork Ventura River and Santa Paula Creek, many of the fish slated to be planted in those streams were diverted to tiny Reyes Creek. So, if you have the patience to make the drive, you can plan on using a lot of Power Bait and catching fish.

Don't expect to find a raging river; Reyes Creek has just enough water to allow for trout stockings. Most of the stockers are caught the week they are planted, with plants typically taking place from January to March when water levels are high. Check the newspaper to make sure it's been stocked, otherwise you won't find any fish.

Leave all your lures at home. Power Bait, nightcrawlers and salmon eggs are the rule here. All the 4,360 fish planted (that's 2,860 more fish than in 1997) are in the seven to nine-inch-class. Best places to fish are upstream from the campground. Once summer arrives, all the trout vanish along with most of the stream, a clear sign its time to move on.

Reyes Creek

If you plan to make the trip, supplies are available in Ojai. A Forest Service Adventure Pass is required to park in the Los Padres National Forest.

Also nearby are Sespe Wilderness, Sespe River, Matilija Creek, Rose Valley Lakes and the North Fork of the Ventura River.

ROSE VALLEY **LAKES**

The Rose Valley Lakes are three small ponds located within a quarter mile of each other. These ponds provide good fishing for stockers.

Rating: 6

Species:
Rainbow Trout, Bluegill and Channel Catfish

Stocked with 8,400 pounds of rainbow trout.

Facilities:
Campgrounds and Restrooms

Need Information?
Contact: Los Padres National Forest (805) 646-4348

Directions: From Highway 33 in Ojai, drive north six miles past Wheeler George Campground to Rose Valley Lakes turnoff. Turn east and continue about three miles to lakes.

Rose Valley Lakes are a popular float tubing spot in the Los Padres National Forest.

Less than a mile from Rose Valley Lakes, Rose Valley Falls pours 300 feet over a cliff (providing there's been sufficient rainfall in the recent past), target shooters unload rounds at the Ojai Gun Club and helicopters takeoff from a nearby heliport. In fact,

Rose Valley Lake No. 3

there is so much going on around Rose Valley Lakes it's difficult to pay any attention to the lakes themselves. Most people don't, but those bait dunkers who do focus their efforts on fishing end up doing pretty well.

The Rose Valley Lakes are three small ponds located within a quarter-mile of each other. These ponds provide good fishing for stockers. However, because they are also loaded with weeds, they are difficult to fish when growth reaches its peak in the spring and summer. With Sespe River, North Fork Ventura River and Santa Paula Creek no longer being planted by the California Department of Fish and Game in an effort to protect native steelhead runs, Rose Valley Lakes plants have nearby doubled.

The view of Rose Valley Lakes from the brink of Lower Rose Valley Falls.

In most years, in addition to the normal trout plants, the lakes are also blessed with 60,000 fingerling rainbow trout, a surprisingly high number for such small ponds. Most of the 23,230 catchable trout stocked are in the seven to nine-inch-class and can be caught on Power Bait, salmon eggs and just about any lure properly presented.

The lakes are planted from late winter through spring, as long as water temperatures stay down and algae growth doesn't hamper fishing. Any spot around these tiny ponds can be productive. Just bring a chair, relax and wait. You won't be the only one there. When the plants begin the crowds come with them.

If you plan to make the trip, supplies are available in Ojai. A Forest Service Adventure Pass is required to park in the Los Padres National Forest.

Also nearby are Rose Valley Falls, Sespe River, Ojai Valley Gun Club, Matilija Creek and the North Fork Ventura River.

Rose Valley Lake No. 1 with Rose Valley Falls in the background.

SANTA PAULA **CREEK**

You need to hike through the college, located a few miles upstream of the county park, to get to the upper reaches of Santa Paula Creek where the best fishing is found.

Rating: 4

Species: Rainbow Trout

Stocks: None

Facilities: Campgrounds, Restrooms and Picnic Areas

Need Information? Contact: Los Padres National Forest (805) 646-4348, Ventura County Parks and Recreation (805) 654-3951

An emerald pool above Santa Paula Canyon Falls.

Directions: From Ventura, drive east on Highway 126 to Santa Paula and exit Highway 150. Drive north to Thomas Aquinas College on the right.

On my way to Sespe Creek, I noticed that there were always a bunch of cars parked out in front of Thomas Aquinas College. I figured the parking lot was full because school was in session, until one day I saw a guy leaving his car with a fishing pole strapped to his backpack. Then, I realized that the cars had nothing to do with the school. Rather, they had to do with hiking and fishing, both of which now go hand and hand at Santa Paula Creek, located in the Los Padres National Forest.

Prior to 1998, every spring the California Department of Fish and Game dumped 6,900 trout into the creek, making fishing relatively easy. But, in an effort to save the steelhead now on the endangered species list, environmental groups demanded that the stocks cease. Because of a dam along Santa Paula Creek, how steelhead could ever get this far up the stream seemed a mystery to almost everyone. However, a fish ladder was recently built to enable the fish to spawn upstream. During high water levels, the steelhead swim from the Pacific Ocean up the Santa Clara River, and then up Santa Paula Creek that joins with the river on the south side of Highway 126 near the city of Santa Paula.

Jerry Weeks used a rope to repel down to Santa Paula Creek.

The recent stoppage of plants has forced anglers to find a new way to fish the creek. The plants used to take place in two places, at Steckel County Park and where Highway 154 rises over the creek near the college. Anglers used to fish for the stockers when the CA DFG planted every other week in the spring and early summer, but since the plants stopped and few fish remain, fishing here has become a thing of the past.

Because there are no longer any plants, the new thing to do is target the creek's wild trout, and that's where Thomas Aquinas College comes in. You need to hike through the college, located a few miles upstream of the county park, to get to the upper reaches of Santa Paula Creek where the best fishing is found. Wild trout from five to 12 inches are abundant in this portion of the creek and are caught on a regular basis.

Snorkeling is popular in the sparkling water beneath Santa Paula Canyon Falls.

The most consistent place to catch big fish is in the pool below Santa Paula Canyon Falls. The falls is also a favorite place for hikers and swimmers, and when people aren't jumping off the top of the falls the fishing can be pretty good. That is, if you know what you're doing. Think about it... these fish are big, right? That means they've been here for a while and they've seen just about every lure invented, so you have to show them something different, and there are no easy answers.

My advice is to leave the big boys alone and either head upstream or downstream to catch smaller fish. For those who don't want to venture back into the small creek located in the mountains above Santa Paula, you can try to fish at Steckel Park, but don't expect to catch many. Another spot to try is just below the bridge that crosses over Santa Paula Creek near the college. The pools below the bridge (on Highway 150) hold some small trout, with one downfall -- the water in them is oily and it makes your line black, so don't bring your good pole with you. Or, even smarter, just don't bother fishing here. You can ruin your gear and there aren't that many fish left in the stream, anyway.

If you plan to make the trip, supplies are available in Santa Paula. There is a fee to enter Steckel County Park.

Also nearby are Happy Valley, Lake Casitas, the Fillmore Fish Hatchery, North Fork Ventura River, Matilija Creek, Lake Piru and Santa Paula Canyon Falls.

REGION 3

Los Angeles County West/Ventura County East

Rancho Simi Park Lake
Hansen Dam Lake
Hansen Ponds
Balboa Park Lake
Reseda Park Lake
Malibu Creek
Century Lake
Troutdale

RANCHO SIMI PARK **LAKE**

This lake is like fishing in a barrel and the catch rates reflect it.

Rating: 5.

Species: Rainbow Trout, Channel Catfish, Bluegill, and Largemouth Bass

Stocked with 2,000 pounds of rainbow trout and catfish periodically

Facilities: Playgrounds, Picnic Areas, A Recreational Area and Restrooms

Rancho Simi Park Lake

Need Information?
Contact: Taylor Tackle (818) 340-2880

Directions: From the 118 Freeway in Simi Valley, exit Erringer and turn south. Continue past Los Angeles Avenue and over the wash to the lake on the west side of the street.

Fishing in a barrel is fun for some people. After all, you know exactly where all the fish are. This lake is like fishing in a barrel and the catch rates reflect it.

Rancho Simi Park Lake is a beautiful pond in the middle of urban Simi Valley. Prior to 1998, the lake received three trout plants a year, one the week of Thanksgiving, another the week of Christmas and the last came prior to the popular Tom Sawyer Fishing Derby, an annual spring event in Simi Valley. However, with the North Fork Ventura River, Sespe River and Santa Paula Creek no longer being stocked, many of the fish slated for those waters have been diverted to Rancho Simi Lake. The lake is now a hot spot with fish being stocked just about every other week in the winter and spring.

It is extremely productive the week it is stocked, kicking out easy limits of trout. All the fish are in the seven to nine inch range. Best baits are small Kastmasters, Panther Martins and Power Bait. An added treat the week of the Tom Sawyer fishing derby is solid plants of catfish. I saw a man catch a 10 pounder a month after the derby. Although a good majority of residents don't even know there are fish in the lake, surprisingly it is mostly fished by locals who want to treat their kids to an evening of fishing.

In the spring, the attention at this tiny park lake turns to the bluegill bite. Although the fish are small, they are fun to catch. Concentrate on fishing where the inlet (artificial and recirculated) empties into the lake. They love bits of nightcrawlers.

Watch out for ducks, they like the fish here too. You don't want to accidentally snag one.

If you plan to make the trip, supplies are available in Simi Valley.

Also nearby are Piru Lake and the Fillmore Fish Hatchery.

HANSEN **DAM**

Although there is no shade around the lake, it provides excellent access for anglers interested in catching stocked rainbow trout and catfish.

Rating: 4

Species: Rainbow Trout, Channel Catfish, Largemouth Bass, Carp and Bluegill

Stocked with 1,100 pounds of rainbow trout.

Facilities: Picnic Areas, Boat Launch, Paddle Boat Rentals, Swimming Pool, Lockers, Showers and Restrooms

Need Information?
Contact: Hansen Dam Aquatic Center
(818) 899-3779

Directions: From the 118 Freeway in Northridge, drive east to the 210

Hansen Dam Lake as seen from the 210 Freeway.

Freeway. Take the 210 Freeway east to the Osborne Street exit in Lake View Terrace and turn right. (You'll actually be on Foothill Blvd., but the road takes you to Osborne.) Just before Osborne, turn left on Stonewall and continue to the Hansen Dam Aquatics Center.

The Hansen Dam Aquatics Center is the newest recreation area in Los Angeles County. Completed in August of 1999, the 20-acre facility, located within the Hansen Dam Recreation Area, has a 1.5-acre swimming pool rated for 1,500 people, and a nine-acre lake. Although there is no shade around the lake, it provides excellent access for anglers interested in catching stocked rainbow trout and catfish.

The California Department of Fish and Game stocks 2,930 rainbow trout during the winter and early spring, providing San Fernando Valley anglers with a close and easily accessible (it's less than a mile from the 210 Freeway) urban trout fishery. After a plant the lake gets crowded, but catch rates remain high despite the crowds. Unlike most urban lakes, Hansen Dam is well aerated, keeping the trout healthy and in feeding mode.

One way to beat the crowds is to bring a boat, canoe or float tube. No gas-powered motors are permitted, but electric trolling motors are allowed. If you do decide to bring a boat, get here early. It's a small lake that only allows 15 boats on the water at a time. Tossing lures, jigging Trout Teasers and soaking Power Bait work well.

Once late spring approaches the water becomes too warm for trout and catfish are stocked. The lake receives 3,000 pounds of cats throughout the summer months. The best time to catch them is in the early morning or just before sunset when temperatures are cooler. The best place to catch the cats is near the artificial waterfall that recirculates the water. They aren't fussy about what they eat, but mackerel and nightcrawlers will catch them the fastest.

Hansen Dam Lake has benefited greatly from the CA DFG's new fish rescue operation. The project relocates fish that aren't wanted in private lakes, as well as fish from lakes that are drained for maintenance, by transporting them to new lakes. Examples of fish from this operation poured into Hansen Dam Lake include: in August of 1999, 200 bass, 10 carp and 20 bluegill were taken from San Gabriel Reservoir; in November of 1999, 20 carp were taken from the Hansen Dam Flood Control Basin; in December of 1999, 20 carp, 10 of which weighed more than 30 pounds, were taken from Fin & Feather Lake in Palmdale. Most recently, in May of 2000, Fin & Feather donated 54 more carp, some of which weighed up to 45 pounds.

The Hansen Dam is a popular place to fish for the residents of the San Fernando Valley.

Frequently, people confuse the Hansen Dam Flood Control Basin with the new lake. Don't get them confused. Although the lake in the flood control basin has many small bass, it's off-limits to fishing. Driving east on the 210 Freeway, you can get a view of both. The lake surrounded by dirt and brush near the large concrete dam is the flood control basin. The closer one located next to the pool is the new lake.

If you plan to make the trip, supplies are available in Sunland. The lake is open from sunrise to sunset.

Also nearby are Hansen Dam Ponds, Little Tujunga Canyon and Upper and Lower Big Tujunga Creek.

HANSEN DAM

HANSEN **PONDS**

Rating: 4

Species: Largemouth Bass, Channel Catfish, Bluegill and Carp

Stocks: None

Facilities: None

Need Information? Contact: Hansen Dam Aquatics Center (818) 899-3779

Fishing with nightcrawlers can be productive at Hansen Ponds.

Directions: From the San Fernando Valley, drive north on the 405 Freeway and exit east on the 118 Freeway. Take the 118 Freeway to the 210 Freeway. From the 210 Freeway exit Wheatland and turn north to Foothill Blvd. Turn right on Foothill and continue over Big Tujunga Wash to Wentworth. Turn right on Wentworth and drive under the freeway to Sharon Ave. Turn right on Sharon Ave., park at the end of the road and walk past the white wooden fence to the trail.

Although the fishing is the pits, Hansen Ponds is one of my favorite places in Southern California. Small and shallow with shorelines covered by trees, bushes and bamboo, these ponds are different than all other lakes in the region. The two ponds, located adjacent to one another inside of the Hansen Dam Recreation Area, receive little fishing pressure. The water is usually almost entirely covered by lily pads, and with the exception of a few horseback riders and myself, nobody seems to care about the place.

Although Hansen Ponds hold largemouth bass, channel catfish, bluegill and carp, I mainly come here for the wildlife. The ponds are one of only a few places were you can sit on a rock and see bullfrogs, crawdads, turtles, salamanders and dozens of species of birds. It's like a small zoo with no cages. Many other lakes do have all of these animals, but not concentrated like this in one area.

The coolest thing I've ever seen here was a giant turtle. I still don't know what kind it was, but it was huge, like one of those sea turtles you see on the Discovery Channel. I watched in awe for about an hour as it cruised around the pond, finally heading into a cove so thick with bushes I couldn't follow.

Hansen Pond

Crawdads and salamanders can be seen along the shoreline all day, but if you're coming to see the bullfrogs, you need to come early in the morning or in the evening. First, listen for the frogs croaking. Then, quietly move in to get a better look. They like to hang in the tules and in shady spots along the bank. Some of the frogs are only about the size of your hand, but I've seen a few as large as an adult's head.

One evening when I was with friends, we were using a fishing net to catch frogs and accidentally caught a bat. We quickly released it without touching it. My friends got a kick out of it when I showed them the bat on video. "Don't those things have rabies?" one asked. I told him I released the bat so fast because I didn't want to find out.

Don't come here expecting to catch big fish because there aren't many. Most of the time the lake is entirely covered in lily pads. When the lily pads don't completely cover the lake, try tossing small Rapalas and silver Kastmasters. The majority of the bass are only six to 10 inches, but they attack the lures with a vengeance. Bluegill can be caught on red worms, but they are tiny, too. If it's catfish or carp you want, try using a nightcrawler.

Hansen Pond No.1 as seen from the 210 Freeway.

One thing I don't like about Hansen Ponds is that there are a lot of poachers around. I saw one guy who'd caught about 50 fish, fishing without a fishing license. He took off before I could approach him. If you see any poachers, please report them to the California Department of Fish and Game by calling the Cal Tip Hotline at 888-334-2258.

Access is also available via Cottonwood Road, which is on your right just past Sharon Ave. The gate is sometimes locked, but if it's open the road takes you directly to the lakes. If going to the lakes from Sharon Road, there's a dirt trail about 20 yards from the road at the bottom of the hill. If you don't see it right away, walk towards the trees near the freeway and stay to your left. The ponds are on the other side of the trees, on the south side of the freeway. If you want to get a look at them before you come, drive east on the 210 Freeway. Just after you pass the sign for Wheatland Ave., get in the right lane and look to your right. You can't miss them.

If you plan to make the trip, supplies are available in Sunland. A fishing license is required to catch any amphibians or reptiles.

Also nearby are Hansen Dam Lake, Upper Big Tujunga Falls and Upper and Lower Big Tujunga Creek.

BALBOA PARK **LAKE**

When the tilapia fishing is on, it's not uncommon to catch over 50 in a short period of time.

Rating: 3

Species: Channel Catfish, Largemouth Bass, Carp, Bluegill, and Tilapia

Stocks: None

Need Information? Contact: Taylor Tackle (818) 340-2880

Facilities: Launch Ramp, Playground, Restrooms, Bike Path, Paddle Boat Rentals and Picnic Areas

Balboa Park Lake

Directions: Heading east on 101 Freeway in Reseda, exit Balboa and turn left. Drive through two stoplights and turn right into the signed recreation area.

Almost every soccer player in the San Fernando Valley has heard of Balboa Park. It's one of a few soccer complexes in the San Fernando Valley that has more than four fields. It's used by numerous soccer leagues for weekend games and weekday practices, as well as major tournaments held each Thanksgiving holiday weekend and in the spring.

Every time I drive by I see people sitting under trees and canopies waiting anxiously for their turn to play. Sometimes they have to kill a few hours between games, but I have a better idea than getting itchy, sitting in the grass. How about going fishing? Balboa Park Lake is across the street, just on the other side of the Los Angeles River.

Jason Fractor gets his line wet at Balboa Park Lake.

Candice Thierry spends an afternoon fishing for catfish at Balboa Park Lake.

The lake was built in the mid-Nineties to create a popular and easily accessible urban fishery. It's usually packed, so the idea was successful. However, the fishing is nothing to brag about. Since its opening in the mid 1990's, poor water quality has kept the California Department of Fish and Game from consistently planting trout and catfish in the lake. Carp, bluegill, catfish and a bundle of bass still roam the 27-acre lake, although there aren't enough of them to catch on a consistent basis.

Ironically, the only fish that really thrive here, tilapia, were introduced illegally. But they are the great hit. When the tilapia fishing is on, it's not uncommon to catch more than 50 in a short period of time. They range from a quarter-pound to a tad over two pounds, and fight better than bluegill. Depending on water temperature their population fluctuates. If the water dips below the mid-sixties there is usually a large die-off. But if it stays warm for long periods of time, the fish multiply fast and infest the lake. Catching them is easy. You don't even need a pole. The kids catch them on sticks with line attached. It's as easy as putting a nightcrawler, red worm or mealworm on a small hook with a light split shot, and casting it directly in front of you. A big hit for the tilapia in the late Nineties was Wonder Worms, but they were replaced with the new Neon Worms. Taylor Tackle can keep you updated on what works the best.

The lake does offer a nice, peaceful setting in an often-crowded park, but the smell of reclaimed water doesn't let you forget you're still in the city.

If you plan to make the trip, supplies are available in nearby Van Nuys. No motorized boats are allowed on the lake.

Also nearby is Reseda Park Lake.

BALBOA PARK **LAKE**

RESEDA PARK **LAKE**

You will always find a few unwitting youngsters trying to outdo the old timers, but all of them are wasting their time.

Rating: 1

Species: Channel Catfish

Stocked: None

Facilities: Playgrounds, Recreational Facilities and Restrooms

Need Information? Contact: Taylor Tackle (818) 340-2880

Reseda Park Lake

Directions: From the 101 Freeway in Reseda, exit Reseda Blvd and travel north. The lake is on your right, just before the wash.

Years ago, tiny Reseda Park Lake was stocked with rainbow trout and channel catfish, but nothing has been stocked there since the mid-Eighties. There are a number of reasons, including an abundance of ducks and geese and poor water clarity and quality. The ducks and geese pooped so much in the water that it polluted the concrete bottom lake.

Even though most anglers know the chance of catching fish dwindled more than decade ago, a few old timers still come here looking for fish. They even manage to pull one out from time to time. You will always find a few unwitting youngsters trying to outdo the old timers, but all of them are wasting their time. They could catch the same amount of fish in a gutter on a rainy day. Don't bother coming here. You'll get skunked!

Locals joke that there are three-eyed fish in the lake caused by the horrid water quality, but I've never seen one. If the water quality remains poor, one might be caught soon.

If you plan to make the trip, supplies are available in Reseda.

Also nearby is Balboa Park Lake.

No fish are stocked at Reseda Park Lake.

MALIBU **CREEK**

Being so close to the San Fernando Valley, Malibu Creek gets heavily visited, but not heavily fished.

Rating: 4

Species: Largemouth Bass, Bluegill, Green Sunfish, Channel Catfish and Carp

Stocks: None

Facilities: Campgrounds, Picnic Areas, Restrooms, Hiking and Biking Trails and a Visitor Center

Need Information? Contact: Malibu Creek State Park (818) 880-0367

Rock Pool is one of the most heavily visited areas of Malibu Creek State Park.

Directions: From Los Angeles, drive west on the 101 Freeway an exit Las Virgenes Road. Turn left and continue to the entrance station for Malibu Creek State Park on your right.

Being so close to the San Fernando Valley, Malibu Creek gets heavily visited, but not heavily fished. Located in the Santa Monica National Recreation Area, much of Malibu Creek runs through Malibu Creek State Park, which is primarily used by visitors as a place to hike and mountain bike. The creek runs from Malibu Lake down through the state park, and follows to the end of Las Virgenes Canyon Road, where it empties first into Malibu Lagoon and then into the Pacific Ocean.

As long as Malibu Lake releases water, the creek stays at a consistent level to hold fish, but fishing here has never been a main attraction. The California Department of Fish and Game used to stock the park with 8,000 rainbow trout per year from winter

A popular rock climbing area of Malibu Creek State Park.

through spring, but that program was canceled in 1989 because of concerns that the trout would interfere with native steelhead runs. Subsequently, the steelhead were put on the endangered species list in 1997 and most coastal streams like Malibu Creek were protected.

It was obvious to biologists that the steelhead couldn't get over the 100-foot Rindge Dam, located about halfway between the park and the Pacific Ocean, up to where the

Malibu Creek hasn't been planted with trout since 1989.

trout are planted. However, they were still concerned about the possibility that the trout might somehow get over the dam and inter-bred with the steelhead. The thought of even one rainbow getting pushed over the dam during high water, and a rainbow trout's genes mixing with a steelhead's, resulted in the cessation of all future trout plants. There's been talk of destroying the dam, but nothing has come of it.

Although no trout are believed to currently be in the stream, there are some small largemouth bass, catfish, carp and bluegill. Despite the fact that the stream has never been planted with fish other than trout, the fish have entered either during high water levels when water flows over the spillway, or when water is released from Malibu Lake.

When the water warms in April, a few anglers fishing with pieces of worms below a bobber have been known to catch bluegill near the visitor center inside the state park. Another popular spot is Rock Pool, just upstream from the visitor center. This pool is large and deep and holds some catfish, bass and bluegill. Downstream, along Las Virgenes Canyon Road, the stream is less accessible and less fished, which means the fishing is going to be better. State park rangers told me that you can even catch bass and carp in Malibu Lagoon, which is partially fresh and partially salt water.

If you plan to make the trip, supplies are available in Malibu or Calabasas. There is a day-use fee.

Also nearby are Troutdale, Pepperdine University and Malibu Pier.

CENTURY **LAKE**

The lake has a stable population of fish, mainly largemouth bass, carp, bluegill, channel catfish and green sunfish.

Rating: 4

Species: Largemouth Bass, Channel Catfish, Carp, Bluegill and Green Sunfish

Stocks: None

Facilities: Picnic Areas

Need Information?
Contact: Malibu Creek State Park (818) 880-0367

Century Lake

Directions: From Los Angeles, drive west on the 101 Freeway and exit Las Virgenes Road. Turn left and continue to the entrance station for Malibu Creek State Park on your right.

More than 250,000 visitors come to Malibu Creek State Park each year, many of whom end up at Century Lake. The lake is only a 2.5-mile round-trip hike from the parking lot, but its scenic, green shoreline makes you feel like you've traveled much farther.

The lake was originally created for recreational use in 1901 by a local country club, but was given its present name when 20th Century Fox used the area as a movie set. One of the most famous shows filmed nearby was the TV show "Mash".

The TV show M.A.S.H. was filmed near Century Lake.

Today, hikers, bird watchers, picnickers and anglers use Century Lake. Because the trail is well maintained and easy enough for hikers of all ages, it is an excellent destination for a family hike. Over the years, silt buildup and over-grown trees and brush have turned the lake into more of a marsh, making it even more popular to the many species of birds that flock here.

The lake has a stable population of fish, mainly largemouth bass, carp, bluegill, channel catfish and green sunfish. To better fishing and hiking access, the state park is looking into making improvements to the lake by removing some of the silt and clearing away brush and overgrown weeds. However, as of October 2000, the project had yet to be approved.

There are no trophy size fish here, but a six-pound largemouth bass was caught a few years back. Most anglers are content catching six to 10-inch bass, by tossing small Rapalas and spinnerbaits near the dam and around submerged trees. Fishing red worms or pieces of nightcrawlers below a bobber is also a popular method. There aren't many catfish in the lake, but if you toss out a juicy nightcrawler and wait long enough you might just catch one.

Century Lake is an excellent destination for a day hike.

To reach the lake, pick up the trail signed for the visitor center at the end of the parking lot. Just before the visitor center, make a right turn, crossing over Malibu Creek. Follow the trail that takes you gradually uphill to the trail's peak, where you veer left and head down to the lake.

If you plan to make the trip, supplies are available in Calabasas and Malibu. There is a day-use fee.

Also nearby are the Malibu Creek State Park Visitor Center, Troutdale, Malibu Pier and Pepperdine University.

TROUT**DALE**

Years back, when I was working at Meadow Oaks School in Calabasas, I went along with a group of fourth graders for their class party and the kids were catching fish on pieces of hamburgers and hot dogs.

Rating: 5

Species: Rainbow Trout

Stocked periodically.

Facilities: Restrooms, Picnic Areas, Bait & Tackle and a Snack Bar

Need Information?
Contact: Troutdale
(818) 889-9993

Directions:
From Los Angeles, drive west on the 101 Freeway (past the San

Troutdale

Fernando Valley) to Kanan Road. Turn left and continue three miles to Troutdale Drive. The ponds are on your left on the corner of Troutdale Drive and Kanan Road. Access is also available from the Pacific Coast Hwy. Turn north on Kanan Road and continue nine miles to the ponds on your right.

Many children from the San Fernando Valley catch their first fish at Troutdale. Conveniently close to the beach, it is the only private stocked trout pond in all of Los Angeles, Ventura and Santa Barbara Counties. There are two major routes for the residents of the San Fernando Valley to get to the beach. One is to take Las Virgenes Canyon Road and the other, which leads you right to Troutdale, is to take Kanan Road. So, after a long day at the beach, what could be better than a little fishing? Wait – let me rephrase that – a little "catching."

Troutdale is a private fishery that requires no fishing license, just a full wallet. Because when you're done paying for your fish, I can assure you won't have any money left for dinner.

Christina Dickens eagerly awaits a bite from a hungry rainbow trout.

However, for most people the combination of a convenient location and watching children catch their first fish makes it worth the money.

Troutdale is made up of two small ponds equipped with aerated units to keep the water cool enough for the trout during the summer when temperatures frequently climb above 100. One pond holds smaller fish (nine to 12 inches) and the other contains fish from 12 to 18 inches, that weigh up to five pounds. The fish in the shallow, swimming pool-size pond shaded by trees are always hungry because they're never fed. Included in the entrance fee is a bamboo pole and bait, usually corn, so you don't need to bring tackle.

Troutdale is a popular spot for birthday parties and field trips. Years back, when I was working at Meadow Oaks School in Calabasas, I went along with a group of fourth graders for their class party and the kids were catching fish on pieces of hamburgers and hot dogs. One kid even hooked one on watermelon.

If you plan to make the trip, supplies are available at Agoura. Troutdale is open seven days a week and charges by the inch for the fish. For an extra fee they will ice and clean them for you.

Also nearby are Malibu Creek State Park, Zuma Beach and the Malibu Pier.

Troutdale

REGION 4

Santa Clarita Valley/Tejon/Tehachapi Area

CALIFORNIA

LAKE **PIRU**

With the California Department of Fish and Game stocking more than 58,000 trout annually, you'd think the trout fishing would be a little better.

Rating: 7

Species: Rainbow Trout, Crappie, Bluegill, Largemouth Bass, and Channel Catfish

Stocked with 33,700 pounds of rainbow trout.

Facilities: Picnic Areas, Campgrounds, RV Hookups, Restrooms, General Store, Snack Bar, Boat Rental, Bait & Tackle, Boat Launch, Fish Cleaning Station, Full Service Marina and RV & Boat Storage

Orange Cripplelure proved to be the hot lure for Phil Freed at Lake Piru.

Need Information? Contact: Piru Lake (805) 521-1500, Marina (805) 521-1231, Campground Reservations (805) 521-1572

Directions: From Interstate 5 in Valencia, take Highway 126 west to the town of Piru. Turn right on Main St. and continue to the lake.

Fed by Piru Creek, the 1,200-acre Piru Lake is about a 15-minute drive from Magic Mountain and five minutes away from the tiny town of Piru. Probably because there aren't enough trophy size fish here, the mile wide and four miles long lake doesn't receive half of the pressure that other large lakes in the Southland get.

Yet, newspaper reports will tell you that the trout bite is "red hot and limits are the rule." So, every time I come to Piru Lake I get revved-up with anticipation and tell my friends what a great fishing day we're going to have. However, my anticipation has never fully paid-off, and catching a limit of trout can take much longer than you'd expect. The going rate I've experienced is about one trout every hour to hour-and-a-half, and that's running four separate lines. Anglers may catch limits, but it could take a full day to do so, a thought not keen to most fishermen.

Michael Taylor caught and released this bass near San Felicia Dam.

The most exciting thing I've seen occur at the lake was when my friend Kayvon Kadjar got our rental boat stuck on the buoy line. While we were trolling near the dam in a pontoon boat, we stalled and a gust of wind pushed us across the buoy line against the rocks on the dam. When we finally got the engine started, our propeller caught the buoy line and it became tangled in the blades. Kayvon was really upset, but I got a kick out of it and so did all the other fishermen. They laughed every time he tried to rev enough force out of the engine to free us up. The buoy line was attached to a tree on a cliff adjacent to the dam, and each time he revved the engine to try to free the boat, it looked like the tree was going to come flying off. Eventually we broke free.

With the California Department of Fish and Game stocking more than 58,000 trout annually, you'd think the trout fishing would be a little better. Shoreline fishing can be productive during the cooler months when the fish are in shallow water and trout can be caught from the dam, marina and boat launch area. As the water warms, you'll need either leadcore line or downriggers to catch fish.

The best areas to troll are near the buoy line, the pumphouse and in the Narrows. If trolling the buoy line, be careful not to troll too close to the buoys. I've seen people hook the chains beneath them and think they've caught a lake record. Then they end up reeling their boat over to the buoys and have to cut their line.

Tony Scalercio and Christian Perez proudly pose with a few trout caught at Lake Piru.

Catfish to 20 pounds can be caught from the north end of the lake in the summer. In spring, the bass bite takes off. Brown, blue and a lighter shade of purple plastic worms should catch you fish. In the coves and along the dropoffs, use crawdads and nightcrawlers. A new lake record 15-pounder was caught in 1999 on a night-crawler, proving there are a few big bass in the lake. Best spots for bass are in Cow Cove and Felicia Cove. As for the rest of Piru Lake, it stays quiet most of the year until late spring and early summer when water-skiers take over.

If you plan to make the trip, supplies are available at the lake. There is a day-use and a boat launch fee.

Also nearby are Santa Paula Creek, Castiac Lake, Castiac Lagoon, Magic Mountain and the Fillmore Fish Hatchery.

LAKE PIRU

BOUQUET CANYON **CREEK**

The best way to fish the stream is to try a few casts and if you don't get any takers, move on. It's better to cover a lot of water than to stay in one place.

Rating: 5

Species: Rainbow Trout

Stocked with 6,200 pounds of rainbow trout.

Facilities: Campgrounds, General Store, Restrooms and Picnic Areas

Need Information?
Contact: Angeles National Forest (661) 296-9710

Peter Bomar shows what he caught after an hour of fishing at Bouquet Canyon Creek.

Directions: From Interstate 5 in Valencia, turn east on Valencia Ave. and continue to Bouquet Canyon Road. Turn north and drive past Saugus High School to the creek. You know you're getting close when you enter Bouquet Canyon.

Bouquet Canyon is more of a trickle than a stream. At no point is the creek wider than three feet or deeper than one foot, but that's not to say that there aren't a lot of fish here. The California Department of Fish and Game mercifully stocks 18,150 trout per year, the equivalent of 6,200 pounds. Sounds like a lot? Well, back in 1997 they stocked another 24,000 fish in the stream. The numbers have been cut back because the stocks have been diverted to urban lakes.

Tom Bomar waits for a willing trout at narrow Bouquet Canyon.

Most of the fish are small, about seven to nine inches. But it's an easy drive here for anglers from the Antelope, San Fernando and Santa Clarita Valleys who want to catch a quick limit and don't feel like trekking up to Bishop. You can leave your lures at home because the stream is too small for them. Dunk Power Bait or salmon eggs, instead. The best way to fish the stream is to try a few casts and if you don't get any takers, move on. It's better to cover a lot of water than to stay in one place. The best holes and pools are easily visible from the road. The stream is stocked from the Texas Canyon Ranger Station upstream to about a mile below Bouquet Reservoir. Fish all the turnoffs, where the stream crosses under the road and in Streamside Campground. Remember, the CA DFG stocks the pools that are most easily accessible to anglers. They don't want to make people work for them.

Bouquet Canyon Creek has been an expensive place for me to fish. When I was 15, my friend David Bina dropped my new video camera in the creek, and as you guessed it wasn't covered by the warranty.

Fed by water released from Bouquet Canyon Reservoir the creek flows year-round. The reservoir is said to hold a lot of bass and bluegill, but it's closed to fishing. If you have a little bit of extra time, take the kids to Bouquet Canyon Falls on the north side of the road about 1.5 miles below the reservoir.

If you plan to make the trip, a Forest Service Adventure Pass is required to park in the Angeles National Forest. Supplies are available at a store just below Streamside Campground.

Also nearby are Big Tujunga Falls, Lake Piru and Castaic Lake.

Rick Spadaro at Bouquet Canyon Falls.

CASTAIC **LAGOON**

Although lunkers are caught on crawdads year-round, the best time to target big bass is after a trout plant when the bass move in towards the boat launch to feed on the helpless little rainbows.

Rating: 7

Species: Rainbow Trout, Channel Catfish, Bluegill, Striped Bass, Crappie, and Carp

Stocked with 16,900 pounds of rainbow trout.

Facilities: Boat Launch, Fishing Piers, Snack Bar, RV Hookups, Picnic Areas, Campgrounds, Playgrounds, Restrooms and Swimming Beaches

Need Information? Contact: Fishing Guide Erik Stepanek (661) 295-1565, Fishing Guide Bob Crupi (661) 424-9315, Castaic Lake Recreation Area (661) 257-4050

Directions: From Interstate 5 in Los Angeles, drive north past the Santa Clarita Valley to the Lake Hughes Road exit. Turn right and drive past the spillway to the lake entrance on your left.

When Castaic Lake's world record bass hype dwindled in the mid-Nineties, Castaic Lagoon's reputation drained away with it. At one time, the Lagoon was thought to have bass close to 20 pounds. But once word got around about the Lagoon's legendary bass, every fisherman in the region hammered it day in and day out, and the pressure took its toll on the fishery. Added to that, a few years back, a combination of warm water and mishandling of fish caused a big die-off of lunkers.

Yielding bass to 14 pounds, the Lagoon kicks out larger fish than the upper lake. March and April are the best time to fish here, because as May approaches the weeds

Castaic Lagoon

grow tall and thick and fishing becomes difficult. Although lunkers are caught on crawdads year-round, the best time to target big bass is after a trout plant when the bass move in towards the boat launch to feed on the helpless little rainbows. Try tossing large trout imitation plugs from shore or a boat.

Darin Phiffer and 12 inch rainbow trout taken from Castaic Lagoon.

Trout are also a big attraction at the Lagoon. The California Department of Fish and Game stocks 32,340 rainbow trout from eight to 14 inches from late October through April, keeping fishing fair throughout winter and spring. After stocks, the trout roam from the wheelchair accessible fishing pier to the spillway. Some anglers set up folding chairs from the boat launch to the fishing pier and toss out an inflated nightcrawler or Power Bait. Others sit on the rocks between the boat launch and spillway. A popular method is the use of Trout Teasers, but the fish have to be in close to shore for that to work.

If you have a boat with an electric trolling motor, you can troll the area near the boat docks and the middle of the lake with Needlefish and silver Kastmasters. No gas-powered boats are permitted. There is also no water-skiing on the lake. You say you've seen water-skiers on the lake? That's because Cal State Northridge has worked out a deal where the school can hold an aquatics course at the lake, however, no other skiing is allowed.

The most popular time to fish the Lagoon is at night. The 180-acre Lagoon is the only lake (besides Quail Lake) in Los Angeles County that allows night fishing. The most consistent bass night producer is a black plastic worm. Catfish fishing off the point near the campground produces fish up to 20 pounds each summer and fall.

The Lagoon has been in the takeover spotlight. In the latter-middle Nineties the owners of Santa Ana River Lakes tried to purchase the lake and turn it into a put-and-take fishery, but the plan never unfolded. It might have been a great thing. Although you would have had to pay to fish the lake, the lake operators would have stocked so many trout that the bass could have grown to enormous proportions again.

If you plan to make the trip, supplies are available in Castaic. There is a day-use and a boat launch fee.

Also nearby are Castaic Lake, Lake Hughes, Elizabeth Lake, Bouquet Canyon Creek, Lake Piru, Piru Creek, Pyramid Lake, Quail Lake and Magic Mountain.

CASTAIC LAGOON

CASTAIC **LAKE**

Although they aren't heavily fished, stripers are the lake's new trophy fish.

Rating: 8

Species: Rainbow Trout, Channel Catfish, Crappie, Bluegill, Largemouth Bass and Striped Bass

Stocked with 30,200 pounds of rainbow trout.

Facilities: Boat Launch, Boat Rentals, Picnic Areas, Restrooms, Bait & Tackle and Snack Bar

Need Information? Contact: Fishing Guide Erik Stepanek (661) 295-1565, Fishing Guide Bob Crupi (661) 424-9315, Castaic Lake Recreation Area (661) 257-4050, Castaic Lake Boat & Marine (661) 257-4140

Erik Stepanek and his father, Bill, caught these stripers at Castaic Lake.

Directions: From Los Angeles, drive north on Interstate 5 to Castaic. Exit Lake Hughes Road and turn east, continuing 2.5 miles to the lake on your left.

Castaic Lake was once known as the best largemouth bass lake in the world. This 2,200-acre lake, located in rolling hill country just north of Los Angeles, was recognized by nearly every bass angler in the country. They flocked to the lake in the early Nineties when Bob Crupi caught his 22-pound largemouth bass (only four ounces from the world record caught in Georgia in 1932). But things have changed at this popular lake.

Crupi, who still guides on the lake, openly admits that there are no longer giant bass here. The explanation simply has to do with competition for food and over-fishing. At the peak of the bass hype there began to be too many bass in the lake and they had to compete for the same food sources. So, less food equaled smaller fish. Also, a striper popula-

Castaic Lake

tion began to develop and the two predators had to compete for the same food, which meant even less food. The larger stripers have appeared to win the battle.

As for over-fishing, this lake has been picked over a million times. The fish have been to hell and back. They've seen every lure in creation and have had to deal with serious water fluctuation. Don't let me mislead you, however. There are still tons of large-mouth bass in the lake, but most are small, one to four pounds. A few anglers still catch largemouths to 14 pounds each year, but that's an embarrassment compared to the 10-15 pounders that were caught daily during the glory years.

When fishing for bass, make sure to use light line. These fish have smartened up over the years and anything over 12- pound test will spook them. The best place to catch bass is in Elizabeth Canyon Arm, on waterdogs in the winter, crawdads in fall and spring, plastics in early summer and shad from mid-summer till fall.

Although they aren't heavily fished, stripers are the lake's new trophy fish. The stripers came in through the Elderberry Forebay, which is fed by the California Aqueduct. The number of large stripers in the lake is staggering. Most of the fish you'll catch are between 15-24 pounds, with a new lake record 40-pounder caught in early 2000. For the last 15 years, stripers lived in the lake untouched as anglers tried to catch the much-hyped, world record bass. This allowed the stripers to multiply and get bigger. Since the late-Nineties, some anglers have started to wise up about fishing for stripers. Fishing guide Erik Stepanek is the most knowledgeable about the fish. He has been fishing for them since the mid-Nineties. With the exception of July and August when water-skiers take over the lake, the striper bite remains good year-round.

Fishing guide Erik Stepanek is Castaic's best striper fisherman.

In April, May and June, fishing near the inlet (forebay) until about 10 a.m. stays good. If they are pumping water into the lake, the bite can be excellent. Anchor some-where between the buoy line and the hills on the other side of the lake. Your best bet is to chum with anchovies to bring in the fish and then use sardines, mackerel or anchovies on light line, with a small split shot, fished right on the bottom. These fish are bottom

From left to right, Bill Stepanek,
Erik Stepanek and Ray Merrill
had a blast catching these
stripers at Castaic Lake.

feeders during the spring season. This same method also works at the other end of the lake, in the channel near the 5-mph buoys.

Although the number of huge stripers is beginning to decline because of over-fishing, there are always going to be huge ones in the lake due to the heavy trout plants. The stripers feed best when the water is clear, but this is rare because the water fluctuates so much. So much water is pumped in and out of the lake that it churns up the water and gives it a discolored look. When the water is being pumped in the lake, trolling the inlet area can be productive. You'll need either leadcore or downriggers to do it, because the stripers hang in 40-80 feet of water. Try using large Needlefish and Krocodiles.

From October to March, the stripers feed on trout plants. This is the time when the large fish are most vulnerable (they aren't as smart when they're chasing trout). The only way shore anglers can get into the striper action is by casting trout imitation plugs from the marina where the trout are stocked, or off the dam. Remember, using a live or dead real trout is illegal and the fine for doing so is hefty.

Catching trout is good for anglers tossing Power Bait, nightcrawler-marshmallow combos or spinners from the dam. The California Department of Fish and Game plants more than 55,000 rainbow trout from eight to 14 inches from October to May. Trollers also do well working the area between the dam and jet ski area.

Although not targeted, bluegill fishing is fair in the back of the coves during the summer using mealworms. Also during summer, catfish can be caught on mackerel in the back of coves, or in deep water all year.

If you plan to make the trip, there is a day-use and boat launch fee. Supplies are available in Castaic. Fishing Castaic is a waste on the weekends because there is too much boat traffic. So, try to plan your trip during the week.

Also nearby are Castaic Lagoon, Pyramid Lake, Bouquet Canyon Creek, Quail Lake, Elizabeth Lake, Lake Piru, Piru Creek and Magic Mountain.

PIRU **CREEK**

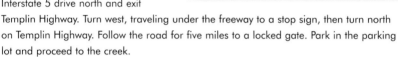

These wild trout love hellgrammites, black insects that look like "pincher bugs" and can be found under rocks along the streambed.

Rating: 6

Species: Rainbow Trout

Stocked with 2,700 pounds of rainbow trout.

Facilities: Restrooms

Need Information? Contact: Angeles National Forest (661) 296-9710

Directions: From Santa Clarita, on Interstate 5 drive north and exit

Piru Creek

Templin Highway. Turn west, traveling under the freeway to a stop sign, then turn north on Templin Highway. Follow the road for five miles to a locked gate. Park in the parking lot and proceed to the creek.

At night Piru Creek is crawling with skunks and crawdads. The skunks are everywhere, but the crawdads are a lot more fun. We often stumble down to the creek with flashlights and buckets to see how many we can catch. My friend, Stephen "Big Bird" Wiessner, holds that record with more than 100 in less than three hours. Surprisingly, the crawdads can exceed eight inches, so don't get your finger pinched if you try it. We always throw them back at the end of the night, but it gives us something to do when there aren't any good movies showing back in the San Fernando Valley.

Rattlesnakes, jiggers and unstable water levels have kept Piru Creek from being one of the most popular trout streams in Southern California. I've encountered a rattlesnake the last three times I've fished here. One was longer than three feet and the others were

The McCullough family enjoys an afternoon of fishing at Piru Creek.

babies coiled up under logs by the stream. None gave me any warning, so I consider myself lucky to not have been bitten.

Piru creek is also known for its jiggers. These small, black flies that thrive on warm weather attack your skin like mosquitoes. There is really no way to keep them from biting unless you cover your hands, neck, face and arms completely with clothing, an almost unbearable task during the warm weather months.

PIRU CREEK

The El Nino rainy season created much havoc on Piru Creek in 1998. With water levels at flood stages, most of the pools were washed away and the river's course was altered. I fished here just after the El Nino season and saw some stripers swimming in the stream that had been washed out of Pyramid Lake. However, the water level has been suitable for trout over the past few years, even though levels continue to fluctuate depending on water releases from Pyramid Lake.

Aside from annoying bugs, dangerous snakes and fluctuating water levels, Piru Creek is one of the best wild trout streams in Southern California, if you're willing to do a little work to land them. Work that involves some difficult hiking! Much of the trail is completely overgrown and some areas require wading to continue downstream.

From the lower section of Frenchman's Flat downstream to Piru Lake, and from the special regulations section upstream from Frenchman's Flat to Pyramid Lake, the fishing is incredible. In these parts of the stream most of the trout are wild, ranging anywhere from six to 18 inches. These wild trout love hellgrammites, black insects that look like

Piru Creek flows out of Pyramid Lake and into Lake Piru.

"pincher bugs" that can be found under rocks along the streambed. Fly fishermen are also successful in these parts of the stream and make up the majority of anglers who fish here.

In addition to the wild trout fishermen, this creek gets a lot of pressure from anglers fishing for stockers. Fishing for the planted fish doesn't require any hiking. When water flows are sufficient and not too warm for stocked trout, the California Department of Fish and Game scatters more than 7,660 trout west of the parking lot for about a mile upstream. If you can't make it the week of the stock, don't bother fishing for the planters. They will be gone. I've fished on a Saturday after a Wednesday stock and all but a few fish had been caught.

In an effort to protect the Southwestern Arroyo Toad, Piru Creek is not stocked during the summer months. Remember, you need a fishing license to catch crawdads.

If you plan to make the trip, supplies are available in Castaic. A Forest Service Adventure Pass is required to park in the Angeles National Forest.

Also nearby are Pyramid Lake, Castaic Lake and Castaic Lagoon.

PYRAMID **LAKE**

The thing I enjoy about using shad is you have a shot at catching large and smallmouth bass, stripers, crappie, trout and catfish with every

Rating: 7

Species: Rainbow Trout, Channel Catfish, Bluegill, Crappie, Largemouth Bass, Smallmouth Bass, Crappie and Carp

Stocked with 20,000 pounds of rainbow trout.

Facilities: Picnic Areas, Snack Bar, Bait & Tackle, Boat Rentals, Boat Launch, Swimming Areas and Restrooms

Keenan Scalercio and a three-pound rainbow.

Need Information? Contact: Fishing Guide Erik Stepanek (661) 295-1565, Pyramid Lake Marina (661) 257-2892, Pyramid Lake (661) 295-1245

Directions: From Los Angeles, drive north on Interstate 5 past Castaic to Smokey Bear Road. Exit west driving under the freeway. Make a left at the stop sign and continue 1.7 miles to the lake.

Got Shad? If you do, fishing Pyramid Lake is a blast. If you don't, it can be a nightmare. Shad are abundant in the lake and can be caught from July through November, but many anglers who have trouble netting them wind-up with an unhappy fishing experience.

Pyramid Lake

Without shad, the lake's largemouth, smallmouth and striped bass can be difficult to catch. In the spring, anglers who can't get shad try using mudsuckers and crankbaits for large and smallmouth bass, and sometimes find success fishing for stripers with anchovies on the bottom of sandy beaches and off points. However, without the shad, catch rates are greatly reduced. The thing I enjoy about using shad is you have a shot at catching large and smallmouth bass, stripers, crappie, trout and catfish with every cast.

Visions of Pyramid's giant stripers that were caught after trout plants are still fresh in anglers' minds, however, things here have changed drastically. No longer are those thirty to forty pound stripers caught on a regular basis. That was the story in the Eighties, but many of those large stripers were caught and put on the dinner table.

Also, in the mid-Nineties, tons of small stripers entered the lake through the aqueduct, competing for the same food source with maturing fish. Even more detrimental was the introduction of smallmouth bass taken from San Gabriel Reservoir in the late Eighties. Then, stripers were forced to compete for food amongst themselves, as well as with the new influx of smallmouths and existing largemouth bass. It all equaled smaller fish, but what hurt the stripers most was the California Department of Fish and Game's decision to halt trout plants in 1993. The stripers relied on the rainbows for much of their diet. Because of all of these factors, today a striper in the low twenties would be considered large.

Fishing Guide Erik Stepanek catches stripers, like this 23 pounder, regularly at Pyramid Lake.

Don't get me wrong, Pyramid is still loaded with stripers, just not the 30-40-pounders that were caught in the Eighties. With a stable smallmouth and largemouth population in the lake, it's questionable whether the stripers will ever return to giant proportions. However, because trout plants were reinstated in 2000, we can still hope.

After seven years of no trout plants, a group of bass anglers sued the Department of Water Resources because of an agreement dating back to the lake's inception in the 1940's. Part of that agreement stated that the operators of the dam would provide a trout fishery for its anglers. The California Department of Fish and Game chose to stop planting the lake because the stripers ate most of the trout before anglers had any shot at catching them. In other words, the trout were basically chumming for striper fishermen.

This pond, located below Pyramid Dam is closed to fishing.

The best bite on stripers is found from September through November, with the most consistent action occurring on live shad off points and in coves. Using light line, six to eight pound test, is best because anything heavier will spook the fish. Also, in July and August, tossing lures into striper boils is effective. At times the striper bite can be hot near the marina. These fish, averaging three-to-five pounds, only move into this area to feed on stocked trout and shad. If there has been a recent trout plant, try tossing from the shore or trolling large trout imitation lures.

Presently, 20,000 rainbows are planted each year, 4,000 more than the previous allotment. They are raised and stocked by the CA DFG, however, they are paid for by the Department of Water Resources. Catch rates for rainbows have improved, with anglers doing well fishing Power Bait and tossing spinners near the marina. As the water warms in the spring and throughout fall, you need leadcore line or downriggers to catch the trout. The 1,360-acre lake can be as deep as 280 feet at full pool and the trout go deep to survive the blazing hot temperatures. There is also a good catfish bite in June for those fishing mackerel in Lost Mine Cove.

For a lake so closely situated to Los Angeles, Pyramid displays some unique wildlife. Deer can be seen roaming the shorelines and sometimes swimming across the lake's main channel out to Chumash Island. What really catches anglers' eyes are the bears. They can be seen in the early morning and late evening near Yellowbar and Bear Trap. If you're lucky, you'll get to see a bear reach out its paw into a striper boil trying to catch a quick snack. My buddy Erik Stepanek, who guides on the lake, said he sees it happen about once a year.

An interesting side note is that the Old Highway 99 which commuters once used to get to the LA Basin ran through Pyramid. When Interstate 5 was built to replace Highway 99, a dam was built and Highway 99 disappeared under the water. There are still remnants of that road near the marina where an old bridge is buried under 40 feet of water. It's a good cat fishing spot.

Stay away from Pyramid on the weekends and during the summer months. The lake is a traffic jam, with boaters, water-skiers, jet skiers and wake-boarders all battling for space. There's no room for fishermen.

If you plan to make the trip, supplies are available in Castaic. Pyramid is open for day-use only. There is a day-use and boat launch fee.

Also nearby are Lake Piru, Castaic Lake, Castaic Lagoon, Piru Creek, Quail Lake, Tejon Ranch and Tait Trout Farms.

QUAIL **LAKE**

Although it's a good 20-minute walk from the parking lot to the inflow (you can see it because it's the only lighted area), fishing is best there at night when water is being pumped into the lake.

Rating: 7

Species: Largemouth Bass, Channel Catfish, Striped Bass, Crappie, Carp and Bluegill

Stocks: None

Facilities: Vault Toilets

Need Information?
Contact: Department of Water Resources (661) 257-3610

Quail Lake

Directions: From Los Angeles, drive north on Interstate 5 past Pyramid Lake to Highway 138. Turn east and continue to the lake on your left.

Quail Lake may be Southern California's last secret water hole, at least until you read this. Off Interstate 5 near Gorman, Quail Lake, which is open 24 hours-a-day, 365 days-a-year to walk-in fishing, is located between the California Poppy Reserve in the Antelope Valley and Pyramid Lake. Used as a holding facility by the Department of Water Resources, water is taken from an aqueduct near Bakersfield and pumped over the Tehachapi Mountains into little Quail Lake at night, when electricity is cheaper. Then, to generate power, the water is released to Pyramid Lake during the day.

Quail Lake is referred to as a power pool, but it's heaven for fishermen. That's because it's loaded with stripers, largemouth bass, catfish, bluegill and crappie, all of which get pushed in from the aqueduct. The lake's extreme fluctuation doesn't seem to bother the fish, either. Those who know what they're doing always catch fish here. And there aren't that many "know how's," because this lake is rarely fished.

I'm guessing the reason people don't come here very much is not just because it's not known. A couple of reasons might be that it's out in the desert, hot and dry with no shade, and the wind always seems to be blowing. There are also no services or facilities nearby and it's a 45-minute drive from the San Fernando Valley. However, those who do come here are not often disappointed by the fishing.

The lake has a large striper and catfish population, and regularly yields big fish. Although it's a good 20-minute walk from the parking lot to the inflow (you can see it because it's the only lighted area), fishing is best there at night when water is being pumped into the lake. That's because the fish congregate in this area and wait for food to be pushed into the lake.

If you use a heavy weight and fish off the bottom, chances are you'll get snagged. There are a lot of rocks down there. Your best bet is to fish nightcrawlers, mackerel or anchovies, anywhere from 18-36 inches below a bobber, and throw it is far as you can towards the middle of the lake or just outside of the current. For the bigger stripers, try tossing trout and shad imitation lures. Stripers over 25 pounds are commonly caught and catfish up to 35 have been recorded. In the evenings and early mornings, there is a good bite on shad, but they can be hard to catch so most people don't bother with them. For anglers less inclined to walk over to the inlet, set up a folding chair anywhere along the shore and toss out some bait. Many anglers have luck with the smaller fish this way.

Stories of giant catfish and stripers come from the lake's outlet pool on the other side of Highway 138, but this area is now off-limits to fishing. The regulations were not created by the California Department of Fish and Game, but by DWR for your protection. At least five people have drowned there. The current is so swift, even professional swimmers can't handle it. All the casualties have been accidental, with people slipping into the water or falling in while trying to net their fish. It's not worth taking the chance. DWR officials tell me if you fall in, expect to be underwater for at least three minutes because of the fierce underwater current. Don't end up another statistic; stay away and stay alive. There are plenty of fish to be caught in other parts of the lake.

There is also a small pond located next to Quail Lake. The pond, known as Kinsey Pond, was named after the man who used to own the white mansion on the south side of Highway 138. It was used for fishing and waterfowl hunting and holds the same species of fish as Quail Lake.

The Pyramid Lake concessionaire considered opening up a small marina with facilities on Quail Lake, but abandoned the idea after discovering how little the lake was used. DWR and the Department of Boating and Waterways have discussed putting a boat launch in to provide for better recreational opportunities, but it's still in the idea stage. Owners of Santa Ana River Lakes also expressed interest in opening a concessionaire here, but for now it's all just speculation.

If you plan to make the trip, supplies are available in Castaic. There are no supplies at the lake. If night fishing, bring your own lanterns and flashlights. There are no lights around the lake, except for the one at the inlet tower. No watercraft is allowed on the lake.

Also nearby are the Antelope Valley Poppy Reserve, Pyramid Lake, Castaic Lake, Castaic Lagoon and Piru Creek.

Quail Lake is used as a holding facility for water headed to Pyramid Lake.

LAKE **HUGHES**

There is still a sprinkle of catfish, bass and bluegill left, but nothing trophy size, and you'll probably have to battle the winds to have any chance at catching them.

Rating: 2

Species: Largemouth Bass, Bluegill, Crappie and Catfish

Stocks: None

Facilities: Picnic Areas, Restrooms, RV Hookups, Boat Launch, Snack Bar, Playground and General Store

Lake Hughes

Need Information? Contact: Angeles National Forest (661) 296-9710, Hughes Lakeshore Park (661) 724-1845

Directions: From Interstate 5 in Castaic, exit Lake Hughes Road and turn east, continuing 20 miles (past Castaic Lagoon and Lake) to County Road N2. Turn right and drive approximately one mile to the lake on the right.

Heading down the Grapevine towards Los Angeles, on your way into Castaic you'll see Lake Hughes Road. Now, many fishermen wonder if there is a Lake Hughes and more importantly if there are any fish in it. The good news is, yes, there is a Lake Hughes and there are fish in it. The bad news is, the fishing is poor.

The California Department of Fish and Game had plans to plant rainbow trout here. However, because local residents were unwilling to share shoreline access with the public at large, the CA DFG was forced to abandon their efforts to stock the lake. (Since the CA DFG is funded by public tax dollars, it is prohibited from stocking fish into lakes with access controlled by private residents.) The lake's fish populations have suffered. For now, the only way for non-residents to fish the lake is to pay a fee and enter through Hughes Lakeshore Park.

There is still a sprinkle of catfish, bass and bluegill left, but nothing trophy size, and you'll probably have to battle the winds to have any chance at catching them. My advice is to skip Lake Hughes and scoot over to Elizabeth Lake where access is free and trout are planted.

Hughes Lakeshore Park

If you plan to make the trip, supplies are available at the lake. There is a day-use fee for public access through Hughes Lakeshore Park.

Also nearby are Elizabeth Lake, Pyramid Lake, Quail Lake and Castiac Lake.

ELIZABETH **LAKE**

Elizabeth Lake provides decent trout fishing in the winter and spring, as well as bass and catfish fishing throughout the summer and fall.

Rating: 6

Species: Largemouth Bass, Channel Catfish, Rainbow Trout, and Bluegill

Stocked with 11,400 pounds of rainbow trout.

Need Information? Contact: Angeles National Forest (661) 296-9710

Elizabeth Lake

Facilities: Boat Launch, Restrooms and a Picnic Area

Directions: From Interstate 5 in Castaic, exit Lake Hughes Road and turn east. Follow the road through the canyon to Elizabeth Lake Road. Turn east and continue approximately three miles to lake.

When the wind is not blowing, Elizabeth Lake is a wonderful place to be. But if there is any wind, stay home because it will shut off the bite. Elizabeth Lake is a small, 90-acre lake nestled in at 3,550 feet in the Angeles National Forest near Gorman. It provides decent trout fishing in the winter and spring months, as well as bass and catfish fishing throughout the summer and fall.

Elizabeth is a natural lake fed by runoff and ground water. An added treat can be snow that sticks to the ground a few times a year, but doesn't last for long. Trout are planted by the California Department of Fish and Game from late fall through spring. Most of the 21,140 trout planted are in the 10 to 12-inch range, with the occasional fish to 15 inches.

Many anglers score limits for about a week after a stock, but fishing can be difficult if you wait longer because a lot of the fish get caught. The best baits are assorted colors of Power Bait fished right near the parking lot. The lake also produces a fair amount of bass, but most are small. In addition to the usual trout plants, 25,200 sub-catchable rainbow trout are planted annually. Best spots to fish are along the sandy beach and to the east of the boat ramp where the fish are stocked. Catch rates can be greatly reduced in the late spring and early summer due to high winds.

One of the lake's downfalls is access. With trees covering 80 percent of the shoreline, good spots are hard to find. Another problem is that almost half the shoreline has been taken over by private homes. If you have a boat you can fish these residential waters as long as you don't anchor on shore. If it's crowded, good luck finding a decent spot to fish. Most of them are taken by 8 a.m.

If you plan to make the trip, a Forest Service Adventure Pass is required to park at the lake. Supplies are available in Lake Hughes.

Also nearby are a 18-hole golf course, Lake Hughes, Pyramid Lake, Quail Lake and Castaic Lake.

TEJON RANCH **LAKES**

Tejon Ranch is an exclusive facility used by members as well as day-use anglers... you can purchase a day permit for $100, at least six times more than other private fisheries in the region.

Rating: 7

Species: Largemouth Bass, Bluegill and Crappie

Stocks: None

Facilities: Boat Launch, Boat Rentals and Restrooms

Need Information? Contact: Tejon Ranch (661) 248-3000

Directions: From Los Angeles, drive north on Interstate 5 over the Tejon Pass to the Fort Tejon exit. Turn right to the ranch.

Castac Lake

For more than 150 years, Tejon Ranch, located off Interstate 5 near Frazier Park, has provided a variety of services to the surrounding community. The ranch has been famous for wild boar, Rocky Mountain elk, turkey, bear and mule deer hunting, but recently they've decided to try something new by opening the ranch to fishing, and they've been successful.

The 272,000-acre ranch, which has been in existence since 1843, covers 425 miles, extending from the San Joaquin Valley to the Antelope Valley and into parts of Lebec and areas north of Castaic. Catch & release only fishing is the newest of the ranch's nine separate operating divisions, which also include: real estate, horse breeding and training, livestock, filming, hunting and game management, oil and minerals, farming, as well as a cement plant.

Although the land has many uses, the wildlife management sector might not be for you unless you have lots of money to dish out to partake in their fishing and hunting programs. Tejon Ranch is an exclusive facility used by members as well as day-use anglers. To become a member it will cost you $1,000 a season, which usually lasts about eight months. Or, you can purchase a day permit for $100, at least six times more than Santa Ana River Lakes, Laguna Niguel Lake and other private fisheries in the region.

Tejon Ranch wants to give its visitors a low-key, high-quality experience, and to management that means keeping away the masses. If you haven't yet gotten the picture, Tejon Ranch is mostly used by lawyers, doctors and other high-class professionals from the Los Angeles area who are willing to pay the high price tag to use its facilities.

The ranch has three major lakes and many smaller ponds to fish. The main 350-acre lake, open to members only, is called Castac Lake on most maps and can be seen on the east side of Interstate 5, just north of Frazier Park. In the past the ranch has had difficulty keeping Castac Lake from drying up during drought periods, but recently they have committed themselves to a plan that will keep the lake full and sustain its fish population.

Although the lake was planted in 1991 with Florida Strain largemouth bass, bluegill and crappie, it has had its problems becoming the quality fishery it is today. In the late Nineties, the wildlife management unit had to contend with a stunted bass population because there were too many bass in the lake and not enough food for them. The ranch made a deal with the California Department of the Fish and Game, exchanging 125 bass from Castac Lake (which were transferred to Belvedere Park Lake) for shad. This exchange resulted in more forage for the bass. The ranch then purchased additional crawdads and small bluegill for the bass to feed on.

Castac Lake as seen driving north on Interstate 5.

The bass population has responded well to both measures. Anglers commonly report 20 to 50 fish days with most weighing two to four pounds. However, bass up to 11 pounds have been checked in. A new proposal to begin stocking trout has been under consideration. However, the lake is only about 25 feet deep and a concern about die-offs has prompted officials to think this project through carefully.

If you plan to make the trip, supplies are available in Frazier Park. Day-use fishing is by reservation only.

Also nearby are Frazier Pound, Tait Trout Farms, Quail Lake and Pyramid Lake.

TEJON RANCH LAKES

TAIT RANCH TROUT **PONDS**

Although the majority of Southland anglers have never heard of Tait Ranch Trout Ponds, it has already been featured in Sunset Magazine and on ESPN Outdoors.

Rating: 7

Species: Rainbow Trout, Brown Trout and Brook Trout

Stocked periodically by private vendors.

Facilities: Cabin Rentals, Restrooms, Picnic Areas and Campgrounds

Tait Trout Ponds

Need Information?
Contact: Tait Ranch (661) 245-6315, Frazier Ski & Sport (661) 245-3438

Directions: From Los Angeles, drive north on Interstate 5 over the Tejon Pass to the Frazier Park exit. Turn left on Frazier Mountain Road and continue for approximately two miles to a sign on your left for the trout ponds. Turn left and drive to the ponds.

Picture this: you, your fly-rod and a fishing guide quietly casting into a small spring fed pond. With every cast you have a chance of catching rainbow trout to seven pounds, brown trout to six and brook trout to three pounds. I must be talking about fishing in Canada or Alaska, right? Not even close. Try Frazier Park. You've heard of it, that small town between Gorman and Lebec, just off Interstate 5. Most people consider Frazier Park a trucker's stop, but Tait Ranch Trout Farms, which recently opened in the summer of 1998, is making Frazier Park known to fishermen.

Tait Ranch Trout Ponds are located on the 400-acre Tait Ranch, about an hour's drive from Los Angeles or a half-hour from downtown Bakersfield. Although the majority of Southland anglers have never heard of Tait Ranch Trout Ponds, it has already been featured in Sunset Magazine and on ESPN Outdoors as a place where you can go catch-and-release fishing for trophy size fish. The

Tait Trout Ponds

Ranch tries to limit fishing to fly-fishermen, but also allows fishing with lures if you use single, barbless hooks. No live bait is allowed.

There are currently five ponds on the ranch, with the largest being 2.5 acres, but a sixth pond is in the works. Float tubing is allowed in the trophy trout pond. The ranch hopes to have a 40-acre bass, bluegill, crappie and catfish pond filled and opened in the near future. Because they pump cool water out of underground springs to fill their ponds, the trout farm is able to remain open daily, year-round, even when air temperatures simmer at over 100.

Clay Worrell caught this two-pound brook trout on a fly.

Rates are charged differently than all other private ponds in the region. Tait Ranch charges by the hour. It's $12 per hour, per person, $45 for a half-day and $80 for the full day. Reservations must be made in advance. No walk-in fishing is allowed. The ranch can also be rented out for parties, used as a picnic area or campground, and there are cabins for rent, but no food and supplies are offered.

If you plan to make the trip, supplies are available in Frazier Park. Fly-fishing courses are also available.

Also nearby are Frazier Pond, Quail Lake and Pyramid Lake.

TAIT RANCH TROUT **PONDS**

Brian Tait and a two-pound rainbow trout.

FRAZIER **POND**

It's so small you can cast your bait across the entire pond with a Snoopy pole. However, the California Department of Fish and Game provides a reason for the locals to fish the pond, stocking 3,000 rainbow trout.

Rating: 5

Species: Rainbow Trout, Channel Catfish, Bluegill, Largemouth Bass and Carp

Stocked with 1,000 pounds of rainbow trout.

Facilities: Picnic Areas, Restrooms, Playgrounds and Baseball Diamonds

Frazier Pond

Need Information?

Contact: Frazier Ski & Pack (661) 245-3438

Directions: From Los Angeles, drive north on Interstate 5 over the Tejon Pass to the Frazier Park exit. Turn left on Frazier Mountain Road and continue for approximately three miles to Monterey Street. Turn left and make a quick right on Park Street, then another right into the county park.

Some Southern California residents have heard of Frazier Park because they see it on the news when the Southland gets snowfall. Less than an hour drive from Los Angeles, it's a great place to bring kids to play in the snow.

Frazier Park's fishing gets much less hype than its snow play area. Operated by Kern County Parks, almost nobody comes from out of town to fish Frazier Pond. It is smaller than one-fourth the size of Arrowbear Lake in the San Bernardino National Forest and Jackson Lake in the Angeles National Forest. It's so small you can cast your bait across the entire pond with a Snoopy pole.

However, the California Department of Fish and Game provides a reason for the locals to fish the pond, stocking 3,000 rainbow trout from eight to 10 inches during the winter and early spring. The fastest way to leave with an easy limit is by using Power Bait and Panther Martins. The middle of the lake is thick with tules, but they do serve a purpose, giving cover to the lake's small bass population. The park's groundskeeper told me he's only seen one bluegill caught in the last 10 years. It was such a big thing it made the local paper. Once summer comes, trout plants cease and the local kids come to try to nab one of the pond's hefty carp from its small carp population.

When the CA DFG publishes their stocking list, they list it as Cuddy Creek Pond. Don't call it that in Frazier Park. People won't know what you're talking about. When I went to the local tackle shop and asked where Cuddy Creek Pond was, they looked at me like I was from another planet.

If you plan to make the trip, supplies are available in Frazier Park.

Also nearby are Quail Lake, Tait Trout Ponds and Pyramid Lake.

INDIAN HILL **RANCH**

You can camp on or near the three smaller ponds, so it's easy to throw out a line with a nightcrawler or chicken liver while cooking dinner and come back later to find a small catfish on the line.

Rating: 5

Species: Largemouth Bass, Bluegill, and Channel Catfish

Stocked periodically by private vendors.

Facilities: Bait & Tackle Shop, Showers, General Store, Campgrounds, RV Park and Picnic Areas

Need Information? Contact: Indian Hill Ranch (661) 822-6613

Scott Wiessner caught this bullhead on a night-crawler from one of Indian Hill's smaller ponds.

Directions: From Palmdale, drive north on Highway 14 to Mojave. In Mojave exit Highway 58 and drive west past Tehachapi. Exit Highway 202 and drive west for 3.5 miles to Banducci Road. Turn west on Banducci Road and drive approximately one mile to the sign for Indian Hill Ranch.

Talk about a secret spot, Indian Hill Ranch, nestled in the hills above Tehachapi, is known almost exclusively by the locals. You ask why it's such a secret? Easy, the owners don't have the money to advertise, nor do they receive plants from the California Department of Fish and Game, so most anglers don't know the place exists.

Ship to Shore, a private vendor, stocks the five small ponds throughout the year with bass, channel catfish and bluegill. Although fishing pressure is generally light, the action is hot in spring and early summer when the bass move into the shallows to spawn. Stay away from the three small ponds and concentrate your efforts on the two larger ponds. Most of the bass are small, anywhere from a half pound to two pounds, but there are some good size fish caught regularly.

No special techniques are needed. Just keep it simple by using nightcrawlers, craw-dads and waterdogs. The bluegill bite is excellent with crappie nibbles scoring you as many fish as you desire. In the early morning and late evening, the catfish bite turns on, but most of the fish are small (one to two pounds). Another plus is you can camp near the three smaller ponds, so it's easy to throw out a line with a nightcrawler or chicken liver while cooking dinner and come back later to find a small catfish on the line. Prior to the year 2000, no fishing license was needed to fish here, but the ranch didn't have the proper permits to be run as a private fishery, so licenses are now required.

If you plan to make the trip, supplies are available at the lake. Check weather conditions ahead of time. The wind can howl here. A fishing fee is charged. At times the lakes are closed to fishing. Call ahead for updates.

Also nearby are Brite Valley Reservoir and the windmill country.

BRITE VALLEY **RESERVOIR**

When water levels are sufficient, the California Department of Fish and Game promptly responds with 19,400 rainbow trout from eight to 11 inches. Catch rates usually remain fair for weeks after a stock.

Rating: 5

Species: Rainbow Trout, Channel Catfish, Largemouth, and Bluegill

Stocked with 10,000 pounds of rainbow trout.

Facilities: Picnic Areas, Campsites, and Boat Launch

Need Information? Contact: Brite Valley Recreation Area (661) 822-3228

Directions: From the 14 Freeway in Palmdale, drive north to Highway 58 in Mojave. From Mojave drive west on Highway 58 for 16 miles and exit Correctional Institution Road. Turn left to Tucker Road. Turn south on Tucker Road and continue to Highway 202. Turn west and drive 3.5 miles to Banducci Road. Turn right at the junction with Highline Road and drive 1.5 miles to the lake.

Located in the Tehachapi Mountains, Brite Valley Reservoir is right smack in the middle of windmill country, but if you get your line wet when the winds aren't howling you should have success. Brite Valley Reservoir sounds like a great and colorful place, but inconsistent water levels keep it from being attractive on a consistent basis and hurt the fishing. This small, 68-acre reservoir located at 4,100 feet in southern Kern County, a few miles from Tehachapi, suffers from extreme water fluctuation, keeping it from developing into a quality fishery.

When water levels are sufficient, the California Department of Fish and Game promptly responds with 19,400 rainbow trout from eight to 11 inches. Catch rates usually remain fair for weeks after a stock. With no gasoline outboard motors allowed, the lake tends to stay quiet. The big problem here is the wind. It almost always blows. The lake's backdrop is complete with rolling hills and grasses that are found along the shoreline.

There are a sprinkle of bluegill and bass in the lake, however, your best bets are catfish. The bottom of the lake is muddy and sandy, and catfish love to play around in it. However, catching them is going to take time. So, throw out some chicken liver, lie down on a blanket, crack open a beer and watch the wind blow the trees around. Chances are you'll hook up, but don't expect any lunkers, the cats that are caught are usually small.

If you plan to make the trip, supplies are available in Tehachapi. Brite Valley Reservoir is closed to fishing from November 1 to the last Saturday in April.

Also nearby is Indian Hill Ranch.

BRITE VALLEY **RESERVOIR**

REGION 5

Antelope Valley/Leeward Side of the San Gabriel

Apollo Park Lake
Aqueduct
Little Rock Reservoir
Little Rock Creek
Big Rock Creek
Jackson Lake
Hesperia Lake
Mojave Narrows Park Lake
Jess Ranch Lakes

APOLLO PARK **LAKES**

Lake Aldrin, Lake Armstrong and Lake Collins are all named after one of the astronauts from the 1969 Apollo 11 Mission, the first manned space mission to land on the moon.

Rating: 5

Species: Rainbow Trout, Channel Catfish

Stocked with 32,500 pounds of rainbow trout and 6,000 pounds of catfish by private vendors.

Facilities: Picnic Areas, Playgrounds and Restrooms

Need Information?
Contact: Apollo County Park
(661) 940-7701

The evening hours are the best time to target catfish at Apollo Park Lake.

Directions: From Lancaster, drive north on the 14 Freeway and exit Avenue H. Turn west and drive 2.5 miles to 50th Street West. Turn right and continue 1.1 miles to the park.

Apollo Park Lake, a grassy park in the heart of the desert, is located next to Fox Airport in Lancaster. It's actually three lakes – 26 acres total– all connected by small bridges, providing residents of the Antelope Valley with a decent fishery. Lake Aldrin, Lake Armstrong and Lake Collins are all named after one of the astronauts from the 1969 Apollo 11 Mission, the first manned space mission to land on the moon.

The park is most popular for its annual fishing derbies. Three derbies are held each year when an additional 5,000 pounds of rainbows are trucked in to keep catch rates high. Adult derbies take place the first Saturday of November and March, and a kid's derby is held on the first Saturday in May.

Each month from November to May, the lake is stocked with 3,000 pounds of Idaho rainbow trout, keeping the trout bite fair before the water warms and the trout die off in mid-May. After early April when the lake begins to get mossy, floating baits are your only chance to catch fish. Power Bait and cheeses give anglers the best prospects for catching fish once the weed growth begins. With temperatures well over 100 on a daily basis, catfish are the only fish you'll be able to catch during the summer.

The lake is open from 6 a.m.-10 p.m. daily, but your best bet is to arrive early in the morning or late in the evening, otherwise the fishing will be horrible due to the unbearable heat.

If you plan to make the trip, supplies are available in Lancaster.

Also nearby are Quail Lake, Elizabeth Lake and the California Poppy Reserve.

APOLLO PARK LAKES

CALIFORNIA **AQUEDUCT**

Bring along a few lanterns, a cooler full of drinks, dinner, and a radio; toss out a line and wait.

Rating: 3

Species: Largemouth Bass, Carp, Channel Catfish and Striped Bass

Stocks: None

Need Information? Contact: California Department of Water Resources, Southern Field Division (661) 257-3610

Directions: From the junction of the 14 Freeway and Highway 138 in Palmdale, drive east on Highway 138. Continue to the town of Little Rock and turn south on 77th Street East. Continue to the Aqueduct.

Fishing is best in the summer months at the Aqueduct.

There are more than 400 miles of open canals, most of which are open to fishing, that are part of the California Aqueduct. Sounds like heaven for anglers, right? Things aren't always as great as they sound. While there are hundreds of thousands of fish in the Aqueduct, they aren't that easy to catch.

Think about it for a second. The Aqueduct is up to 200 feet wide, with a maximum depth of 33 feet, and has a swift current, which means the fish don't stay in one place. So, you have to cast your line and hope a hungry fish is swimming by, exactly at the place where your bait lands.

The odds are slim, yet many anglers do well fishing the Aqueduct. The key is patience. It can take a lot of time to catch a fish, but there are lunkers to be caught.

WALK-IN FISHING ONLY NO BICYCLES NO VEHICLES

Stripers, largemouth bass, channel catfish and carp inhabit these waters and are commonly caught from May through October when the water warms.

Drawing water from the Delta, the Aqueduct begins at Banks Pumping Plant and travels roughly a mile and a half to Bethany Reservoir. Here, some water is diverted to the South Bay Aqueduct. The rest is gravity fed south 63 miles to O'Neill Forebay. From O'Neill, gravity takes the water 87 miles south to Kettleman City, where some water is diverted to the Coastal Branch Aqueduct. The Aqueduct continues south to the Buena Vista Pumping Plant. From Buena Vista, the water is pumped over the Tehachapi Mountains and released into the Tehachapi Afterbay. At this point, the Aqueduct breaks into two branches, the West and East. The West Branch descends to Quail Lake and the East into the Antelope Valley, which brings us to this fishing site, at 77th Street East in Little Rock.

There are four other fishing sites along the Aqueduct in the Antelope Valley: Munz Ranch Road Site, 70th Street West Site, Avenue S Site and Longview Road Site. Located on dry, arid dirt lands with no vegetation, they all look alike and get blazing hot in the summer. In the evening, when the fishing is best, the winds can howl, too.

A section of the Aqueduct in the Antelope Valley, near Little Rock.

While some anglers fish all day, night fishing is the most popular method. Bring along a few lanterns, a cooler full of drinks, dinner, and a radio; toss out a line and wait. It's the only way to go. Use anything stinky, like mackerel, anchovies, chicken and beef liver, nightcrawlers and sardines, and also use heavy line. Chances are you are going to have to battle the fish as well as the current. I've fished here through the twilight hours three nights in a row and didn't get a single bite. Other nights, they've come every half-hour. You really have to get lucky to catch a lot of fish here.

If you plan to make the trip, supplies are available in Little Rock. Swimming is not permitted in the Aqueduct. Stay out and stay alive.

Also nearby are Little Rock Reservoir and Big Rock Creek.

CALIFORNIA AQUEDUCT

LITTLE ROCK **RESERVOIR**

*If I were you, I'd plan to arrive between January and June when snow
runoff is at its peak and Little Rock Creek is flowing fast. Then,
the reservoir is high and the lake can be stunning.*

Rating: 6

Species: Rainbow Trout,
Largemouth Bass and Bluegill

Stocked with 7,000 pounds of rainbow trout.

Facilities: Picnic Areas, Boat
Launch, General Store, Restrooms,
Row Boat Rentals and Campgrounds

Depending on the time of year Little Rock Reservoir can be full or a mud puddle, as seen here in October.

Need Information? Contact: Little Rock Lake Resort (661) 533-1923

Directions: From the 14 Freeway in Palmdale, exit Pearblossom Highway (138) and continue
6.5 miles to the town of Little Rock. Turn south on Cheseboro Road and continue to the lake.

Depending on the time of year, Littlerock Reservoir can leave two completely different
impressions on visitors. Because the reservoir is used as a flood control basin
for the leeward side of the San Gabriel Mountains, it sometimes experiences extreme
drawdowns and can look either like a dried out wash or a beautiful mountain lake. If I
were you, I'd plan to arrive between January and June when snow runoff is at its peak
and Little Rock Creek is flowing fast. Then, the reservoir is high and the lake can be
stunning. If you come any other time of the year, all you'll see is a mud puddle, some
tumbleweeds and a lot of dust. Not a good experience, to say the least.

Set at 3,200 feet in the foothills above the town of Littlerock, the 100-acre lake
(when full) provides a decent fishery for stocked trout. It receives more than 21,500
rainbow trout from the California Department of Fish and Game, ranging from seven to
12 inches. There's not much fishing pressure on the lake and many anglers limit fairly
quickly. The key is in knowing where to fish.

Because it is very steep and difficult to fish, shore anglers have written off the east
side of the lake, but it can be productive with a boat. Most anglers fish near the launch
ramp or by the dam. Locals who fish the lake weekly swear by Power Bait, but for a few
days after a stock tossing lures will catch you fish, too.

Lake operators will tell you there is a good population of bluegill, bass and catfish in
the lake, but I'd be more likely to believe it if the drawdowns weren't so severe. Most
years, Little Rock Reservoir receives a bonus plant of 25,200 fingerlings in November.
The CA DFG hopes to grow these into catchable size before the lake is sucked dry.

If you plan to make the trip, there is day-use fee. Call ahead to check water
conditions. Only electric trolling motors are permitted.

Also nearby are the California Aqueduct, Big Rock Creek, Little Rock Creek
and Jackson Lake.

LITTLE ROCK **CREEK**

Three thousand acres in all have been closed, and the California Department of Fish and Game has suspended trout stocks.

Rating: N/A

Species: Rainbow Trout

Stocked: Stocks have been suspended.

Facilities: Campgrounds

Need Information? Contact: Angeles National Forest (661) 944-2187

Little Rock Creek was closed to fishing in 1997.

Directions: From Los Angeles, drive north on Interstate 5 to Highway 15 east. Exit Highway 138 in Palmdale and drive 6.5 miles east to Cheseboro Road. Turn south and continue six miles (just past the reservoir) to where the road parallels the creek.

On the leeward side of the San Gabriel's, Little Rock Creek used to provide the residents of littleRock and Pearblossom with their own, secluded mountain trout stream. But in order to protect breeding grounds of the fast deteriorating Southwestern Arroyo Toad, now a member of the endangered species list, the area has been closed to the public. Anglers will have to wait until at least 2002 to see if it will be returned to them.

The creek closure stretches from where it enters Little Rock Reservoir (Santiago Crossing) all the way to the top of Angeles Crest. Three thousand acres in all have been closed, and the California Department of Fish and Game has suspended the stocking of 2,100 rainbow trout until the area is re-evaluated and the US Fish and Wildlife Service okays the reopening of the creek. These rainbows will be diverted to Big Rock Creek and Little Rock Reservoir until Little Rock Creek reopens.

For now, all of the wild rainbow trout that populate the creek (and the stockers that swim up from the reservoir) will have a chance to grow and multiply, which will make for great fishing, if and when the creek reopens.

If you plan to make the trip, call ahead for the latest updates on the Southwestern Arroyo Toad.

Also nearby are Little Rock Reservoir, Big Rock Creek, the Aqueduct and Jackson Lake.

BIG ROCK **CREEK**

It's difficult to imagine snowy shorelines in a Southern California fishing spot, but every year you can see anglers dressed in parkas and snow boots fishing the shores of Big Rock Creek.

Rating: 7

Species: Rainbow Trout

Stocked with 2,700 pounds of rainbow trout.

Facilities: Campgrounds

Need Information?
Contact: Angeles National Forest
(661) 944-2187

Directions: From the 14 Freeway in Palmdale, exit Pearblossom Highway (138) and drive east through the town of Littlerock to Pearblossom. Follow signs in Pearblossom to Big Rock Creek.

Clear water makes fish easy to spot in Big Rock Creek.

For those living in the Antelope Valley, Big Rock Creek has been their own private fishing spot. They thought it was a secret, but that "secret" was taken away in 1998 when nearby Little Rock Creek was closed to protect the Southwestern Arroyo Toad, now on the Endangered Species List. Anglers who spent time at Little Rock Creek needed to find a new fishing hole, and most of them found Big Rock Creek. Since then, this creek, situated in a beautiful area shaded by large alders in the Angeles National Forest, has received increased fishing pressure. This added activity has caused local fishermen to wish that more than the allotted 7,660 rainbow trout were stocked here by the California Department of Fish and Game.

Big Rock Creek is a small stream that provides quality fishing during the winter and spring months for anglers fishing in the foothills of the San Gabriel Mountains. Due to storms and high runoff, Big Rock Creek, on the leeward side of the San Gabriel, changes its course almost yearly. I've been fishing the river for more than ten years now and have never found the same pool to fish two years in a row. I look at this as a good thing because it challenges fishermen each year to search for a new favorite fishing spot.

Fish are stocked in various pools scattered from the base of Big Rock Creek Road all the way up to Big Rock Creek Camp, with the general vicinity around the Angeles National Forest sign providing the best action. Most of the planted fish are in the eight to nine-inch class, with some running about 12 inches. Limits are common, but crowds can be a problem on weekends, so try to fish the creek during the week.

After a winter snowstorm this entire area is covered with snow, and I think that makes the fishing even more interesting. Most Southern California anglers have never fished a creek with snowcapped pines and ice along the shorelines. It's difficult to imagine snowy shorelines in a Southern California fishing spot, but every year you can see anglers dressed in parkas and snow boots fishing the shores of Big Rock Creek.

The creek also holds small wild rainbow trout. Fishing is best for wild trout above Big Rock Creek Camp where the stream is less fished. The further you hike, the better the fishing. Best baits here are various colors of Power Bait, salmon eggs, size 1/30 Panther

Big Rock Creek is the best trout stream on the leeward side of the San Gabriel Mountains.

Martins and Roostertails. Keep in mind, about a mile north of Sycamore Campground, which is situated alongside the creek, is a workstation for delinquents. Problems are rarely reported, but it would be a good idea to watch your kids.

If you plan to make the trip, supplies are available seven miles away in Pearblossom. A Forest Service Adventure Pass is required to park in the Angeles National Forest.

Also nearby are Devils Punchbowl, Jackson Lake, Little Rock Creek, Little Rock Reservoir and the Aqueduct.

BIG ROCK CREEK

JACKSON **LAKE**

If you're a skier who's headed up to Wrightwood, chances are you've driven right past Jackson Lake and not even known it exists.

Rating: 6

Species: Rainbow Trout, Largemouth Bass, Large Goldfish, and Bluegill

Stocked with 4,800 pounds of rainbow trout.

Need Information? Contact: US Forest Service, Valyermo District (661) 944-2187

Facilities: Campgrounds, Restrooms and Picnic Areas

Jackson Lake

Directions: From the 14 Freeway in Palmdale, exit Pearblossom Highway (138) and continue east through the towns of Littlerock and Pearblossom to Highway 2. Turn south and continue 10 miles to Big Pines. Turn left on County Road N4 and continue three miles to the lake.

You'd think that most fishermen would remember the great trout fishing, the mountain air or the beautiful scenery when they think about Jackson Lake. Most don't. Believe it or not, it's the lake's large goldfish that are most memorable. The lake is infested with them, and you don't need a line or bait to catch them. Just your hands (although catching fish with your hands is illegal) will do. Anyway, I've never caught one with a hook because they don't bite. They're about five to eight inches long and fat, and sit in the water all day, lazily looking at each other doing nothing.

But the lake has more to offer than oversized goldfish. If you're a skier who's headed up to Wrightwood, chances are you've driven right past Jackson Lake and not even known it exists. Nestled at 6,500 feet in the Angeles National Forest, at only five acres Jackson Lake is really more of a large pond.

Jackson Lake freezes over in the winter.

Although it often freezes over in the coldest months of winter, after ice-out the Department of Fish and Game plants it every other week in the spring and early summer. Many of the 10,070 fish planted here are longer than 12 inches with some occasionally over 16. This is because it's stocked by the Mojave River Hatchery which stocks larger fish than the Fillmore Fish Hatchery that normally plants waters in Los Angeles County.

Limits are common after a stock. Many anglers use Power Bait and salmon eggs, but I've had good luck with size 1/16 Panther Martins. Fishing slows down here in the summer and fall as the water temperature rises. The best places to fish for bass are on the west side of the lake near the weeds. Trout are found adjacent to the road and in the beach area near the parking lot. Small bluegill are scattered around the lake.

At five acres Jackson Lake, is more of a large pond, however, trout fishing can be great in the spring and early summer.

Jackson Lake is not only a great place to fish, it's a beautiful place to bring the family for a fun-filled day of sledding in the winter months or hiking and picnicking during the warmer months. If you are sledding one of the larger hills around the lake, use caution and don't pick up too much speed. Once I saw a guy and his sled boogie right into the lake. Buurrr.

If you plan to make the trip supplies are available in Wrightwood. A Forest Service Adventure Pass is required to park in the Angeles National Forest.

Also nearby are Big Rock Creek and Wrightwood.

JACKSON LAKE

HESPERIA **LAKE**

Hesperia Lake, run by the Hesperia Recreation and Parks District, receives stocks of catfish year-round, and rainbow trout during the cooler months.

Rating: 6

Species: Rainbow Trout, Channel Catfish, Largemouth Bass, Sunfish, Bluegill, Crappie and Carp

Stocked with 12,000 pounds of rainbow trout and 29,000 pounds of channel catfish.

Facilities: Picnic Areas, Playgrounds, General Store, Bait & Tackle, RV Hookups, Showers, Horseshoes, Campgrounds, and Restrooms

Twelve-acre Hesperia Lake in summer of 2000.

Need Information? Contact: Hesperia Lake (800) 521-6332 or (760) 244-5951

Directions: From Interstate 10 in Ontario, drive north on Interstate 15 for 23 miles to the Cajon Junction (Highway 138). Exit Highway 138 and drive east continuing to Arrowhead Lake Road. Turn left on Arrowhead Lake Road and follow the road to the lake on your right hand side.

I arrived at Hesperia Lake, just southwest of Apple Valley, about an hour before sunset on a warm, breezy June evening. I was prepared to do a little catfish fishing when I encountered something I wasn't prepared for. There was a derby going on and the lake was packed with wall-to-wall anglers. But it wasn't the crowds that bothered me as much as what they were doing.

I walked along the shoreline to talk to some anglers so I could get a feel for the lake, and I couldn't get a straight answer from any of them. They were all too drunk or too busy smoking cigarettes. It looked more like a heavy metal concert than a catfish derby. I can't recall if beer was for sale at the general store, but it seemed to be everywhere, as well as wine coolers, hard liquor, cigars, cigarettes and chewing tobacco. It's amazing people put down their beers long enough to reel their fish in.

Peace and quite? There was none. Boom boxes were blasting all over the lake, competing to see who could play the loudest. I think rap music won, but country and heavy metal put up a good

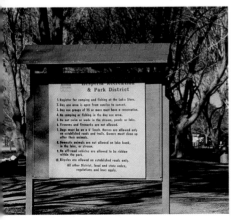

fight. What amazed me the most was that there were no problems. Everybody respected each other and recognized that all people enjoy different things. All in all, I'd think twice about bringing kids here, at least on derby night. Despite all the commotion, people caught fish all night. Lake employees told me that the lake only gets over crowded for derbies, on holidays and right after a stock.

Hesperia Lake, run by the Hesperia Recreation and Park District, receives stocks of catfish year-round, and rainbow trout during the cooler months. The 12-acre lake with a one-mile circumference, located at the base of the leeward side of the San Gabriel Mountains, is the only water hole in the city of Hesperia. The lake is not stocked by the California Department of Fish and Game. Therefore, no fishing license is required, but there is a fee to recompense the operators for the heavy fish plants.

Hesperia Lake provides excellent access for shorline anglers. No boating is allowed.

Chicken liver, beef liver and anchovies, any of which are dipped in Hog Wild, will catch catfish or mackerel. A new lake record catfish was caught and released (35 pounds) in March of 2000. Try casting towards the island for the larger fish, but your best luck comes at night during special night fishing hours.

Once trout plants commence in November, the store quickly begins selling lots of Power Bait as anglers rush to try to catch one of the larger fish that are trucked in from Whitewater Fish Hatchery. Most of the planted fish are just over a pound, but fish to 15 pounds are caught on a monthly basis. The largest trout to date was a 17 pounder. With no boats or float tubes allowed on the water, it makes it easy for anglers to cast and retrieve lures like green Cripplelures, black and red Panther Martins and gold Kastmasters.

If you plan to make the trip, there is a fee to fish the lake. Unless you catch bass or use barbless hooks, no catch & release is allowed. With the exception of worms, live bait is not permitted. Check with the lake for night fishing hours.

Also nearby are Lake Silverwood, Jess Ranch Lakes, Big Rock Creek, Jackson Lake and Mojave Narrows Park Lake.

MOJAVE **NARROWS**

The best spots on Horseshoe Lake are by the weeds around the island, while Pelican Lake kicks out limits everywhere.

Rating: 5

Species: Largemouth Bass, Bluegill, Channel Catfish, and Rainbow Trout.

Stocked with 12,600 pounds of rainbow trout and periodically with channel catfish.

Mojave Narrows Regional Park from Ridgecrest Road.

Facilities: Campgrounds, Horse Corrals, Boat Rentals, Wildlife Trails, Restrooms and Picnic Areas

Need Information? Contact: Mojave Narrows Regional Park (760) 245-2226

Directions: From Interstate 15 about four miles south of Victorville, take the Bear Valley cut-off four miles east, then turn north on Ridgecrest Road. Follow signs to the lake on the left.

Back in the mid-Nineties, Mojave Narrows Park Lake was being compared to the lakes of Bishop, but those days are long gone! Its lakes used to be planted with monster trout shipped in from Utah, however, those plants have since been discontinued and the hype has disappeared with them. Mojave Narrows has gone back to being just another San Bernardino County Park lake stocked with regular California Department of Fish and Game and from private Whitewater Trout Farms.

Mojave Narrows is split up into two small ponds, Horseshoe and Pelican Lakes. These heavily stocked lakes receive 25,000 trout per year as well as catfish in the summer. Plants from both the state and the county ensure quality fishing year round.

Fly & bubble combos, Power Bait, nightcrawlers and lures work well here. Located in Victorville near the Mojave River Fish Hatchery, it can get very cold at this lake in the winter, and hot and windy during the summer. So, come prepared. The best spots on

Horseshoe Lake

Horseshoe Lake are by the weeds around the island, while Pelican Lake kicks out limits everywhere. Don't overlook the feeder streams, either. You'd be surprised how many fish are yanked out of them.

If you plan to make the trip, there is a day-use and fishing fee. Supplies are available in Victorville.

Also nearby are Jess Ranch Lakes, Hesperia Lake and Silverwood Lake.

JESS RANCH **LAKES**

The $10 permit allows you to keep a combination of five bass, catfish or trout, as well as 15 bluegill.

Rating: 5

Species: Rainbow Trout, Channel Catfish, Bluegill and Largemouth Bass

Stocked with 26,000 pounds of rainbow trout and 5,000 pounds of channel catfish.

Facilities: Bait & Tackle, Restrooms and Picnic Areas

Jess Ranch Lakes

Need Information? Contact: Jess Ranch Lakes (760) 240-1107

Directions: From Interstate 15 in Ontario, drive north over the Cajon Pass to Victorville and exit Bear Valley Road. Turn right and continue for approximately seven miles. Turn right on Apple Valley Road and continue seven-tenths of a mile to the sign for the lakes on your left. After you pass a stop sign, Apple Valley Road becomes Country Estates Road.

If you had ever been to Jess Ranch in the past when it was used as a turkey ranch, you might not recognize it today. It is now known as Jess Ranch Estates and it looks like a mini Palm Desert. Located in Apple Valley, with its own golf course, church, community center and RV Park, Jess Ranch Estates is a fairly new desert resort community.

These are the only lakes in the Antelope, Apple and Victor Valleys that can sustain trout year-round. This is because Jess Ranch Lakes employs four wells to pump 1.5 million gallons of cold water a day from the lakes to irrigate parts of the community and keep its own golf course and parkways green.

Although it hasn't been open for more than 10 years, at one time Jess Ranch operated the largest fish hatchery in the state. Today, it is made up of five private, stocked lakes. Two are opened to shore fishermen, one to catch & release fishing from float tubes and the last two are closed to fishing. One ton of rainbow trout is stocked in two of the lakes every other week, year-round. Most of these fish weigh in at a pound to a pound-and-a-half, but many live to grow heavier. Trout are best caught using Power Bait or by tossing lures along the shoreline.

They stock catfish as well. Fishing for bass up to 10 pounds is also fair, but with consistent trout action not many anglers come for the bass.

If you plan to make the trip, supplies are available in Apple Valley. No fishing license is required, but a $10 fishing permit is required. The $10 permit allows you to keep a combination of five bass, catfish or trout, as well as 15 bluegill. A second permit can be purchased. The lakes are open Friday, Saturday and Sunday.

Also nearby are Hesperia Lake and Mojave Narrows Park Lake.

REGION 6

San Gabriel Mountains (West)

Lower Big Tujunga Creek
Upper Big Tujunga Creek
Arroyo Seco Creek
Santa Anita Creek
San Gabriel River (West Fork)
San Gabriel River (North Fork)
Crystal Lake
San Gabriel River (East Fork)
San Gabriel Reservoir
San Dimas Reservoir

LOWER BIG TUJUNGA **CREEK**

Remember, you need to get here early following a stock because locals who fish this area have a good idea when the CA DFG truck comes and where it stocks, so later in the day the fish will be gone.

Rating: 5

Species: Rainbow Trout

Stocked with 2,800 pounds of rainbow trout.

Facilities: Picnic Areas and Restrooms

Need Information?
Contact: Angeles National Forest (818) 899-1900

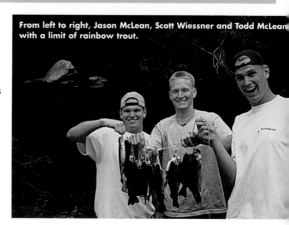
From left to right, Jason McLean, Scott Wiessner and Todd McLean with a limit of rainbow trout.

Directions: From the 210 Freeway in Sunland, exit Sunland Blvd. and turn east. (Sunland Blvd. turns into Foothill) Continue east on Foothill to Oro Vista. Turn left and continue to Big Tujunga Canyon Road (Oro Vista becomes Big Tujunga Canyon Road. Drive north to Ottie Road and make two quick rights to the day-use area, or continue north on Big Tujunga Canyon Road to Wildwood or Stonyvale day-use areas.

The last time I visited Lower Big Tujunga Creek was on a Friday afternoon in early May. Talk about a stream for locals! When I arrived, the place was full of anglers but no one had their poles out. Instead, they were all cooking on barbecues. I asked them what the story was and they told me they were waiting for the Fish and Game truck to show up. It was about noon and they all thought it would arrive in the next hour or so. Sure enough, about 1 p.m. the truck came rolling in. The fishermen grabbed their poles and the fishing began.

When Big Tujunga Creek, located in the Angeles National Forest, used to get heavy plants from the California Department of Fish and Game, I used to limit here in less than a half-hour. However, with the advent of the "Fishing in the City" project in the early 1990's, more fish got planted in urban areas and the plants here suddenly dwindled. Nowadays, despite over 8,100 fish stocked, limits are much harder to come by. James Adams, Director of the CA DFG Hatchery in Fillmore, insists that they are stocking the same poundage of fish. He said the fish are just larger in size, so less go in the stream. In the past, the fish weighed one-third of a pound and now they are stocking half pounders, so numerically less fish are being stocked, but the overall total allotment of fish stocked in the stream is the same.

The creek is only stocked in two day-use areas, both directly off Big Tujunga Canyon Road. Vogel Flats is stocked upstream from the bridge for about a quarter-mile. Ottie Road is stocked upstream from the parking lot for about one-fourth of a mile. Wildwood used to be planted as well, however, the day-use area has been temporarily closed. The closure began in the summer of 2000 when the Santa Anita sucker fish, a member of the endangered species list, was found in its waters. There is still no word on if and when it may reopen. The best way to catch fish here is with Power Bait and salmon eggs. Small Panther Martins also work very well. However, there are a lot of trees on the shoreline and that can make fishing difficult.

You can forget about fishing this area after mid-May because the stream turns into a trickle and becomes bombarded with picnickers and waders. Don't bother fishing here after a storm, either. The rain turns the water in the creek milky and the stream becomes unfishable. Remember, you need to get here early following a stock because locals who fish this area have a good idea when the CA DFG truck comes and where it stocks, so later in the day many of the fish will be gone. The day-use areas also become crowded following a stock. Because of its close proximity to the San Fernando and San Gabriel Valleys, Lower Big Tujunga provides a good fishing experience if you beat the crowds. That's when you can catch plenty of fish.

Sunsets can be breathtaking at Lower Big Tujunga Creek.

If you plan to make the trip supplies are available in Sunland. A Forest Service Adventure Pass is required to park in the Angeles National Forest.

Also nearby are Upper Big Tujunga Creek, Upper Big Tujunga Creek Falls, Cooper Canyon Falls and Buckhorn Falls.

LOWER BIG TUJUNGA **CREEK**

UPPER BIG TUJUNGA **CREEK**

Upper Big Tujunga Creek not only provides a decent trout fishery, it is also one of the few secret places (until now) left in the Angeles National Forest that offers peace and quiet.

Rating: 6

Species: Rainbow Trout

Stocked with 600 pounds of rainbow trout.

Facilities: Primitive Campsites

Need Information?
Contact: Angeles National Forest
626-574-5200

Skies clear after a brief snow storm at Upper Big Tujunga Creek.

Directions: From Pasadena, drive west on the 210 Freeway to Highway 2 (Angeles Crest Highway) and turn north. Drive for nine miles to Clear Creek Ranger Station and turn west on County Road N-3. Continue 12 miles to Angeles Forest Highway and turn southeast. Continue to Upper Big Tujunga Road and turn right. Drive Approximately three miles to a sign for Colby Camp. Turn right and follow the winding road to the stream.

When I first heard about Upper Big Tujunga Creek, a friend told me about a secluded stream filled with trout, surrounded by the natural beauty of the Eastern Sierra, right in Los Angeles County. I'll tell you, it was pretty hard to believe him. Well, it turns out he was right. Upper Big Tujunga Creek not only provides a decent trout fishery, it is also one of the few secret places (until now) left in the Angeles National Forest that offers peace and quiet.

Upper Big Tujunga Creek also receives much less fishing pressure than most other streams in LA County. Fed by snowmelt from the San Gabriel Mountains, the stream is fairly large in the spring, with water crashing onto boulders, alder trees blended in with a few pines covering the banks and wild trout mixing in with the stockers. It's a place where

A wild trout from Upper Big Tujunga Creek.

Southern Californian anglers can get their lines wet before trout season opens in the Eastern Sierra.

Most of the fish planted are in the seven to nine-inch class, but anglers don't come here for size. They come for a quick getaway from city life. Unless you are an experienced angler and are confident casting between trees and bushes, stay away from using spinners. There is a lot of brush along the shoreline and trees overhanging banks, so using Power Bait and salmon eggs are the easiest way to go. The fish are picky though, so make sure you bring different colors of Power Bait. Until you find the color of the day, the trout won't bite. White is usually their favorite color. Don't bother to fish here unless it's between January and April, because that's the only time water levels are sufficients to carry fish. During late spring and throughout summer, the water flow slows down to a trickle and the plants stop.

I first surveyed the area in November of 1997 when the creek was dry, but after El Nino in 1998, high water levels made the creek unfishable until late May. Lets hope the rains keep coming though, because if the rains don't come, neither do the plants. When water levels are high, the creek is stocked in three places. First, it is stocked for about 50

Upper Big Tujunga Creek

yards above and below the bridge that crosses over the creek near Colby Camp. It is also stocked near the fire station a few miles further southeast along Upper Big Tujunga Road at an area called Shortcut, and when water levels are sufficient the stream is also planted a few miles up Upper Big Tujunga Road where Alder Creek crosses under the road. For more than 20 years the stream used to be stocked in Old Wickiup Campground, but the California Department of Fish and Game was forced to cease plants there in an effort to protect the Southwestern Arroyo Toad, a member of the Endangered Species List that lives along the stream.

Best spots to catch fish are at the Colby Camp access site, from the pool below the bridge all the way to the waterfall. What? There's a waterfall, too! Yes. It's less than a thirty-minute walk downstream from the bridge, and there are fish in the pool below. The falls is only about 20 feet high, but in this area any waterfall is worth your trip.

If you plan to make the trip, supplies are available in Hidden Springs. A Forest Service Adventure Pass is required to park in the Angeles National Forest. If there are heavy rains the week the CA DFG plans to stock, the stocks are usually postponed because of swollen water levels. Call the Forest Service before making the trip.

Also nearby are Strawberry Peak, Upper Big Tujunga Creek Falls, Cooper Canyon Falls and Big Tujunga Dam.

ARROYO SECO **CREEK**

Arroyo Seco Creek is one of the most heavily used day-use areas in all of Southern California. Hikers heading to Switzer Falls walk over the stream on their way to the falls.

Rating: 6

Species: Rainbow Trout

Stocked with 1,000 pounds of rainbow trout.

Facilities: Picnic Areas and Restrooms

Need Information?
Contact: Angeles National Forest
(818) 790-1151

Directions: From the 210 Freeway in La Canada, exit Angeles Crest Highway (2) and continue north for nine miles to Switzer Day Use Area. Walk or drive through the locked gate on the paved road and continue a quarter mile to the creek.

Arroyo Seco Creek in winter of 1999.

Arroyo Seco Creek is one of the smallest streams in the Angeles National Forest. It's so shallow and narrow, most anglers don't believe there are any fish in it at all. There are plenty of fish in the stream, but the window of opportunity to catch them is short.

The stream is fed by snow and rain runoff from high elevations in the San Gabriel Mountains, so if there isn't much precipitation during winter, the stream suffers. By late spring continuing through the fall, the stream slows to a trickle. Many anglers who think they are knowledgeable about the trout in the stream believe they all die-off. What these anglers don't realize is that further downstream there are pools that stay cold enough to sustain trout year-round.

Arroyo Seco Creek is one of the most heavily used day-use areas in all of Southern California. Hikers heading to Switzer Falls walk over the stream on their way to the base of the falls, which are located about 1.8 miles downstream of the fishing area. Most of these hikers also don't realize there are fish in the stream.

The last time I fished here there was a group hikers heading down to 50-foot Switzer Falls. They stopped and looked puzzled as they watched me fish. "What are you doing?" asked one of the hikers. "Fishing," I replied.

The man chuckled and yelled to a few of his friends that were still in the parking lot, "You guys have to see this. Some guy's fishing in the stream. I guess he doesn't know there are no fish here." "Really? What are all those then?" I said, as I pointed to about 20 rainbow trout swimming in a pool. The hikers were stunned. "How did those get there?" asked one of the others.

I explained to them that the California Department of Fish and Game stocks about 3,000 trout, Typically from February till late March. I also explained that the planted fish are small, usually seven to nine inches. But the hikers didn't mind. They lived in Pasadena, only about a twenty-minute drive away, and were excited to hear there were fish in the stream. Half of the group shined the hike and went home to get their poles.

Later that day I ran into Forest Service ranger William Shaw who told me that they have been having problems with poachers. He said that he's been ticketing anglers who get frustrated when the trout don't bite and show up with nets to catch fish.

There's no need for nets. Just make sure you have Power Bait or salmon eggs, because the water level is too low for lures. White and rainbow Power Bait have always proved to be the best for me. The streambed is dark with large trees shading anglers at

Arroyo Seco Creek is one of the
most popular day-use areas in all
of Southern California.

all times, so you'll need bright colored baits that stand out. Another tip is to arrive early in the week because the stockers are usually gone by the Saturday after the stock.

Arroyo Seco Creek is a great place to bring youngsters to catch a lot of fish, because the fishing pressure is low compared to other streams in the region. Kids also enjoy the sight of deer that commonly stroll through the campground.

The CA DFG stocks the fish in the stream along the immediate vicinity of Switzer's Picnic Area. The best places to catch fish are at the far north of the campground where the path crosses the creek, near the end of the parking lot and in the various pools where the trail turns from cement to dirt on the way towards the falls.

If you plan to make the trip, supplies are available in La Canada. When water flows are sufficient, the creek is also stocked at Gould Mesa Campground. A Forest Service Adventure Pass is required to park in the Angeles National Forest. Switzer's Picnic area is open for day-use only.

Also nearby are Mt. Wilson, Upper and Lower Big Tujunga Creek, Switzer Falls, Cooper Canyon Falls and Mt. Waterman.

ARROYO SECO CREEK

SANTA ANITA **CREEK**

With its numerous small waterfalls there are a ton of large, but shallow pools suitable for both trout and (providing the water isn't too cold) wading.

Rating: 5

Species: Rainbow Trout

Stocked with 500 pounds of rainbow trout.

Facilities: Restrooms, Hiking Trails and Picnic Areas

Need Information? Contact: Angeles National Forest (626) 335-1251

Directions: From the 210 Freeway in Pasadena, drive seven miles east to Arcadia and exit Santa Anita Ave. Drive six miles north to the road's end

Sturtevant Falls

at Chantry Flat. The trailhead to the stream is at the locked gate near the parking lots.

For years, Santa Anita Creek has been a favorite spot for Southern California waterfall lovers who come to see two of Los Angeles' most known falls, Hermit and Sturtevant. However, recently the California Department of Fish and Game has given anglers a reason to come to the creek by planning to stock rainbow trout. The program was supposed to commence in spring of 2000, but road construction on Santa Anita Ave. blocked the plants. Plants began in spring of 2001. When water levels are sufficient, usually from January through May, about 1,500 rainbow trout from eight to 10 inches are stocked.

Located in the Angeles National Forest, Santa Anita Creek is shaded by alders and oaks and runs year-round. However, for those who like to park your car next to the stream and fish, you might want to pass on Santa Anita Creek. Although the walk is short, the trek to the stream is a butt-kicker, straight down on the way in and straight up on the way out. The trail is paved for the first six-tenths of a mile before you cross a bridge over Winter Creek (which may be dry), and then it's a short walk around the bend down to the creek.

Now that it is being stocked Santa Anita Creek provides a lot of fun for local anglers of the San Gabriel Valley. With its numerous small waterfalls there are a ton of large, but shallow pools suitable for both trout and (providing the water isn't too cold) wading. Make sure to bring along some Power Bait. The stream is too small for lures.

If you plan to make the trip, supplies are available in Arcadia and Sierra Madre. A Forest Service Adventure Pass is required to park in the Angeles National Forest. In wet weather the road to the stream is commonly closed due to mud slide threats.

Also nearby are Arroyo Seco Creek, Switzer Falls, Eaton Canyon Falls, Monrovia Canyon Falls and Millard Canyon Falls.

SANTA ANITA CREEK

WEST FORK SAN GABRIEL **RIVER**

For those looking for more of a challenge or interested in a little fly-fishing, there is a special regulations section of the river.

Rating: 8

Species: Rainbow Trout

Stocked with 4,100 pounds of rainbow trout.

Facilities: Picnic Areas and Restrooms

Need Information?
Contact: Angeles National Forest
(626) 335-1251

Jeff Oakerman fishes river's one of San Gabriel Rivers large pools.

Directions: From the 210 Freeway in Pasadena, drive east to Azusa Ave. and turn north. Continue on Azusa Ave., which becomes San Gabriel Canyon Road, for approximately 11 miles to the West Fork Bridge. Park either in the dirt lot just before the bridge or in the paved lot after crossing the bridge.

Every time I think of the West Fork of the San Gabriel River a certain story comes to mind. Back in the mid-Nineties I used to fish the river all the time. I spent a lot of time with some retired guys, meeting them each week on the river. One day they told me a story about how a California Department of Fish and Game warden busted a few deer poachers in the area. How the warden accomplished it was what I found most amusing.

He placed a fake deer up in the mountains just off San Gabriel Canyon Road, took cover behind some trees and waited for poachers to come by and take a shot at it. Deer season was over, but these hunters were still shooting deer anyway. They took five or six shots before they realized the deer was a decoy. About a month later, a warden I talked to confirmed that the story was true. Then a blurb appeared describing the event a few months later in an outdoor magazine. They kept shooting at the decoy even after it didn't move when their bullets just missed it. I think that should have tipped them off it wasn't real.

San Gabriel River drainage does offer hunting, but most people come here to fish. Located in the Angeles National Forest, about a 15-minute drive from the 210 Freeway in Azusa, with pine and alder trees along its shorelines, the West Fork of the San Gabriel River is quite beautiful. It also has a lot of mistletoe. I know this for a fact because I fell out of one of the trees while trying to get some for a New Years Eve party a few years back. The fall was worth it. I placed the mistletoe just above the front door and insisted that all the women kiss me before entering. (Well, not exactly all, just the pretty ones.)

Aside from the Los Angeles River after a rainstorm and the Colorado River, the West Fork of the San Gabriel River is the second largest river in Southern California, with the Santa Ynez River being the largest. It is also one of the most popular and heavily fished rivers in Southern California. Unlike most of the rivers in Los Angeles County that become cloudy and muddy after rainfall, the West Fork remains clear and fishable. With consistent flows, deep pools, free-flowing water and large trees that keep you shaded from the sun, the West Fork is a fisherman's paradise. Unfortunately, along with paradise comes crowds, and unless you fish the river from Monday through Thursday, you'll be miserable, fighting with other anglers for the best spots.

The CA DFG stocks the river with 11,630 rainbow trout from eight to 10 inches, but it doesn't seem to be enough. Even if you get here a few days after a stock, a majority of the fish will be gone. This is because CA DFG makes it so easy for you to catch them. Where? They start stocking at the bridge near where you park, then continue up the paved road along the river, stocking every pool that can hold fish. Most people fish the two largest pools right near the parking lot, but fishing tends to improve the further upstream you walk.

The stream is stocked from the point where the road crosses over the river, upstream to the second bridge near the confluence with Bear Creek, a popular backpacking spot with small, wild rainbow trout. Power Bait is an all-time favorite here, with salmon eggs coming in a close second. I've always had my best luck on small yellow or white Panther Martins.

For those looking for more of a challenge or interested in a little fly-fishing, there is a special regulations section of the river. It begins at the second bridge and extends upstream to Cogswell Reservoir, which releases the water that forms the river. This section of the river is loaded with willing wild trout to 18 inches, but only artificial lures with barbless hooks are allowed, and all fish must be caught and released. The further upstream you go, the better fishing is. Another option is to ride a bike along the service road that parallels the river. No vehicular traffic is permitted.

Once mid-spring comes around, the river algae and moss begin to take over the stream making for difficult fishing. Just a sign it's time to put the rods away and wait until fall to return. From May through October, it's impossible to fish, with people wading in pools and having barbecues all along the shoreline. Even the fish scatter for cover.

If you plan to make the trip, supplies are available in Azusa. A Forest Service Adventure Pass is required to park in the Angeles National Forest.

Also nearby are the North and East Forks of the San Gabriel River, an off-road vehicle area, San Gabriel Reservoir, the Bridge to Nowhere, Soldier Creek Falls and Crystal Lake.

West Fork San Gabriel River

NORTH FORK SAN GABRIEL **RIVER**

With the bigger and more heavily stocked West and East Forks nearby, nobody pays much attention to the North Fork, but those who do are greatly rewarded.

Rating: 6

Species: Rainbow Trout

Stocked with 2,100 pounds of rainbow trout.

Facilities: None

Need Information?
Contact: Angeles National Forest
(626) 335-1251

North Fork San Gabriel River

Directions: From Pasadena, drive east on the 210 Freeway and exit Azusa Avenue (Highway 39). Turn north and continue on Azusa (which turns into San Gabriel Canyon Road) for approximately 10 miles to the creek on the north side of road. The creek begins just after cross the West Fork Bridge. From this point the stream parallels the road.

With the bigger and more heavily stocked West and East Forks nearby, nobody pays much attention to the North Fork, but those who do are greatly rewarded. The North Fork kind of reminds me of a used car dealership in between Lexus and Lincoln dealerships. You can get a great deal at the used car lot, but everyone desires the status and reputation of those more classy cars. It's the same with the North Fork of the San Gabriel River, which is the smallest and most neglected of the three forks, but it provides good fishing after a stock and shouldn't be overlooked.

The fish planted here are the same size as those dumped in the West and East Forks, and they're even planted the same day. The stream, located at 1,800 feet in the Angeles National Forest, is planted with 6,000 rainbow trout by the California Department of Fish and Game, beginning at the West Fork Bridge and continuing for about three miles upstream. The best place to fish is the mile or so upstream right after you cross over the bridge.

You can see the stream on your right driving up Highway 39. Further upstream, where cabins line the shore, residents watch the creek closely to make sure there are no poachers. Don't forget your license. Game wardens patrol this area heavily. With rock pools built to hold the fish, the entire stream is accessible and provides easy fishing. Best baits here are Power Bait or salmon eggs. Small spinners are also productive in some of the larger pools.

If you plan to make the trip, supplies are available in Azusa. A Forest Adventure Pass is required to park in the Angeles National Forest.

Also nearby are Crystal Lake, Soldier Creek Falls, the East and West Forks of the San Gabriel River, Cogswell Reservoir, San Gabriel Reservoir and an off-road vehicle area.

CRYSTAL **LAKE**

Situated atop the San Gabriel Mountains deep in the Angeles National Forest, surrounded by tall pine trees, it is a favorite to many anglers, picnickers and other outdoors lovers.

Rating: 7

Species: Rainbow Trout, Largemouth Bass, Bluegill and Channel Catfish

Stocked with 7,000 pounds per year.

Need Information? Contact:
Angeles National Forest (626) 335-1251, Crystal Lake (626) 910-1133

Neal Karchem holds up a nine-inch rainbow trout caught on Power Bait.

Facilities: Camp Store, Campgrounds, Restrooms and a Picnic Area

Directions: From the 210 Freeway in Azusa, exit Azusa Ave. (39) and turn north. Follow Azusa Ave. (which turns into San Gabriel Canyon Road) for 26 miles to the campground.

It's no secret that Crystal Lake is as close as you're going to get to the Eastern Sierra in Los Angeles. Situated atop the San Gabriel Mountains deep in the Angeles National Forest, surrounded by tall pine trees, it is a favorite to many anglers, picnickers and other outdoors lovers. And when stocked, it provides some of the best trout fishing in LA County.

Crystal Lake is actually a large pond that is replenished with fish in the eight to 12-inch class from November through May, as well as fingerlings in early spring. Your best bets here are Power Bait, Kastmasters and Panther Martins. The easiest way to catch the willing rainbows is by float tubing, although shore fishing can also be productive.

The lake gets its share of snowfall in winter, and at higher than 5,500 feet it has been known to partially freeze over, making it difficult to fish. But anglers who don't mind the snow are often rewarded with beautiful scenery to compliment their fishing.

The chance of catching a bass or catfish increases in spring when the snow melts, however, there are only a few of them in the tiny lake. Limits are common for trout fishermen during the week when fishing pressure is low, but are harder to come by on the weekends when the lake is surrounded by anglers.

In addition to the 14,000 catchable trout planted here, Crystal Lake is also stocked with 20,000 subcatchable rainbow trout each year to ensure good fishing through the summer months. Fish are caught all around the lake, with the south shore being the most popular spot. Catch rates slow by summer, an indication it might be time to plan a trip to the real Sierra's where you have a chance at hooking into a big rainbow.

If you plan to make the trip supplies are available at the lake's general store. There is a day-use fee. No motorboats are permitted on the lake. Check with Caltrans (1-800-427-7623 -- remember to put in 39 for the highway number) to make sure the narrow, winding road is open. Chains are sometimes required.

Also nearby are the West, North and East forks of the San Gabriel River, San Gabriel Reservoir, Cogswell Dam and Soldier Creek Falls.

EAST FORK SAN GABRIEL **RIVER**

The East Fork of the San Gabriel River is nowhere near as beautiful as the West or North Forks, but it does provide good fishing and easy access.

Rating: 6

Species: Rainbow Trout

Stocked with 8,700 pounds of rainbow trout.

Need Information? Contact: Angeles National Forest (626) 335-1251

Facilities: General Store, Campgrounds, RV Hookups and Restrooms

Todd McLean a limit of trout caught in Camp Follows.

Directions: From the 210 Freeway in Azusa, exit Azusa Ave (Hwy 39) and travel north. Continue on Azusa (which turns into San Gabriel Canyon Road) for approximately nine miles to East Fork Road. Turn right and travel approximately three miles to Follows Camp or continue another two miles to Camp Williams. Fish are stocked from Follows Camp to Cattle Canyon Guard Station.

When I first arrived at the East Fork of the San Gabriel River I thought I was in the wrong place. More people were mining for gold than fishing. They had on wetsuits and air tanks and were actually finding minute strands of gold.

As the story goes, there used to be a small mining town on the East Fork of the San Gabriel River that was washed away in a flood years ago. Rumor has it there was a safe that was filled with gold that was washed away with the town. That safe has never been recovered, but the miners are positive it will turn up some day in this stretch of the river. While some people continue to pan for the gold, others fish for their own type of gold in the form of rainbow trout.

The East Fork of the San Gabriel River is nowhere near as beautiful as the West or North Forks, but it does provide good fishing and easy access. The East Fork is the second most heavily stocked river or stream in Southern California. (Santa Ana River gets the most.) It receives 7,170 more trout than the North and West Forks combined, even though its stocks have been reduced over the last five years. In 2000, 24,770 trout were stocked, substantially less than the 33,000 that were trucked in during the 1997 season.

The river flows well during the winter and early spring, but slows down in the summer and becomes covered in algae. Best baits are Panther Martins, Power Bait and salmon eggs. The best spots to find schools of fish are at Camp Follows from the bridge to the east end of the campground. At Camp Williams, fish are planted near the camp store. For those who prefer wild trout, you can hike up the East Fork back into the Narrows.

If you plan to make the trip, supplies are available at Camp Williams or Follows Camp. A Forest Service Adventure Pass is required to park in the Angeles National Forest.

Also nearby are West and North Forks of the San Gabriel River, Fish Fork Falls and the Bridge To Nowhere.

SAN GABRIEL **RESERVOIR**

You can come for the trout if you want, but this remote reservoir, nine miles north of the 210 Freeway, is known for its bass.

Rating: 5

Species: Largemouth Bass, Smallmouth Bass, Rainbow Trout, Bluegill, and Channel Catfish

Stocked with 25,000 subcatchable rainbow trout.

Facilities: None

Need Information?
Contact: Angeles National Forest
(626) 335-1251

Directions: From the 210 Freeway in Azusa, exit Azusa Ave. (Highway 39) and continue north for nine miles (the road becomes San Gabriel Canyon Road) to the reservoir on your right. For the ORV Station, continue another three miles on Highway 39.

Driving up San Gabriel Canyon Road just north of Azusa, you pass two good-sized reservoirs, first Morris and then San Gabriel. Morris Reservoir

San Gabriel Reservoir can suffer from drawdowns. Take note of the bridge in the middle on the right. It's the same one shown on the picture on the next page.

was once used as a naval testing facility, so it's closed to fishing. However, San Gabriel Reservoir is fair game. Because few people know it's legal to fish here, the lack of fishing pressure has bolstered the fish population. Ssshhh, it's all a big secret.

Each year San Gabriel Reservoir is drawn down in late spring and early summer. Then it's filled again from late winter through spring, when the East, West and North Forks of the San Gabriel River carry runoff from the San Gabriel Mountains down into the reservoir. Because access is poor and extreme drawdowns make the once full reservoir look like a barren canyon, hardly anybody knows about the stable fish population here.

For trout, it's strictly a put and grow fishery, with the California Department of Fish and Game stocking more than 25,000 subcatchable rainbow trout in January. You can come for the trout if you want, but this remote reservoir, nine miles north of the 210 Freeway, is known for its bass.

With numerous coves, good shoreline structure and a consistent food supply brought in from the East and West Forks of the San Gabriel River, bass thrive here. The regulars (and there are only a few of them) consistently catch bass in the three two five pound-range. Don't expect to catch a lot of fish. This reservoir is about quality not quantity. Spinnerbaits and nightcrawlers are favored, but since the water is rarely fished, the bass will attack just about anything.

There are only a few ways to get down to the reservoir. The easiest is a paved road just south of the East Fork Road on the east side of San Gabriel Canyon Road. The gate is locked so you have to walk about 100 yards to the shoreline. The only other routes are driving down the San Gabriel River from the San Gabriel Canyon Off Road Vehicle station a few miles away, or scaling down one of the steep, loose cliffs to the remote and rugged shoreline. There is no access on the east side of the reservoir.

The East Fork Bridge and San Gabriel Reservoir in spring.

Recently, in August of 1999 the CA DFG fish relocation project took 200 largemouth bass, 20 bluegill and 10 carp out of the reservoir and placed them in Hansen Dam.

If you plan to make the trip, supplies are available in Azusa. A Forest Service Adventure Pass is required to park in the Angeles National Forest.

Also nearby are the East, West and North Forks of the San Gabriel River, Fish Fork Falls, Crystal Lake, the Bridge to Nowhere and Soldier Creek Falls.

SAN GABRIEL RESERVOIR

SAN DIMAS **RESERVOIR**

Fewer than three miles from urban San Dimas, there's a beautiful, peaceful fishing hole that takes your mind away from the smog and cars that plague nearby city life.

Rating: 6

Species: Rainbow Trout and Largemouth Bass

Stocked with 1,600 pounds of rainbow trout.

Facilities: None

Fishing from the east shore of San Dimas Reservoir.

Need Information? Contact: Angeles National Forest (626) 335-1251

Directions: From Foothill Blvd. in San Dimas, turn north on San Dimas Canyon Road and continue three miles to the reservoir.

The city of San Dimas became nationally known in 1989 when it was featured in the hit comedy Bill and Ted's Excellent Adventure. Southern Californians have long known San Dimas as the home of Raging Waters Theme Park. But very few know it's a good place to fish.

Fewer than three miles from urban San Dimas, there's a beautiful, peaceful fishing hole that takes your mind away from the smog and cars that plague nearby city life. That fishing hole is the narrow 36-acre San Dimas Reservoir located partially in the Angeles National Forest. Finding the reservoir is easy, but unfortunately getting down to its banks can be a bit tricky. There is no access on the dam itself or on the west shoreline, which is far too steep.

There are basically two ways to get down to where the water is. If you plan to fish near the dam, park near the building signed "San Dimas Reservoir" just past the dam on your left and walk up the road to the end of the fence. Walk through the opening and follow the paved road down to the water. At the end of the road you'll come to a sandy beach that many fisherman use to set up lines. This is the same place trout are planted in the lake, so it's a productive spot. On the beach they use Power Bait, but if you want to use spinners, wander up and down the steep fisherman's trail that runs along the lake's shoreline in an attempt to find a few hungry rainbows cruising the lake.

Another option is to fish the reservoirs' inlet. When flows are high in late winter and early spring, the fish station themselves here and wait for food to flow down into the lake. To reach the inlet, drive past the reservoir to the fire station, park your car and follow the stream down towards the dam. It sounds like a long way, but it's not.

As for the fishing, it always remains fair. The California Department of Fish and Game stocks about 2,900 rainbow trout in the cooler months, keeping the morning and evening bites active. At times the lake is also stocked with subcatchable rainbow trout.

If you plan to make the trip, supplies are available in San Dimas. No watercraft is allowed. A Forest Service Adventure Pass is required to park in the Angeles National Forest.

Also nearby are Puddingstone Reservoir, the Santa Fe Dam, San Gabriel River, Raging Waters and San Gabriel Reservoir.

REGION 7
San Gabriel Mountains (East)

CALIFORNIA

Mt. Baldy Trout Pools
Cucamonga Creek
Cucamonga/Guasti Park Lake
Green Mountain Ranch
Lytle Creek
Glen Helen Park Lake

MT. BALDY TROUT **POOLS**

Remember that lure you love that's been sitting in your tackle box looking brand new because you've never caught anything on it? Bring it. I'll guarantee you'll have no problem catching fish with it.

Rating: 5

Species: Rainbow Trout

Stocked weekly by private vendors.

Facilities: Restrooms, Picnic Areas, Fish Cleaning and Packaging, Bait and Tackle and a Snack Bar

Need Information? Contact:
Mt. Baldy Trout Pools (909) 982-4246

Mt. Baldy Trout Pools

Directions: From Interstate 10 in Upland, exit Mountain Ave. and turn north. Continue approximately 12 miles to the ponds on your right.

Mt. Baldy provides hikers with the tallest peak in the San Gabriel Mountains, waterfall lovers with a free-falling waterfall coming down its face (San Antonio Falls), outdoor enthusiasts with ski and snow play areas, but the fishermen feel left out. It seems there is something for everyone but them. There are no lakes, rivers or streams that hold fish nearby. There is, however, one alternative – Mt. Baldy Trout Pools.

Open since 1953, most fishermen don't consider Mt. Baldy Trout Pools real fishing because the fish are so easy to catch. They refer to it as "catching." Sounds easy? Well, it should. Fishing at the trout pools is like fishing in a trash can for fish that aren't fed.

Located in Mt. Baldy Village, the ponds are a tourist attraction that is constantly replenished to ensure that your bait is chomped on each cast. It's that simple? Yes, but there is a catch, besides the fish. Each fish will cost you the minimum of a McDonald's value meal, and that's if you catch the smallest fish in the pond. There are two separate ponds, one for the larger, more expensive fish (at a minimum of $7.40 per fish), and one for smaller, less expensive fish (minimum $2). There is also a third pond, but it's used to raise fish, and fishing is not allowed.

So how do you catch fish here? Simple, use anything you want. Remember that lure you love that's been sitting in your tackle box looking brand new because you've never caught anything on it? Bring it. I'll guarantee you'll have no problem catching fish with it.

Mt. Baldy Trout Pools doesn't stay open year-round. However, it's always open on the weekends and during the week in July and August. To be safe, call ahead for updated hours.

If you plan to make the trip, there is a fishing fee.

Also nearby are San Antonio Falls, Cucamonga Creek, Cucamonga-Guasti Regional Park Lake and Mt. Baldy Ski Area.

MT. BALDY TROUT **POOLS**

CUCAMONGA **CREEK**

Salmon eggs or white Power Bait fished above or below where the stream crosses the road should catch you fish.

Rating: 5

Species: Rainbow Trout

Stocked with 1,000 pounds of rainbow trout.

Facilities: None

Need Information?
Contact:
San Bernardino National
Forest (909) 887-2576

Brett Ermilio exhibits three rainbows caught on a Panther Martin.

Directions: From Interstate 10 in Upland, drive east and exit Euclid Ave. Turn north and drive three miles to 19th Street. Turn east and drive 1.5 miles to Sapphire Street. Turn left and drive north for three-fourths of a mile to Almond Road. Turn west and drive one fourth of a mile to Skyline. Turn right. In one-tenth of a mile, you'll enter the San Bernardino National Forest and will be traveling on Forest Service Road IN34. Continue for 1.3 miles to Forest Service Road IN35 and turn left. Take the rough dirt road for about a mile to the stream crossing.

Finally, the residents of the Pomona Valley have their own small trout stream to brag about. Ironically, these same residents had the stream years ago. However, in 1989 when the California Department of Fish and Game discovered that poachers were illegally catching fish with gill nets and trapping them with their hands, they ceased trout plants at Cucamonga Creek. In the mid-Nineties, the CA DFG decided to give residents another chance at fishing responsibly and began stocking 1,000 rainbow trout between May and August. So far, there haven't been any problems reported, and anglers have been catching easy limits.

This heavily shaded stream which flows year-round through San Bernardino National Forest does, however, have one downfall -- the Forest Service road leading to it is not maintained and can be extremely rough, especially after winter storms. It's one of those roads you drive at 10-mph and still feel like the wheels are going to pop off your car. Just a small price to pay for catching fish. Salmon eggs or white Power Bait fished above or below where the stream crosses the road should catch you fish.

If you plan to make the trip, supplies are available in Upland. The road is sufficient for two wheel drive vehicles, but can get rough after heavy rains. A Forest Service Adventure Pass is required to park in the San Bernardino National Forest.

Also nearby are Mt. Baldy Trout Pools, San Antonio Falls, Lytle Creek and Green Mountain Ranch.

CUCAMONGA/GUASTI PARK **LAKE**

The urban lakes are shallow, only 20 feet deep in the middle, and the air gets blazing hot and smoggy in the summer, making early morning and evening fishing the only option.

Rating: 4

Species: Rainbow Trout, Channel Catfish, Bluegill, Largemouth Bass, Carp

Stocked with 34,000 pounds of rainbow trout.

Facilities: Paddle Boat Rentals, Bait & Tackle Shop, Snack Bar, Wheelchair Access, Waterslides, and Swimming Pools

Cucamonga/Guasti Park Lake

Need Information? Contact: Cucamonga-Guasti Regional Park (909) 481-4205

Directions: From Interstate 10 in Ontario, exit north on Archibald Ave. and drive three-tenths of a mile to the park entrance on the right.

It seems like every urban city has its own, stocked park lake, and Ontario is no exception. Located a few minutes from the Ontario Mills Mall and the Ontario Airport (less than a minute from the I-10), Cucamonga-Guasti Regional Park Lake provides fishermen and the residents of Ontario, Rancho Cucamonga and Fontana with an easy to get to, decently stocked fishery.

There are actually two small ponds here, both lined with grassy shorelines and shaded by large trees. Throughout much of the Nineties a fishing license wasn't needed to fish the lake because it was not stocked by the California Department of Fish and Game. However, the CA DFG resumed plants in 2001 and a license is again required. The lake also gets plants of rainbow trout from San Bernardino County each week in the winter. The CA DFG stocks trout once a month during the cooler months, but catch rates remain just fair.

All the trout from the county are between one and 14 pounds, with most in the two-pound range, the CA DFG fish are smaller than a pound. The urban lakes are shallow, only 20 feet deep in the middle, and the air gets blazing hot and smoggy in the summer, making early morning and evening fishing the only option. Trust me, the fish just won't bite during mid-day.

From mid-April to late September the lake is stocked weekly with 1,000 pounds of catfish. As a special treat for anglers, the lake stays open for midnight catfish fishing on Saturday nights.

Although you have to share it with ducks and geese, shoreline fishing is your only option. No float tubes or watercraft are allowed. While you are waiting for a bite, take a view of the scenery. You can see Mt. Baldy and Big Bear from here.

If you plan to make the trip, supplies are available at the lake. There is a parking and fishing fee.

Also nearby are Lytle Creek, Glen Helen Park Lake, San Antonio Falls, Bonita Falls.

GREEN MOUNTAIN **RANCH**

Rating: 4

Species: Rainbow Trout
and Channel Catfish

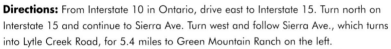

Stocked periodically by private hatcheries.

Facilities: Diner, Bait and Tackle & Restrooms

Need Information? Contact: Green Mountain Ranch (909) 880-1125

Directions: From Interstate 10 in Ontario, drive east to Interstate 15. Turn north on Interstate 15 and continue to Sierra Ave. Turn west and follow Sierra Ave., which turns into Lytle Creek Road, for 5.4 miles to Green Mountain Ranch on the left.

Less than a quarter-mile from Lytle Creek, Green Mountain Ranch is located in the San Bernardino National Forest. Heavily stocked with rainbow trout year-round, it provides anglers who are willing to spend a few extra bucks with sure catch rates. The trout cost a minimum of $1.95 for a nine-incher, up to $13.60 for fish that are 18 inches. I can assure you there aren't many fish fewer than 12 inches in this pond.

A little smaller than an Olympic size swimming pool and about five feet deep, Green Mountain Ranch is different than other stocked trout ponds in the area (Alpine, Whitewater, Mt. Baldy Trout Pools, Oak Tree Village) because it also has catfish. The ranch planted catfish more than seven years ago and few have been caught.

Considering that the pond is so small and so heavily fished, you'd think it would be easy to catch the cats, but catfish fishing here is tricky. The reason is because it's almost impossible to get your bait to rest on the bottom where the cats hang out. The trout snatch the bait before it gets anywhere near the catfish. I thought about using a large piece of mackerel that was bigger than the trout. Then I talked to the guy at the fish cleaning station who told me that all the catfish are at least 20 pounds, and at $3 a pound it would have cost me a minimum of $60 to catch one. I decided I didn't want to spend the money. On second thought, that might be a good idea for a birthday present. Where else can you catch a 20-pound catfish without having to wait an entire day to get a bite like you do at most larger lakes?

Green Mountain Ranch is most famous for being the lone diner of the Lytle Creek drainage. They commonly host weddings and large parties. Can you image having your wedding on the patio next to the trout pond? I can picture it now... "Hold on honey. Before I say 'I do,' I want to catch one more trout." For you fishing fanatics the idea might not be so far-fetched. I've actually thought about getting married at a place like this myself, but if I were going to get married at a lake, I'd rather do it shaded by towering pines in the Eastern Sierra. It's much prettier.

If you plan to make the trip, supplies are available at the ranch. No fishing license is required. There is a fishing fee. The ranch is open Friday through Sunday.

Also nearby are Lytle Creek and Bonita Falls.

LYTLE **CREEK**

Concentrate your efforts about half a mile upstream from the point at which the Middle Fork Road becomes a dirt road. Power Bait and salmon eggs will get the job done here.

Rating: 6

Species: Rainbow Trout

Stocked with 2,300 pounds of Rainbow Trout.

Facilities: Campgrounds, General Store, Lodging, Restrooms, RV Hookups and Picnic areas.

Need Information?
Contact: San Bernardino National Forest (909) 887-2576

Lytle Creek

Directions: From Interstate 15 in Rancho Cucamonga, drive 7.6 miles north to the Sierra Highway-Lytle Creek Road exit. Turn west and continue three miles to the Middle Fork turn-off. Turn left. The stream is stocked for one mile upstream from the point at which the pavement turns to dirt. The stream is also stocked on Lytle Creek Road at Applewhite Campground.

Many people believe that finding a good trout stream in close proximity to the Inland Empire is near impossible, but Lytle Creek should put all their doubts to rest. Located at 3,000 feet in the San Bernardino National Forest, Lytle Creek is a medium-size trout stream that is heavily fished by anglers. During the spring, the creek is stocked twice a month with rainbow trout, providing consistent action as long as water flows remain at suitable levels.

Many fishermen get skunked here, but that's not because of the lack of fish. Good streamside access and the ability to fish in large pools, makes it easy for anglers to achieve limits. The California Department of Fish and Game stocks 4,040 rainbow trout in this stretch of water. The key is in knowing where to cast your line.

The fish are split between the North and Middle Forks, with the Middle Fork getting the bulk of the trout. (The North Fork only gets 660 fish.) Concentrate your efforts about half a mile upstream from the point at which the Middle Fork Road becomes a dirt road. Power Bait and salmon eggs will get the job done here.

As for the North Fork, plants have been greatly reduced over the years because of a lack of public access. The majority of the stream is lined with private residences and private campgrounds. The North Fork is stocked exclusively at the RV Park on Lytle Creek Road across from Applewhite Campground.

If you plan to make the trip, supplies are available at a general store just past the Middle Fork turn-off. A Forest Service Adventure Pass is required to park in the San Bernardino National Forest.

Also nearby are Bonita Falls, Glen Helen Park Lake and Cucamonga Gausti Park Lake.

GLEN HELEN PARK **LAKE**

Last time I fished the lake I saw a guy boasting that he was hooked up on a 10-pound trout, when five minutes later he was disappointed to see a five-pound carp.

Rating: 5

Glen Helen Park Lake

Species: Rainbow Trout, Channel Catfish, Black Bass, Carp and Bluegill

Stocked with 12,200 pounds of rainbow trout and weekly seasonal plants of catfish.

Need Information? Contact: Glen Helen Regional Park (909) 880-6211

Facilities: Campgrounds, Waterslides, RV Hookups, Nature Trails, Restrooms, Playgrounds, Swimming Areas and a Snack Bar

Directions: From the 215 Freeway near San Bernardino, exit Devore Road and turn west. Continue eight-tenths of a mile to the park entrance on Glen Helen Road. Turn south into the park.

Many people get Glen Helen Park Lake confused with Glen Helen Blockbuster Pavilion located within Glen Helen Regional Park, but the two have dramatic differences. One involves dancing, screaming, cheering, hot dogs, pretzels, beer and listening to loud music and the other requires you to get your hands dirty and smelly while fishing. Another difference is that while the Blockbuster Pavilion puts on some of the best concerts in Southern California, you can't say that Glen Helen Park Lake offers some of the best fishing.

Just minutes from the 15 and 215 Freeways, Glen Helen Park Lake, in the city of Devore, can best be described as two small, weekly-stocked ponds that can require a lot of patience to fish. The lakes can get crowded, hot and smoggy during the summer. With the water normally discolored, still fishing is usually the only option, which means you have to sit back, shoulder-to-shoulder with everybody else, and wait.

The larger, seven-acre pond is used for trout, and a smaller three-acre pond is set aside for catfish. The fishing always remains fair here. Weekly plants from both county and state hatcheries (which occur in all the San Bernardino County Park Lakes) guarantee it. More than 25,000 trout are planted in the winter and early spring, with catfish coming from late spring through fall. Surprisingly, at this shallow, cement bottomed lake, anglers land huge rainbows, up to 13 pounds, almost always on Power Bait. Remember, the water is too murky for lures.

Crowds fill the shorelines with bait dunkers, scoring limits in a few hours. Carp often shock anglers who think they are reeling in a trophy trout. Last time I fished the lake I saw a guy boasting that he was hooked up on a 10-pound trout, when five minutes later he was disappointed to see a five-pound carp. A few anglers target the small bass and bluegill in the lake.

If you plan to make the trip, supplies are available in Devore. There is a day use and fishing fee.

Also nearby are Lytle Creek, Silverwood Lake and Bonita Falls.

REGION 8

Los Angeles/Orange County Metro Area

Echo Park Lake
Sante Fe Reservoir
Puddingstone Lake
Centennial Park Lake
Irvine Lake
Santa Ana River Lakes
Anaheim Lake
Laguna Niguel Lake
Trabuco Creek
San Juan Creek

CALIFORNIA

Barstow
Needles
Santa Barbara
Pasadena
San Bernardino
Los Angeles
Riverside
Indio
Long Beach
Escondido
San Diego
El Centro
Colorado River

ECHO PARK **LAKE**

*So unpack your lunch, set up the lounge chair, turn on the radio,
listen to the baseball game, throw out some Power Bait
and wait. It's going to be a while.*

Rating: 4

Species: Rainbow Trout, Channel Catfish,
Bullhead, Carp and Largemouth Bass

Stocked with 7,100 pounds of rainbow trout
and 3,000 pounds of catfish.

Facilities: Picnic Areas, Gas, Restrooms
and Food

Echo Park Lake is one of Los Angeles'
most popular urban fisheries.

Need Information? Contact: California
Department of Fish & Game (562) 590-5151

Directions: From downtown Los Angeles, drive north on the 101 Freeway to Glendale
Blvd. Turn north and continue a half-mile to the park.

If you're a fan of professional baseball, chances are you've driven by Echo Park Lake
and had no idea that the 15-acre lake had any fish in it. Well, the good news is that it
does. Echo Park Lake is a small and shallow urban fishery that people drive by regularly
when taking Glendale Blvd. to Dodger Stadium. In contrast to the urban sprawl
surrounding it, the grassy shorelines and palm trees make the scenery appealing. The
bad news is that the fishing is the pits.

Although the California Department of Fish and Game stocks 15,470 rainbow trout
here in the cooler months and 3,000 pounds of catfish in the summer, catch rates are
low. The planted trout are small and require time and patience to catch because you
have to use Power Bait
or nightcrawlers. Lures
don't work well because
the water is usually discolored. So, unpack your
lunch, set up the lounge
chair, turn on the radio,
listen to the baseball
game, throw out some
Power Bait and wait. It's
going to be a while.

If you plan to make
the trip, supplies are available in Los Angeles.

Also nearby is
Dodger Stadium.

Echo Park Lake

SANTA FE **RESERVOIR**

All the smart anglers write this place off and head over to the San Bernardino Mountain lakes where it's cool enough for trout to live in the hot summer months.

Rating: 4

Species: Rainbow Trout, Largemouth Bass, Bluegill, and Channel Catfish

Stocked with 13,600 pounds of rainbow trout and 6,000 pounds of channel catfish.

Inspite of heavy plants, fishing is generally poor at Santa Fe Reservoir.

Facilities: Boat Launch, Boat Rentals, Snack Bar, Bait & Tackle, Picnic Areas, Restrooms, Playgrounds, and a Bicycle Path

Need Information? Contact: Santa Fe Dam Recreation Area (626) 334-1065

Directions: From the 210 Freeway in Irwindale, exit south on Irwindale Ave. Continue to First St. and turn right. Then turn right on Peckham Rd. into the county park.

The Bermuda Triangle and Santa Fe Reservoir have much in common. They both seem to lose objects. In the case of the Bermuda Triangle it's a few ships, but Santa Fe seems to lose a lot more fish. My friends jokingly refer to the reservoir as the "black hole," because the California Department of Fish and Game dumps tons of rainbow trout and channel catfish into the lake but hardly anybody seems to catch anything. People read in the newspapers that the lake is being stocked and they rush out to get skunked over and over again. You ask where all the fish are going? I wish I could tell you. It's a mystery to me, too!

Aside from the absence of trout and catfish, Santa Fe Reservoir is a small 80-acre lake located in a flood control basin in the San Gabriel Valley near the convergence of the 210 and 605 Freeways. The reservoir is stocked every other week with trout in the cooler months, and catfish as water temperature increases. But don't expect to catch any lunkers here. The 27,930 trout stocked barely peek above a pound, while the catfish range from one to three pounds. As for the small bass and bluegill that roam the lake, they'll provide much more action than the trout and catfish, and they're a lot easier to catch. Just throw out a piece of a nightcrawler and you're in business.

Located in a park that is dominated by family picnics, birthdays, bike riding and other recreational activities, Santa Fe Reservoir is not a fisherman's paradise. As you might have guessed, it's not a popular fishing hole, either. Once the heat and smog of summer arrives, the fish go searching for that "black hole" in the bottom of the lake. All the smart anglers write this place off and head over to the San Bernardino Mountain lakes where it's cool enough for trout to live in the hot summer months.

If you plan to make the trip, there is a day-use fee. No gasoline motors are permitted. Also, check for boat length regulations.

Also nearby are Puddingstone Reservoir and Peck Road Park Lake.

PUDDINGSTONE **RESERVOIR**

The lifeguards are constantly busy here. One told us they call the lake "NFL," short for "no fun lake."

Rating: 6

Species: Largemouth Bass, Red Ear Sunfish, Crappie, Bluegill, Carp, Channel Catfish, and Rainbow Trout

Stocked with 24,000 pounds of rainbow trout and 3,000 pounds of channel catfish.

Facilities: Boat Launch, Snack Bar, Picnic Areas, Restrooms, Swimming Beach and Fishing Piers

Need Information? Contact: Bonelli Regional Park (909) 599-8411

Directions: From Interstate 10 in Pomona, exit Ganesha Drive. Drive north for one mile to Puddingstone Drive. Turn left and continue to the lake.

When you have a lake so close to an urban area, the fishing almost always suffers from lake overuse. This is definitely the case with Puddingstone Reservoir. Located just minutes from the congested and smog infested San Gabriel Valley, in Frank G. Bonelli Regional Park near Raging Waters Theme Park, the 250-acre reservoir is bombarded by boaters, recreationists and fishermen on a daily basis.

We tried to fish it on a weekend in June and it looked like Lake Havasu during spring break. Way too many boats, some pulling water-skiers, sailing, fishing, sightseeing, all causing large wakes everywhere on the lake, perhaps only to the delight of the wakeboarders. The lifeguards are constantly busy here. One told us they call the lake "NFL," short for "no fun lake." It is so crowded they have to keep the rules extra tight to prevent accidents. No tubing is allowed and no swimming is permitted, except for the swimming beach.

There are surprisingly a lot of fish in the lake, but with all the traffic they can be difficult to catch. The most prized fish here are largemouth bass. Bass can grow more

Trolling for rainbow trout can be productive near the dam from December through April.

than 10 pounds in this shallow, crowded, over-fished lake. Most of them are caught in the bushy coves, off the many fishing piers, and near the cliffs between the dam and the boat launch. Another productive spot is off the point near the swimming beach. Rat-L-Traps are a favorite here, but plastics do well, too.

For shore anglers, the trout bite is fair to good from November to March when the fish are in shallow water. But as the water warms in late March and April, the only way to catch trout is trolling near the dam with leadcore or downriggers. All of the trout die off by mid-May.

The red ear sunfish and bluegill bite stays decent throughout the summer months, with most of the fish caught in shallow water on pieces of worms and crappie jigs. Action of catfish bites pick up in May when plants begin and last until October when the water starts to cool.

Puddingstone Reservoir is heavily used by both boaters and anglers.

If fishing for any type of fish, your best bet is to get on the lake early. Before 10 a.m. there is a 12-mph speed limit, which keeps the lake free of major traffic. But from 10 a.m. to an hour before sunset, the lake's speed limit switches to 35-mph in the speed zone and the bite turns off completely.

If you plan to make the trip, supplies are available in San Dimas. There is a day-use and a boat launch fee.

Also nearby are the Santa Fe Reservoir, Peck Road Park Lake, San Dimas Reservoir and the San Gabriel River.

PUDDINGSTONE **RESERVOIR**

CENTENNIAL PARK **LAKE**

Catfish fishing is a game of patience here. If you have it, you'll catch fish.

Rating: 4

Species: Rainbow Trout, Channel Catfish, Bluegill and Carp

Stocked with 4,600 pounds of rainbow trout and 3,000 pounds of catfish.

Facilities: Picnic Areas, Restrooms, Playgrounds and Recreational Facilities

Need Information? Contact: Orange County Recreational Facilities (714) 771-6731

Directions: From the 405 Freeway in Santa Ana exit Fairview Street. Turn north and drive 2.5 miles to Edinger Avenue. The lake is on the west side of the street.

Centennial Park Lake is one of many urban fisheries in Orange County. The 10-acre lake, surrounded by grassy areas and shaded by large trees, serves as a quick getaway from city life for the residents of Santa Ana, Fountain Valley and Costa Mesa.

From December to February, the lake is stocked by the California Department of Fish and Game with about 15,000 rainbow trout from eight to 10 inches. Runner up to Tri-City Lake, which receives about 500 more trout, Centennial Park Lake is the second most heavily stocked public urban lake in Orange County. Each year the lake also gets a bonus plant of 30 trout that weigh two pounds or more. Due to murky water, the use of lures can be difficult. Most anglers set up a lounge chair along the shore, use Power Bait and wait for a nibble.

Once the water begins to warm and the trout die off, plants of catfish are poured into the lake. The lake is stocked with 3,000 pounds of channel catfish each year, making it the most heavily stocked public urban catfish lake in the county. Catfish fishing is a game of patience here. If you have it, you'll catch fish. If you don't, you'll go home unhappy. It's all about tossing out a nightcrawler, anchovies or mackerel and waiting for a bite. To keep you occupied, you might want to bring along a portable radio and listen to the ballgame while waiting. The bite is best in the morning and evening, and if you wait long enough you'll catch one. No night fishing is allowed.

If you plan to make the trip, supplies are available in Santa Ana.

Also nearby are Mile Square Park Lake, the Orange County Swap Meet and Newport Beach.

IRVINE **LAKE**

Irvine Lake is a popular lake and the shoreline can get mighty crowded. I've seen it look like opening day at Dodger Stadium.

Rating: 6

Species: Blue Catfish, Channel Catfish, Rainbow Trout, Bluegill, Common Carp, Crappie, Largemouth Bass and Wipers

Stocked periodically by the lake.

Facilities: Launch Ramp, Tackle Shop, Boat Rentals, Fish Cleaning Station, Picnic Areas and Restrooms

Need Information? Contact: Irvine Lake Hotline (714) 649-2168, Tackle Shop (714) 649-9111

Freedom McCullough displays a trout caught on a mini jig from Irvine Lake's catch-out pond.

Directions: From Interstate 5 in Anaheim, drive south to 22 Freeway. Drive east to the 55 Freeway. Drive north on the 55 Freeway, exit Chapman (East) and follow it for seven miles to lake.

Every fisherman has read the stories of the giant fish in Irvine Lake. How many actually catch those fish is a whole other story. When you read the fishing report, it sounds like Irvine Lake kicks out limits to everybody, but that's not how it works. Not even close. The way I see it, one person gets lucky and catches a huge fish over 10 pounds, then the lake management takes their picture and plasters it on the cover of outdoor publications. Fishermen flock to the lake thinking they'll catch the fish of a lifetime, but in reality few do.

With continuous plants year around you'd think the action would never stop, but on my last five occasions my bait remained untouched. To tell you the truth, in the five times I've been there I've only snagged one carp. Most of the time, there are just a few fishermen catching fish while the rest patiently wait on the shore. Every time I go to the lake, the guys in the tackle shop tell me that the fishing is "red hot and limits are common." But when I walk the shoreline to do a survey, only a few anglers have fish.

Putting all my bad luck aside, the lake management insists that they stock 150,000 pounds of trout from November to May, and 30,000 pounds of catfish from May to November. With the catch rates I've witnessed, it's hard to believe. The trout are shipped from Mt. Lassen Trout Farms in Northern California and the catfish are raised in Blythe. All the fish stocked are said to be over a pound, but I've seen a lot of half-pounders.

The lake record for trout is 22.55 pounds. While the largest cat recorded is 89.6 pounds, but word of mouth has bigger ones swimming the lake. The lake also has large-mouth bass, but they aren't heavily targeted. The lake record is 14.7 pounds, and that fish is still in the lake. Fishing for bass, crappie, bluegill and wipers is strictly catch & release. The lake planted hybrid bass, called wipers, a few years ago.

Trout and catfish are stocked year-round in the kid's pond.

Irvine Lake is a popular lake and the shoreline can get mighty crowded. I've seen it look like opening day at Dodger Stadium. Although I haven't personally seen many anglers catch fish, with all the fish the lake advertises it stocks there should be a good chance you'll hook into one.

Best bet for trout is inflated nightcrawlers or rainbow Power Bait fished in Sierra Cove and along the West Shore. Catfish are caught on chicken or beef liver and mackerel. The best time to hook into a lunker is during all night fishing in the summer. Concentrate you efforts around Santiago Flats and the east shore.

Irvine Lake has experienced problems with water levels over the last few years, so call ahead for launch conditions and make sure you get the right information! I dragged my boat two hours to the lake after they told me the launch ramp was in good shape, and when I got there I was told I couldn't launch.

If you plan to make the trip, there is a $12 per person charge to fish at Irvine Lake. Boats are also available as well as food, tackle and a kids fishing pond (which costs extra).

Also nearby is Santa Ana River Lakes.

IRVINE LAKE

SANTA ANA RIVER **LAKES**

SARL is one of the most heavily stocked waters in the entire state.

Rating: 9

Species: Rainbow Trout, Bluegill, Crappie, Channel Catfish and Sturgeon

Stocked with 152,600 pounds of rainbow trout and 12,765 pounds of channel catfish.

Facilities: Bait & Tackle, Snack Bar, Restrooms, Boat Launch and Boat Rentals

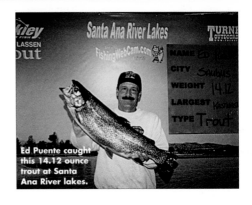

Ed Puente caught this 14.12 ounce trout at Santa Ana River lakes.

Need Information? Contact: Santa Ana River Lakes (714-632-7830)

Directions: From Interstate 5 in Santa Ana, drive north to the 57 Freeway. Continue on the 57 to the 91 Freeway and drive east. Exit Tustin Ave., turn north and continue to La Palma. Turn right and continue to the entrance.

Lets start by saying it's very difficult to make money running your own pay fishing lake, but you can make anglers happy. At least the owners of Santa Ana River Lakes will tell you it's true any day. These owners get carried away stocking fish, maybe too many. SARL is one of the most heavily stocked waters in the entire state, probably the country.

Where else can you go where more than 152,000 pounds of rainbow trout are stocked? Can you imagine, some anglers have the audacity to complain about having to purchase a fishing permit? If you knew how much the owners were paying for the fish, you'd be willing to pay more. Think about how expensive rainbow trout are in your local grocery store. And these trout that Santa Ana River Lakes stocks are much bigger than the ones you see behind the glass in the seafood section. Most of the fish planted are from one to three pounds, but fish up to 23-pounds are planted each year.

SARL has kicked out two fish (a 23.76 and 23.25 trout) that are larger than the California state-record rainbow trout. During the 1999-2000 trout season, eight rainbows more than 20 pounds were checked in at SARL and Corona Lake (which is also owned by SARL). Not enough big fish for you? How about this? A whopping 5,000 trout over 10 pounds were also caught that season!

Surprisingly, the owners say business is slowing a bit; they only draw 2,000-5,000 anglers a week now. Back when the lakes first opened in the mid-Eighties, at least 1,000 people a day flocked to them. The explanation is simple – back in the Eighties, SARL was the only lake that had big fish, but now many other lakes import them, too. Yet, SARL still imports twice the amount of lunkers than other lakes.

In the late Nineties, SARL and competitor Irvine Lake battled for customers in what was referred to as the "Trout Wars." Each lake tried to outdo the other by offering better prizes and more money at derbies, and by stocking more and larger fish. SARL called themselves the "Home of the Super Fish." However, a recently published article in the Orange County Register reported that Irvine isn't going to try to outdo SARL anymore. The "Trout Wars" are through, and SARL has claimed victory. But is it really a victory? This is a business, remember, and SARL isn't making much money. Trout are too expensive and catfish prices recently shot up in the spring of 2000.

With three stocked ponds and continuous plants, SARL is a favorite spot for many anglers in Southern California. There are two trout lakes, one 15-acres and the other 90, and a 35-acre catfish pond. On weekends and holidays, and when the bite is on, the lake gets crowded, but most anglers still leave with their limits. This is a Power Bait and inflated nightcrawler lake, with anglers who use a sliding sinker rig enjoying success. Tossing Panther Martins or using Trout Teasers salso catch fish. SARL recently gave some new flavor to trout fishing by stocking "Lightning Trout." The trout are a bright orange colored fish with flashes of pink and yellow.

Santa Ana River Lakes owner Greg Elliott releases a trout into the lake.

A hidden gem in the lake is large sturgeon. At last count, there were 23, but over Thanksgiving Weekend of 2000, another 1,000 pounds of the dinosaur looking fish, all from 5-7 pounds, were planted. Many fishermen catch them by accident. They aren't targeted because most people don't know they exist in these lakes.

To give anglers some action when the trout die off in late May, SARL is stocked with 12,765 pounds of channel catfish in early June. Operations at SARL are shut down in the summer and moved to Anaheim Lake.

SARL is used as a reservoir for Orange County's drinking water and is drained and cleaned each year. When SARL is drained, all the fish are taken out and transported to Anaheim Lake.

Remember to hold on to your pole. If one of those sturgeons takes your bait you could be going in with it!

If you plan to make the trip, supplies are available at the lake. There is a fishing and boat launch fee. No fishing license is required.

Also nearby are Disneyland, the Arrowhead Pond and Anaheim Lake.

ANAHEIM **LAKE**

The trick to fishing Anaheim Lake is using a marshmallow/ mealworm combo. It works even better than mackerel!

Rating: 7

Species: Channel Catfish, Crappie, Bluegill and Sturgeon

Stocked with 85,250 pounds of channel catfish.

Facilities: Bait & Tackle, Snack Bar, Picnic Area, Restrooms, Fish Cleaning Stations, Boat Launch and Boat Rentals

Need Information? Contact: Anaheim Lake (714) 996-3508

Directions: From Interstate 5 in Los Angeles, drive south to the 91 Freeway east. From the 91 Freeway exit Tustin Ave. and drive north to East Mira Loma Ave. The lake entrance is on East Mira Loma Ave. just west of Tustin.

Each year, when Santa Ana River Lakes closes in June for maintenance, operations move to nearby Anaheim Lake. Located in the city of Anaheim the 75-acre lake with 2.5 miles of shoreline was opened as an urban reservoir in 1969 by the Orange County Water District. SARL, which also runs Corona Lake, leases the reservoir from late June to early October, running it as a successful put-and-take fishery.

Although the reservoir is drained twice a year, it remains full during the summer when 82,250 channel catfish are stocked. No trout plants are made. The lake also inherits fish taken from the drained SARL, including some big catfish, bluegill, crappie and 26 sturgeon weighing at least six pounds each (at the time of this writing). It is popular with anglers because you can park your vehicle anywhere around the lake and fish out of your back seat if you want, although most people go with the more traditional folding chairs.

There are also three islands, all split by a deepwater channel where the largest fish hang. A couple of other good fishing spots are the Bubble Hole, where water is pumped into the lake and near the boat docks. The trick to fishing Anaheim Lake is using a marshmallow/mealworm combo. It works even better than mackerel! Other traditional baits like nightcrawlers and chicken liver work, too.

As soon as October comes, they haul away the rental boats and truck what's left of the fish back over to SARL. Then trout season begins and Anaheim Lake is once again drained.

If you plan to make the trip, supplies are available at the lake. There are boat launch and fishing fees.

Also nearby are Santa Ana River Lakes, Disneyland and the Arrowhead Pond.

LAGUNA NIGUEL **LAKE**

Surrounded by the hills of Laguna Niguel, the park makes you feel like you're somewhere far away from the city.

Rating: 10

Species: Rainbow Trout, Channel Catfish, Largemouth Bass, Bluegill, Carp, White & Black Crappie

Stocked with 45,000 pounds of rainbow trout and 34,000 pounds of channel catfish.

Facilities: Boat Rentals, Bait & Tackle, Picnic Areas, Restrooms, Fish Cleaning Station and Snack Bar

Rick Mendoza, owner of Laguna Niguel Lake regularly catches rainbow trout like this five-pounder.

Need Information? Contact: Laguna Niguel Lake (949) 362-3885

Directions: From Interstate 5 in Mission Viejo, drive south and exit La Paz Road. Turn right and continue approximately four miles to the park entrance on your right.

Laguna Niguel Lake is a place most communities would love to have. The 44-acre lake, located in Laguna Niguel Regional Park, is peaceful, quiet and clean, with excellent fishing and a family atmosphere. The lake is close enough to a variety of urban centers that people can enjoy it before or after a long day at work. Surrounded by the hills of Laguna Niguel, Orange County residents don't need to drive hundreds of miles away to get the full outdoor experience because the park makes you feel like you're somewhere far away from the city. That feeling is only heightened as you walk to the creek inlet and see kids trying to catch turtles, bullfrogs, crawdads and ducks with their hands. This is the kind of stuff you don't normally get to see in the city.

The lake usually stays quiet (except when someone catches a huge fish) -- at times so quiet you can hear people on the other side talking. Unlike most pay lakes in Southern California (Corona, Santa Ana River Lakes and Irvine Lake), the park doesn't generally get overcrowded. But when the fishing gets hot, there is no controlling the crowds. When people are catching lots of fish, word gets out fast and anglers rush to the lake to get in on the action.

The trout at Laguna Niguel are an experience you can't find anywhere else in Southern California. Raised in natural, spring-fed creeks and purchased from the Boulder Mountains in Utah, they are more lively and fight better than other trout stocked in Southern California lakes. They jump out of the water when caught. Most fish planted in local rivers and lakes by the California Department of Fish and Game have half tails from being too closely quartered in growing tanks, and scales that come off after you touch them. These fish look big, beautiful and natural. Their bright colors, and the hook jaws on the males, grab you and keep you coming back for more. And best of all, they have pink meat and taste great!

Trout season begins the day after Thanksgiving and lasts until early May. The lake is stocked regularly, on schedule (every other Tuesday), so you have a better chance of going out right after the stock and catching one of the big ones. They stock 60,000 pounds of rainbow trout, but that doesn't mean that 60,000 fish are planted because they are all larger than a pound. Most of the fish are in the three to six pound class, with some up to 15 pounds. Your chances of catching big fish are good.

As a matter of fact, there are more big fish here than in most of the Eastern Sierra lakes. Catching these lunkers is all about knowing what lures and bait to use. The easiest, but least known method is by trolling Norman crappie crankbaits. The lake has a tremendous amount of bass fry that trout love to feed on, and the Norman lures imitate that fry.

The best troll is from about 30 yards out from the boat dock to the dam. Trolling small Rapalas and Panther Martins also work well around the island and creek inlet area. Bait fishing is also popular along the shoreline near the aeration units located around the boat docks, and near the dam and the creek inlet. Although nightcrawlers and Power Bait work, the most popular bait is using a single salmon egg hook and a small split shot.

Curt Gibson holds a double limit of trout caught trolling Norman crappie crankbaits in May of 2000.

Once the water gets too warm for trout, the lake begins stocking catfish. About 2,000 cats are stocked for the opener and another 1,200 on each Friday morning from May to November. The best place to catch the cats is near the dam and inlet areas. Catfish fishing is best during night fishing hours, but night anglers are required to use lanterns. Call ahead for specific night fishing hours.

In the mid-Nineties, 5,000 adult bass were stocked in the lake from Lake Matthews. Bass to 18 pounds are known to be in the lake, but they aren't heavily targeted. All bass fishing is catch & release.

In the spring of 2000, the lake's crappie population was bolstered with a plant of 2,000 crappie from Lake Cuyamaca. There are also about 30 carp over 30 pounds in the lake, but they are hard to catch. The best way to hook them is if you accidentally snag one. I don't think the lake operators would mind. They want them out of the lake.

Laguna Niguel Lake treats their guests differently than other pay lakes in the region. Fishing is based on trust. You aren't stopped at an entrance station and forced to pay a fishing-fee whether or not you are fishing. Anglers are simply asked to come to the office before leaving to pay.

I'm convinced that Laguna Niguel Lake is still a secret. If it weren't, the lake would be full of anglers, daily. Once the word gets out, this place could turn into a crowded nightmare like other pay lakes in the region. Do yourself a favor and come here before it gets that way.

Laguna Niguel Lake imports trout, like this eight pounder from the Boulder Mountains in Utah.

If you plan to make the trip, there is a fee to enter Laguna Niguel Regional Park. No fishing license is required, however, there is a fishing fee. No private boats are allowed, but float tubes are permitted. All the boat rentals have electric powered trolling motors. No gas-powered motors are allowed on the lake. Supplies are available at the lake.

Also nearby are San Juan Creek, San Juan Falls, Trabuco Creek and the Pacific Ocean.

LAGUNA NIGUEL **LAKE**

TRABUCO **CREEK**

I was miserable, and let's just say the fishing was about as much fun as the drive.

Rating: 4

Species: Rainbow Trout

Stocked with 700 pounds of rainbow trout.

Facilities: None

Need Information?
Contact: O'Neill Regional Park
(714) 858-9365, Orange County Department of Park and Recreation (714) 771-6731

Trabuco Creek is the only stream stocked with trout in Orange County.

Directions: From Interstate 5 in San Juan Capistrano, drive nine miles north to the El Toro Road turnoff and turn northeast. Continue for 7.1 miles to Live Oak Canyon Road and bear right. Follow the road for 3.3 miles to Trabuco Canyon Road. Turn northeast and continue one mile to the stream on your right.

You need a high tolerance for the hazards that accompany hard to reach places like Trabuco Creek. My normally high tolerance was shattered the night before when I ordered a Charleston Chicken Ranch Sandwich from Denny's in San Clemente. They didn't have any ranch for my sandwich, to dip my fries in or for my salad! Being a ranch freak, I was still ticked-off when I arrived at Trabuco Creek, and I had little patience for what the creek was about to put me through.

The dirt road that parallels the creek is one of the most poorly maintained, heavily used roads I've ever encountered. I was driving less than 5-mph in my Suburban and the ride was unbearable. Things were falling off my dashboard, my head was bouncing off the ceiling and the fishing poles in back of the car sounded like they were snapping every time I stepped on the gas. It felt like I was in an airplane that was about to crash! I was miserable, and let's just say the fishing was about as much fun as the drive.

This small stream, located at 1,000 feet in the Cleveland National Forest, is only stocked with 1,340 trout from February to May. That is, providing it has enough water to support fish. The stream is only a few miles from Orange County, so when there are a number of good-sized pools a lot of anglers fish here, keeping catch rates low. If you still want to brave it, stick to Power Bait or salmon eggs. The fish that hold in small pools are easily spotted, so don't bother fishing where you don't see any fish. If you arrived late, somebody else already caught 'em all.

If you plan to make the trip, supplies are available in Mission Viejo and Rancho Santa Margarita. A Forest Service Adventure Pass is required to park in the Cleveland National Forest.

Also nearby are Laguna Niguel Lake, Falls Canyon Falls and Holy Jim Falls.

SAN JUAN **CREEK**

As a coastal stream, San Juan Creek was viewed as a possible area in which steelhead could spawn, and the California Department of Fish and Game was forced to stop stocking rainbow trout in the stream.

Rating: 2

Species: Rainbow Trout

Stocks: None

Facilities: Restrooms, Picnic Areas and Campgrounds

Need Information?
Contact: Cleveland National Forest (909) 736-1811, Ortega General Store (909) 678-2774

Trout plants have ceased at San Juan Creek.

Directions: From Interstate 5 in San Juan Capistrano, drive east on Highway 74 to the Upper San Juan Picnic Area.

In 1997, many Southland rivers and streams were taken off the trout planting schedule when the US Fish & Wildlife Service put the steelhead on the endangered species list. As a coastal stream, San Juan Creek was viewed as a possible area in which steelhead could spawn, and the California Department of Fish and Game was forced to stop stocking rainbow trout here. The thought of steelhead even making it to an elevation as far up the creek where the rainbows were stocked is far-fetched, but the concern is that the stockers will somehow swim downstream to the ocean and mix with the native steelhead.

The plants last took place in 1997, when the CA DFG stocked 300 pounds of rainbow trout (580 fish). Yet, in the summer of 2000, when I called the local Forest Service office, they told me the stream gets planted every spring. They said it was only planted once in 2000 because of low water levels. Wrong! It wasn't planted at all and will no longer be planted unless the steelhead is taken off the endangered species.

However, even if the steelhead is taken off the list, San Juan Creek may have another problem to deal with. The Southwestern Arroyo Toad, also a member of the endangered species list, is found here too. Although the toad has been found at the creek and several of its tributaries from February through April, recent studies have shown that it's just passing through and doesn't use this area as its breeding ground. Despite those studies, the USFWS may shut down Upper San Juan Campground to all traffic in order to protect the species.

The whole thing is bad news for fishermen, most of whom have stopped coming to the area because there are no stockers and only a few wild trout left in the stream.

If you plan to make the trip, a Forest Service Adventure Pass is required to park in the Cleveland National Forest. Supplies are available at the Ortega General Store near Upper San Juan Campground.

Also nearby are Trabuco Creek, Lake Elsinore, San Juan Falls and Ortega Falls.

REGION 9

San Bernardino Mountains

CALIFORNIA

CLEGHORN **CREEK**

Don't bother bringing lures. The creek isn't big enough to cast and retrieve them. Come prepared with all the Power Bait and salmon eggs you have. These fish love them.

Rating: 4

Species: Rainbow Trout

Stocked with 800 pounds of rainbow trout.

Facilities: Campgrounds, Picnic Areas, and Restrooms

Need Information? Contact: Silverwood Lake Park Office (760) 389-2281, Silverwood Lake Camping Information (760) 389-2282

Directions: From Interstate 10 in San Bernardino, turn north on Interstate 15 and continue approximately 23 miles to the Cajon Junction, also known as the Silverwood Lake

Cleghorn Creek

exit (Highway 138). Exit Highway 138 and drive east for 11 miles to the Silverwood Lake Recreation Area exit. The off-ramp crosses the creek and the road parallels it.

Cleghorn Creek, located on the west side of the Silverwood Lake Recreation area, has a rocky base and suffers from low water levels. There are only sufficient flows to hold fish from February to early May. However, when flows are consistent, it is stocked with 1,900 rainbow trout from the California Department of Fish and Game, and doesn't receive a lot of pressure from anglers because there are so many better places nearby for anglers to spend their time, like Gregory and Big Bear Lakes.

Cleghorn Creek actually becomes the West Fork of the Mojave River before it empties into Silverwood Lake, but nobody pays much attention to the boundary. All that anglers care about is that there are fish in the stream. By late April rattlesnakes become a problem and you'll understand why if you ever visit and see all the fallen trees and dead brush along the streambed.

At 3,378 feet in the San Bernardino National Forest, the stream is just below the transition zone. It's still in the dry foothills, below the pine trees that greet you higher up the mountain, about another 1000 feet of elevation towards Crestline.

As for the fish, they are easy to catch. Don't bother bringing lures. The creek isn't big enough to cast and retrieve them. Come prepared with all the Power Bait and salmon eggs you have. These fish love them.

If you plan to make the trip, supplies are available at Silverwood Lake. Call ahead to check on water conditions.

Also nearby are Silverwood Lake, Cleghorn Creek, Heart Rock Falls, Lake Arrowhead, Lake Gregory and Hesperia Lake.

SILVERWOOD **LAKE**

As for the fishing, it remains good year-round, providing you dodge the winds that usually hit the lake by 10 or 11 a.m.

Rating: 7

Species: Blue Catfish, Channel Catfish, Rainbow Trout, Largemouth Bass, Crappie, Red Ear Sunfish, Brown Trout, Bluegill and Striped Bass

Stocked with 26,100 pounds of rainbow trout.

Facilities: Full Service Marina, Bait & Tackle Shop, General Store, Boat Launch, Boat Rentals, Gas, Campgrounds, Picnic Areas, Restrooms, Swimming Beach, Hiking and Biking Trails and Showers

Need Information?

Contact: Silverwood Lake Entrance Station (760) 389-2303, Park Office (760) 389-2281, Marina and Boat Rentals (760) 389-2299, Campground Reservations (800) 444-7275

Blake Lezak fooled this crappie with a Rapala.

Directions: From Interstate 10 in San Bernardino, drive north on Interstate 15 for 23 miles to the Cajon Junction, also known as the Silverwood Lake exit (Highway 138). Turn east on Highway 138 and continue 12 miles to the lake.

Tucked away at 3,378 feet on the leeward side of the San Bernardino Mountains, Silverwood Lake doesn't get as much fishing pressure as other lakes in the region. The 1,000-acre reservoir is the highest lake under the jurisdiction of the California State Water Project, and can provide good fishing for anglers when the winds aren't howling. The lake came into existence with the construction of the dam from 1969-72, blocking off the West Fork of the Mojave River and creating one of the most popular boating reservoirs in the region. It also provides water to San Bernardino and Rialto, and transports water to Perris Lake.

Silverwood Lake can be thought of as huge fish tank. So much water is pumped in and out of the lake that it recycles itself every two to three weeks, leaving the water extremely aerated. The lake came under recent controversy when from 1995-97 the Department of Water Resources drew the lake down to build an earthquake resistant intake tower. This drawdown killed off a lot of the lake's fish population, including the largemouth bass, which fared the worst.

Soon after, the Southern California Bass Council sued DWR specifically because of the heavy toll the drawndown took on the bass, and also cited a lack of fish habitat and structure on the lake. The SCBC won the battle in a San Bernardino Superior Court, and part of the settlement forced DWR to plant about 4,000 bass and 70,000 trout. In 1999, DWR paid about $15,000 to plant 3,400 four-inch bass, 400 seven-to-eight-inchers and another 400 from nine to 15 inches. In addition, the DWR paid for the stocking of 68,000 rainbow trout from nine to 13 inches.

Although the SCBC won the court battle, they'll feel the repercussions of the work on the dam for years to come. For example, Silverwood used to be one of the best striper fisheries in the state but the striper population has already begun to decline. Part of the problem has to do with the way water now flows into the lake. Water coming from the

Silverwood Lake's striper fishery has suffered from work done to the intake tower that changed the way water from the Aqueduct entered the lake.

aqueduct used to pour through an intake, free-falling down a chute into the lake. This free flow of water constantly replenished the lake with stripers, carp, goldfish and shad. However, since 1998, the hydroelectric power plant at the bottom of the dam began forcing water through turbines to get electric power, chopping up the fish in the turbine blades. Every so often they let the water flow in the old way through the inflow tower allowing stripers into the lake without being chopped up by the turbine blades, but to fishermen it's not often enough.

As for the fishing, it remains fair year-round, providing you dodge the winds that usually hit the lake by 10 or 11 a.m. There are still a fair amount of stripers in the lake, but with the decrease in the striper population the trout don't get eaten as often. Trout fishing is hot for bank anglers who throw white Roostertails or Panther Martins near the marina or in Cleghorn and Miller Canyons. That's because the stockers stay in these areas within 10 feet of the shore to avoid predators. The CA DFG plants a total of more than 50,000 rainbow trout in October and November, and also in March, April and May.

In addition, the lake has a stable population of holdovers, but you'll need either leadcore line or downriggers to catch 'em. These fish, which get as large as eight pounds, hold near the dam in depths of water anywhere from 50 to 200 feet.

A surprise to most anglers is that there are also browns in the lake. When the water levels are high enough, the browns swim in through Miller Canyon and Cleghorn Creeks. In April and May, the crappie bite turns on. Anglers who find rocky coves with calm water can catch anywhere from 50 to 100 a day. The crappie bite stays hot until the water begins to warm. Then the bluegill and red ear sunfish bite picks up and lasts throughout the summer.

Although there aren't many large bass in the lake today, there will be once the fish planted by DWR grow to adult size. At times, catching bass can be difficult because there is so much forage in the lake, including stocked trout and shad, and goldfish and shrimp that flow in from the aqueduct. During the winter, the bass are suspended off points at depths ranging from the lake's bottom to 10 feet below the surface. Using crawdad colored (or brown and black) jigs, with a waterdog hooked through the bottom of the lip, or jigging spoons, should catch you fish. During the spawning period, plastics like salt and pepper, smoke and pepper as well as green weenies work well. Once fall comes, a slower presentation is needed. Most anglers use plastic lizards with a splitshot above.

Catching the stripers is best in the fall. Either troll shad-patterned lures early in the morning or late evening, working the dam area intake and outtake. Another option is to anchor near the dam and fish with anchovies or sardines. The most successful anglers wait till sundown, wade out into the water as far as they can in Miller Canyon and Cleghorn arms, and cast trout imitation lures.

Wind usually kicks up around 10 or 11a.m. at Silverwood Lake.

The catfish bite picks up in the summer. Recently some large fish have been caught, probably because of a goof-up back in 1997 when blues were stocked instead of channels for a kid's derby.

If you plan to make the trip, supplies are available at the lake. There is a day-use and a boat launch fee to enter Silverwood State Recreation area.

Also nearby are Miller Canyon Creek, Cleghorn Creek, Heart Rock Falls, Hesperia Lake, Lake Arrowhead, Lake Gregory and Deep Creek.

SILVERWOOD LAKE

MILLER CANYON **CREEK**

Miller Canyon Creek is stocked in April and May by the California Department of Fish and Game with about 2,500 trout in the eight to 10-inch class.

Rating: 4

Species: Rainbow Trout

Stocked with 1,180 pounds of rainbow trout.

Facilities: Campgrounds, Restrooms and Picnic Areas

Miller Canyon Creek

Need Information? Contact:
Silverwood Lake Recreation Area (760) 389-2281

Directions: From Ontario, drive east on Interstate 10 to Interstate 15. Drive north on Interstate 15 over the Cajon Pass to the Silverwood Lake exit at the Cajon Junction. Exit Highway 138 and turn east. Continue 15 miles to Pilot Rock Conservation Camp and turn left. You'll cross the stream in less than a quarter mile.

Miller Canyon Creek, located just below the pine tree line in a dry foothill area of the San Bernardino National Forest, is a tributary to Silverwood Lake. It is actually the West Fork of the East Fork of the Mojave River and is fed from runoff from the Gregory, Crestline, Arrowhead and Big Bear areas.

It does have more water than its neighbor Cleghorn Creek, which enters Silverwood on the west side of the lake. However, what first caught my attention about the stream had nothing to do with water levels or fishing. Next to the creek, I noticed this sign for the Pilot Rock Conservation Camp, a.k.a. a state prison facility, that uses prisoners to fight fires and do work in the area. The sign said for our safety not to continue past this sign. I thought, "Would I really want to bring kids here?" In fact, there is no reason for anyone to spend time here. After all, there are many better places to fish in the San Bernardino Mountains, places with no prison facilities next to them.

If you must come fish the creek, do so from late winter till early spring, and make sure there is sufficient water in it. It is stocked in April and May by the California Department of Fish and Game with about 2,500 trout in the eight to 10-inch class. The only way to fish the stream is with Power Bait or salmon eggs. It's not deep or wide enough for lures. The best area to fish is from where the creek crosses under the road on down towards the lake. It's also further away from the prison facility.

If you have some extra time, there are some nice swimming areas down at Devil's Pit. To reach this spot, which also occasionally has a few fish in it, continue down the road to the lake and look for a sign on your left.

If you plan to make the trip, there is a day-use fee.

Also nearby are Silverwood Lake, Cleghorn Creek, Lake Gregory, Lake Arrowhead and Hesperia Lake.

LAKE **GREGORY**

Rating: 9

Species: Rainbow Trout, Channel Catfish, Largemouth Bass, Bullhead and Bluegill

Stocked with 18,100 pounds of rainbow trout.
Also receives a bonus of trout from San Bernardino County.

Lake Gregory

Facilities: Boat Rentals, Bait and Tackle Shop, Snack Bar, Swimming Beach, Picnic Areas, Waterslides, Banquet Rooms, Paddle Board Rentals, Restrooms, Paddle Boat Rentals, Restaurant, Campgrounds, Horseshoe Pits, and RV Hookups

Need Information? Contact: Lake Gregory (909) 338-2233, Camp Switzerland (909) 338-2731, Lake Gregory Boat House (909) 338-2233

Directions: From San Bernardino at the junction of Highway 18 and 30, drive north on Highway 18 for 12 miles to Highway 138. From Highway 138 follow the signs for Lake Gregory, driving one mile to Lake Drive in the city of Crestline. From Lake Drive turn east and continue one mile to the lake.

With kids playing on sandy beaches, fishing from rowboats and swimming in the lake, picnic tables full of food and pine trees surrounding the peaceful, pretty wooded mountain area, Lake Gregory is one of the few lakes in Southern California with a family atmosphere. It reminds me of the old Ernest Goes to Camp movies. A place you'd like to send your kids to summer camp to have the time of their life.

Set at 4,500 feet in the San Bernardino National Forest, Lake Gregory has it all, except for that mythical summer camp. There is something for everyone to do. There is so much to do you are robbing yourself if you don't plan to spend a full day here. Not only are there numerous activities at the lake, the surrounding cities of Lake Gregory Village and Crestline are like miniature Big Bears (more the size of Running Springs, Arrowhead, Julian or Idyllwild), with small shops, restaurants and hotels. Aside from all the other activities, the fishing almost always remains good for shore and boat anglers. It is quiet and peaceful because there are no private boats allowed on the lake. However, float tubes can be used, and rowboats, with or without electric motors, can be rented at the boathouse.

In the late Eighties, the lake was one of the few in Southern California that was stocked with brown trout, but those plants ceased almost as soon as they began. Park rangers say there are no browns left in the lake, but one was caught in the summer of 1999. With the browns most likely all gone, the focus has turned to rainbow trout. The

California Department of Fish and Game stocks more than 37,300 rainbow trout, and the county of San Bernardino adds larger fish (to 12 pounds) to supply extra excitement for the fishing derbies.

Like its neighbor Big Bear Lake, Lake Gregory is easy to fish. The water stays cool enough year-round to sustain trout. Although there are a lot of small fish in the lake, there are plenty of larger holdovers from years past that provide weekly catches of fish over eight pounds. Shore anglers do well dunking Power Bait near the fountains, along the dam and just about anywhere along the shore.

Lake Gregory is a good destination for a family trip.

Trolling is also effective and doesn't require any special skills because it works anywhere on the lake. In spring and fall when the fish are on the surface topwater trolling monofilament line with firetiger Rapalas, frog (or copper color) Needlefish and copper Super Dupers works well. As summer approaches, the fish begin to move deeper and leadcore line is needed. For the most consistent troll, follow the point just east of the boat docks all the way to the east side of the lake. There is a shelf there that the fish congregate around, and if you hit it right you'll catch fish all day. Trolling from the fountains down the middle of the lake or from the baseball field to the dam is also productive.

In the winter, the boathouse shuts down and most vacationers, fishermen and swimmers stop coming to the lake, but shoreline fishing remains fair. The shorelines are sometimes covered in snow, and ice can develop near the banks, but the lake has never frozen over. This is the best time for shore anglers to hook up on the larger rainbows as they move into shallow water. During the summer, fishing for bluegill, catfish and bass picks up, but in order to maintain a stable fishery it is recommended that those species are released.

If you plan to make the trip, there is a fishing fee. Supplies are available at the lake and in Crestline. In winter, call ahead for road conditions. Chains may be required.

Also nearby are Heart Rock Falls, Silverwood Lake, Miller Canyon Creek, Cleghorn Creek, Holcomb Creek, Arrowbear Lake, Deep Creek, Bear Creek, Lake Arrowhead and Big Bear Lake.

LAKE **ARROWHEAD**

Although the lake is surrounded by dream homes with breathtaking views of the clear, blue lake, complete with snowy vistas in the winter, it's probably not worth buying property just for the fishing.

Rating: 5

Species: Rainbow Trout, Carp, Largemouth Bass, Bluegill and Catfish

Stocked by private vendors with rainbow trout.

Facilities: Full-Service Marinas, Restrooms, Boat Tours, Gas, Lodging, Food and Shopping

Need Information? Contact: Arrowhead Lake Association (909) 337-2595, For Lake Arrowhead Boat Tours, Leroy's Sports (909) 336-6992

Directions: From Interstate 10 in San Bernardino, drive north on Highway 30 and continue five miles to Highway 330. Exit Highway 330 and drive north for approximately 13 miles to Highway 18 at Running Springs. Turn northwest on Highway 18 to Highway 173. Veer right (north) on Highway 173 continuing to the lake.

Located between Big Bear and San Bernardino, at 5,100 feet in the San Bernardino National Forest, Lake Arrowhead is known as an upscale tourist hot-spot, not for its fishing. The lake's south shoreline is the main tourist area, providing families with dining and shopping along a boardwalk, and boat tours on the lake.

Surrounded by pine trees, clean air, blue skies and million dollar houses, Lake Arrowhead may be the prettiest lake in the San Bernardino Mountain range, but it's off limits to the public. The lake is entirely private. And to fish it you have to be a member of

Lake Arrowhead is a popular tourist trap in the San Bernardino National Forest.

the Lake Arrowhead Association. You can do that either by owning a house on the lake or in the Arrowhead Woods. In other words, Lake Arrowhead is a high-class place with a pricey cost of entrance. Advertised as "The Alps of Southern California," the lake is surrounded by dream homes with breathtaking views of the clear, blue lake, complete with snowy vistas in the winter, but it's probably not worth buying property just for the fishing. One reason is that fishing is much better at other San Bernardino Mountain lakes open to the public, like Green Valley, Big Bear and Gregory.

In recent years, an outbreak of carp has hurt the rest of the fish population, although the ALA stocks some trout and bass to keep the resident fishermen happy. The easiest way to hook up on the trout is by trolling Needlefish or Kastmasters along the shoreline from late fall through spring.

As for the carp, there is always a school of about 50, between five and 30 pounds, that hang out near the boardwalk area where tourists feed them. If you are a member

Lake Arrowhead doesn't allow fishing to the general public.

of the ALA, bring your boat close to shore, tie on a treble hook, wrap a piece of bread around the hook, attach a bobber about 18 inches above the hook, and toss it as close to the fish as you can. You should have a fish in seconds.

Boat tours aboard the Arrowhead Queen are the only way for non-ALA members to get on the lake, and they can provide a relaxing afternoon with the family.

If you plan to make the trip, supplies are available at the lake. No fishing license is required.

Also nearby are Arrowbear Lake, Deep Creek, Bear Creek, Big Bear Lake, Lake Gregory, Silverwood Lake, Deep Creek Falls and Heart Rock Falls.

DEEP **CREEK**

Deep Creek

Rating: 7

Species: Rainbow Trout and Brown Trout

Stocks: None

Facilities: None

Need Information? Contact: San Bernardino National Forest (909) 337-2444

Directions: From Interstate 10 in San Bernardino, turn north on Highway 30 and continue five miles to Highway 330. Drive north for approximately 13 miles to Highway 18 at Running Springs. Turn northwest to Highway 173 and veer right (north), continuing to Lake Arrowhead. Drive along the east shore of Lake Arrowhead to Hook Creek Road and turn right. Follow Hook Creek Road, which becomes Road 2N26Y, and veer right on Road 3N34. Continue to where the road crosses the creek.

Deep Creek is a popular wild trout stream in the San Bernardino National Forest near Lake Arrowhead. The creek is one of only a few streams in the entire southern part of the state that is home to brown trout. From its headwaters near Running Springs, the creek flows towards Lake Arrowhead and then joins forces with the Mojave River. Like its neighbors Bear Creek and the Santa Ana River, Deep Creek flows year-round, however, its flows are greatly diminished during the summer. Spin fishing is popular, but most anglers come here to fly fish. Fishing tends to be best from late winter through spring when water levels are high.

The creek has multiple personalities. It is too wide to cross without getting totally

soaked in some places, and so narrow you can rock-hop across it in others. Its waters can be either deep or shallow, and in some places it flows fast while in others it creeps along. There is a small section with hot springs and another with small waterfalls. Some areas have large boulders that can be used as jumping beams and others are lined with sandy beaches that can be used as tanning salons.

Identified by the California Department of Fish and Game as a wild trout stream, it has special regulations year-round. There is a two fish limit, the fish must be at least eight inches and only artificial lures with barbless hooks are allowed.

However, your biggest concern should not be catching fish because there are plenty of those to go around. The problem is that there are also plenty of rattlesnakes, and they're what you need to worry about. Almost every fisherman I've talked to has seen one while fishing the creek. As a matter of fact, when I called the local Forest Service to check on the water levels, the first thing the lady said to me was, "Keep an eye out for those rattlers."

Deep Creek near its headwaters in Running Springs.

When fishing Deep Creek, use the smallest Panther Martins you can find because the fish won't hit the larger sizes. Your best bet is fly-fishing the larger pools. Most of the fish you'll catch will be six to 10 inches, but I've seen rainbows and browns up to 16 inches.

If you plan to make the trip, call ahead for road conditions. The road to the creek is commonly closed due to construction. During the winter, chains may be required. Supplies are available in Lake Arrowhead. A Forest Service Adventure Pass is required to park in the San Bernardino National Forest.

Also nearby are Lake Arrowhead, Deep Creek Falls, Bear Creek, Lake Silverwood, Gregory Lake, Green Valley Lake and Big Bear Lake.

DEEP CREEK

ARROWBEAR **LAKE**

The key to catching fish is showing up at the right time and knowing where to fish, because the lake freezes over in winter and is only stocked in the spring.

Rating: 6

Species: Rainbow Trout

Stocked with 1,000 pounds of rainbow trout.

Facilities: None

Need Information? Contact: San Bernardino National Forest (909) 337-2444

Arrowbear Lake

Directions: From Interstate 10 in Redlands, take Highway 30 north for five miles to Highway 330 (City Creek Road). Follow Highway 330 northeast for 13 miles to Highway 18 in Running Springs. Follow Highway 18 east for 2.3 miles to Arrowbear Drive and turn right. The lake is on your right.

If you show up at the right time and know where to fish, Arrowbear provides some of the surest trout fishing in the region. I polled about 100 visitors in Big Bear Lake and asked them if they'd ever heard of Arrowbear Lake. Not one said yes. Arrowbear Lake should be thankful. After all, at only five acres at full pool, just a bit bigger than Doane Pond in Palomar Mountain State Park near San Diego, and about one-third the size of Crystal Lake in the Angeles National Forest, Arrowbear isn't big enough to accommodate large numbers of visitors.

Literally a minute's drive from Running Springs and Highway 18, it's amazing more people don't know that Arrowbear provides some of the best trout fishing in the region. At 6,100 feet up in the San Bernardino National Forest, snow can cover the shorelines into April, adding another incentive for your trip.

The key to catching fish is showing up at the right time and knowing where to fish, because the lake freezes over in winter and is only stocked in the spring. However, anglers who fish the lake inlet or who can get their bait into the middle of the lake where the water is deeper, often limit quickly. With a float tube or canoe you can almost be assured of some action, but be forewarned that no powerboats are allowed.

The California Department of Fish and Game stocks some 3,000 rainbow trout here, and these trout aren't picky. In 2000, trout plants resumed after they were halted from 1996-99 because of public access issues. Power Bait, nightcrawlers and just about any trout lure will score fish. If you get bored with the trout, there's a large population of half-pound goldfish, but good luck getting them to bite. They are about as active as a pet turtle stuck in a cage.

If you plan to make the trip, supplies are available in Running Springs. Call ahead in winter to check road conditions. Chains may be required.

Also nearby are Green Valley Lake, Deep Creek, Lake Arrowhead and Bear Creek.

GREEN VALLEY **LAKE**

An interesting side note is that the lake used to be crystal clear, but now only has a 10-foot visibility due to all the leaves that have fallen off oak trees and darkened the bottom.

Rating: 8

Species: Rainbow Trout, Channel Catfish, Largemouth Bass, Bluegill and Crappie

Stocked with 15,000 pounds of rainbow trout.

Facilities: General Store, Bait & Tackle, Rowboat, Canoe, Kayak and Paddleboat Rentals, Swimming Beach, Volleyball Courts, Picnic Area and Restrooms

Green Valley Lake

Need Information? Contact: Green Valley Lake Information (909) 867-2009, Cozy Cabin Rentals (909) 867-5335

Directions: From Interstate 10 in Redlands, turn north onto Highway 30 and drive five miles to Highway 330 (City Creek Road). Follow Highway 330 northeast for 13 miles to Highway 18 in the city of Running Springs. Continue on Highway 18 past Running Spring for seven miles to the Green Valley Lake turnoff on your left. Turn left on Green Valley Lake Road and drive four miles to the lake.

Green Valley Lake used to be a meadow that cows grazed in, with a small stream running through. A dam was constructed for recreational purposes in 1926, and by 1928 Green Valley Lake was filled and stocked with trout for the first time. Now, the lake is a popular put-and-take fishery tucked away in the tiny, remote town of Green Valley Lake.

The lake is owned by Green Valley Mutual Water District, which in turn is owned by the property owners of Green Valley. Each property owner gets one share of the lake, and from this group of shareholders a board of shareholders is elected to run the lake. The lake is not used as a source of income for the community. They just try to break even each year and provide visitors with an opportunity to get away from the busy city life. In order to keep the lake operational, there is a small fee to fish. Even residents have to pay it.

At 6,750 feet in the San Bernardino National Forest, it is the highest lake in the San Bernardino Mountains. Lake operators try to keep it as quiet as possible. They want to keep a low-key, family atmosphere, free of trash, loud music and rowdiness. Thus far, they've been successful. It's one of those places where you holler across the lake and everybody can hear exactly what you're saying.

The lake used to be 60 feet deep, but with recent sediment accumulations at the bottom, it's only about 45 feet deep now. An interesting side note is that the lake used to be crystal clear, but now only has a 10-foot visibility due to all the leaves that have fallen off oak trees and darkened the bottom. There have been rumors that ice-skating is allowed when the lake freezes over in the winter, but they're false. The lake has underground springs that seep up from beneath the ice and weaken its surface, making it unsafe for ice-skating.

Because there are so many fish concentrated in such a small lake, fishing tends to be good. Green Valley Lake receives plants from both the California Department of Fish and Game and Whitewater Trout Farms. The CA DFG contributes 14,250 small, eight to 12 inch trout, and Whitewater follows with another 10,000 fish from one to 12 pounds.

With no gas motors, trolling motors or personal watercraft permitted, the lake remains quiet, with bait fishing as well as casting and retrieving the rule. I saw a few guys trolling, but they had to row to do it. The small, 10-acre lake is so narrow that in many places you can cast clear across it. Instead of risking being tangled in other's lines, most anglers cover their hooks in Power Bait and wait for the big one to bite. Your best chance at catching a big one is using red and gold, or silver Thomas Buoyants and orange Cripplelures.

There is no hot spot to fish; the lake isn't big enough for one. It will be obvious where the fish are because you'll be able to see a flurry of boats anchored around 'em. Two of the most popular spots are near the dam and the boat dock. One downfall is the lake isn't open year-round. To cut costs, it closes in early October. The lake thaws by early April, but again, to save money, it doesn't reopen until mid-May. In the winter, this area is used by cross-country skiers, but doesn't have to accommodate the same crowds that nearby Big Bear does.

If you plan to make the trip, supplies are available in Green Valley Lake. In winter, call ahead for road conditions. Chains may be required. There is a fishing fee.

Also nearby are Lake Arrowhead, Arrowbear Lake, Deep Creek, Bear Creek and Snow Valley.

Green Valley Lake

GREEN VALLEY LAKE

BEAR **CREEK**

Most anglers simply don't want to deal with the exhausting, demanding and physically draining climb. One year, the US Forest Service counted only 15 anglers that fished the creek. Yet, the brave souls who do dare

Rating: 9

Species: Brown Trout
and Rainbow Trout

Stocks: None

Facilities: None

Need Information?
Contact: Big Bear Sporting Goods
(909) 866-3222, Big Bear Discovery
Center (909) 866-3437

Directions: From Interstate 10 in
Redlands, turn north onto Highway 30
and continue five miles to Highway
330 (City Creek Road). Follow
Highway 330 northeast for 13 miles to
Highway 18 in the city of Running
Springs. Turn east and drive 18 miles
to the lake. From the Big Bear Lake
Dam, backtrack exactly 1.9 miles to Forest Road 2N15 and turn left. Continue to the sign
for Glory Ridge Trail. Park,
and walk to the trailhead.

Bear Creek

Located just south of Big Bear Lake in a steep and remote canyon of the San
Bernardino National Forest, Bear Creek is the best brown trout fishery in Southern
California. This wild trout stream with headwaters at 6,700 feet, loses more than 3,000
feet before it empties into the Santa Ana River, and is seldom fished because of the
obstacles that fishermen have to overcome getting to it.

Locating the stream itself is difficult enough, but if you can find it, it's a brutal and
exhausting hike down to its banks. Even those physically fit have great difficulty making it
down to and out of the creek bed. So, if you're still up to it, before even getting into the
creek's "specks" let's first work on finding it.

Start at the Big Bear Lake dam and backtrack (towards Running Springs) exactly 1.9
miles on Highway 18 to an old, logging road on the south side, referred to as Road
2N15. Turn left and drive slowly, carefully dodging the large potholes and fallen rocks
that work their way onto the road. Continue down the poorly maintained road that
begins as cement and then turns to dirt as it winds around the canyon. In 1.5 miles, you
should see a sign on a lone pine tree (it's clearly marked) for the Glory Ridge Trail.
There'll be a parking lot on the right. If you have a two-wheel drive vehicle, park here

and continue walking down the road. Those with four-wheel drive can continue about 200 yards to an open area on the left that looks like a mesa. All vehicular traffic stops here. Now, walk down the road to where it ends. You'll recognize it by a pole with fishing regulations posted.

Congratulations! You made it to the trailhead. That's the easy part. If you dare to continue, you will descend 1,100 feet over the course of the next mile on your way down to the creek. Or, if you prefer, the creek can also be accessed by scaling down the mountainside near the stream's headwaters at Big Bear Lake dam. However, it's not recommended. For one thing, the fishing's no good there because the water flows are kept to a minimum in this area. Big Bear Lake Dam only releases the equivalent of the amount of water that used to seep out of the lake before the dam was repaired in 1991.

If you go two miles further downstream, where the Glory Ridge Trail meets the stream, two feeder streams have joined Bear Creek and its flows are sufficient year-round for fishing there. The Siberian Pass Trail is one more possible route to reach the creek, but there's an elevation change of 3,000 feet, so most people avoid it.

If you make it down to Bear Creek, it's important to mark your route because the trail is so narrow that after a day of fishing you might not be able to find your way back out. Rarely will you see another human at the creek. Most anglers simply don't want to deal with the exhausting, demanding and physically draining climb. One year, the US Forest Service counted only 15 anglers that fished the creek. Yet, the brave souls who do dare are never disappointed.

In the early Nineties, the California Department of Fish and Game did a study and found approximately 5,000 browns per mile living in the stream. In the late Eighties, rainbows that came over the spillway from the lake used to inhabit the stream as well, but in 1991 a fish screen was put on the dam to inhibit them from being sucked out of the lake and down into the creek.

Although you are only allowed to use artificial lures with barbless hooks and keep two fish over seven inches, Bear Creek is a wonderful wild trout fishery. There is a possibility of catching browns to 18 inches, but most are in the 11-12 inch range. Keep in mind that Bear Creek's browns are smart, so if you spook them, move to another pool. For spin fisherman, use the smallest Panther Martins, Kastmasters or Phoebes you can find. Fly-fishermen have luck with ant, gnat and mosquito patterned flies.

Bear Creek from Big Bear Dam.

If you plan to make the trip, supplies are available in Big Bear. Backpacking is permitted at Bear Creek. There are no supplies at the creek. In winter, call ahead for road conditions, chains may be required. A Forest Service Adventure Pass is required to park in the San Bernardino National Forest.

Also nearby are Big Bear Lake, Holcomb Creek, Alpine Trout Farms, skiing, Deep Creek and Arrowbear Lake.

BIG BEAR **LAKE**

Big Bear provides excellent trout fishing throughout a good portion of the year and offers a good bass bite when the trout bite slows down.

Rating: 8

Species: Rainbow Trout, Channel Catfish, Largemouth Bass, Bluegill, Carp, and Sunfish

Stocked with 65,250 pounds of rainbow trout.

Phil Freed and a two-pound rainbow trout

Facilities: Launch Ramps, Restrooms, Visitor's Center, RV Hookups, Full-Service Marinas, Campgrounds, Fuel, Boat Rentals, Food, Picnic Areas, and Lodging

Need Information? Contact: Big Bear Lake Marina (909) 866-3218, Big Bear Charter Fishing (909) 866-2240, Cantrell Guide Service (909) 585-4017, Holloway's Marina & RV Park (800) 448-5335, Pleasure Point Landing (909) 866-2455, North Shore Landing (909) 878-4386 For Camping: US Forest Service (877)-444-6777

Directions: From Interstate 10 in Redlands, turn north onto Highway 30 and continue five miles to Highway 330 (City Creek Road). Follow Highway 330 northeast for 13 miles to Highway 18 in the city of Running Springs. Turn east on Highway 18 and continue 18 miles to the lake.

You fishermen who don't like hunters need to grind your teeth for a minute, because it was a hunter who set the stage for Big Bear Lake to be created. In 1860 while hunting for bears, William Holcomb discovered gold in Bear Valley, prompting the largest Goldrush ever to occur in the southern part of the state. People poured into the valley hoping to strike it rich. When the hype petered out, residents decided to build a dam in Bear Valley, in 1884, creating what we now know as Big Bear Lake. Ironically, Bear Valley, which earned it's name in the mid 1840's due to its plentiful bear population, no longer has problems with bears, but it does provide great fishing.

Over the years, Big Bear Lake has turned into Southern California's busiest mountain community. It combines outdoor recreational activities such as skiing, fishing and boating in a mountain resort community set at 6,750 feet in the San Bernardino National Forest. With most of the bears gone years ago, bald eagles have taken over as the lake's biggest wildlife attraction. It is common to see the eagles dive for fish and soar across the lake.

A year-round fishery, located in the middle of one of only a few mountain resort cities in the southern portion of the state, Big Bear Lake is a special place. It provides excellent trout fishing throughout a good portion of the year and offers a good bass bite when the trout bite slows down. With 23 miles of shoreline and 3,000 acres, Big Bear Lake is more heavily stocked than any other body of water south of Bakersfield. It is stocked from early spring through fall with 26,460 subcatchable Eagle Lake trout; 109,300 half pounders; 100,860 fingerlings; and another 28,000 subcatchables from the California Department of Fish and Game's Mojave River Hatchery. For an added bonus, Whitewater Trout Hatchery stocks a bundle of trout from four to 12 pounds each year for derbies.

Trout fishing for both trollers and shore anglers remains excellent throughout the year, as catch rates and angler satisfaction are high. Trollers have no problem catching limits here. Trolling is productive anywhere on the lake, but favorite spots are in the middle, near the dam, just off Observatory Point, and in Boulder Bay. Best lures to troll are orange Cripplelures, white Phoebes and just about any Needlefish.

Despite the fact that private residences and marinas take up much of the shoreline, the lake does have good shore fishing with access provided at Stanfield Cutoff, near the dam and near the boat launches on the north side of the lake. Power Bait is your best bet from shore, although some anglers score limits tossing lures. Even though the lake is stocked with a lot of dinkers, there are a ton of large rainbows, with the lake record at 14.11 pounds caught in 1995.

Big Bear Lake is the most heavily stocked trout lake in Southern California.

Still fishing from boats can also be productive if soaking Power Bait in Boulder Bay or anchored off Observatory Point. In the summer when the trout move to deeper water, leadcore or downriggers are a necessity. Despite the lake being only 72 feet deep at its deepest point near the dam, it remains cool enough for trout to survive year-round. They congregate in the deepest holes they can find. This is a sign to target the bass. Bass fishing has improved over the years and, combined with a decent catfish and crappie bite, anglers are kept busy all day.

There are rumors of silver salmon in the lake, but they are false. There were salmon stocked in 1982, but without being able to reproduce, and a life expectancy of only six years, they are all gone by now. It is believed that over time the salmon crossbred with the trout, and many anglers mistakenly go home thinking they caught a salmon when in reality it's just a holdover trout with pink meat.

If you plan to make the trip, call ahead in the winter to make sure the lake is ice-free. The campgrounds on the lake close after Thanksgiving and don't reopen until spring.

Also nearby are ski slopes, Green Valley Lake, Deep Creek and Bear Creek.

HOLCOMB **CREEK**

The window of opportunity to fish it is short, usually only in February and March when snowmelt puts water in the stream.

Rating: 4

Species: Rainbow Trout

Stocked with 200 pounds of rainbow trout.

Facilities: Campgrounds

Need Information? Contact: Big Bear Discovery Center (909) 866-3437, For Camping Information (877) 444-6777

Directions: From Interstate 10 in Redlands exit Highway 30 and drive north. Drive five miles to Highway 330 (City Creek Road). Drive northeast on Highway 330 for 13 miles to Highway 18 in the city of Running Springs. Turn east on Highway 18 and drive 18 miles to the lake. Once at the lake continue driving straight (don't turn right to Big Bear City) to the city of Fawnskin. In Fawnskin turn left on Forest Service Road 3N14. Continue 4.2 miles to the Holcomb Creek crossing. Forest Road N393 parallels the creek.

Named after William Holcomb, Holcomb Creek has a lot of history to it, but not a lot of excitement. Holcomb was the man who discovered gold in Bear Valley, now known as Big Bear Lake, and stirred up the largest gold rush in Southern California back in 1860. The influx of people from that gold rush formed the roots of what we now call Big Bear City. Ironically, all Holcomb got out of it was his name on a small creek on the other side of the mountain. Heck, they named the valley after him too, but in an area rich with lakes and large streams, I think Holcomb got robbed.

Holcomb Creek is located at 6,700 feet in the San Bernardino National Forest. It is one of the smallest streams in the region and usually the first to dry up. The creek, about five miles north of Fawnskin, is a tributary to nearby Deep Creek. One interesting note is that the Pacific Crest Trail, which runs from Mexico to Canada, parallels the creek near where it is stocked.

Stocked? This stream is stocked? Yes, it is, but the window of opportunity to fish it is short, usually only in February and March when snowmelt puts water in the stream. The California Department of Fish and Game stocks about 500 trout during that two-month period, but in poor rain years it won't be stocked at all.

If you hit it right you'll catch plenty of fish because not many people bother to come up here. There's too much else to do nearby. Don't forget your Power Bait. That's all these fish seem to eat.

If you plan to make the trip, call ahead for the latest water conditions. Chains can be required at any time during the winter. A Forest Service Adventure Pass is required to park in the San Bernardino National Forest.

Also nearby are Big Bear Lake, Bear Creek, Alpine Trout Farms and the Big Bear ski areas.

ALPINE TROUT **LAKE**

So you can drink up and forget about getting skunked at Big Bear. Heck, you'll be the only one that knows because you'll leave Alpine Trout Lake with a full cooler of trout.

Rating: 7

Species: Rainbow Trout

Stocked weekly by private vendors.

Facilities: Picnic Areas, Snack Shop, Bait & Tackle Store, Restrooms and Barbeques

Alpine Trout Lake

Need Information? Contact: Alpine Trout Lakes (909) 866-4532

Directions: From Interstate 10 in Redlands, turn north on Highway 30 and continue five miles to Highway 330 (City Creek Road). Follow Highway 330 northeast for 13 miles to Highway 18 in the city of Running Springs. Turn east and drive 18 miles to Big Bear Lake. From the east end of Big Bear City, turn south on Catalina Road off Big Bear Blvd. and continue one-fourth of a mile to the pond your right.

Fed by Rathburn Creek, Alpine Trout Lakes is less than a five-minute drive from Big Bear Lake. It is the only private stocked trout pond in Southern California that is spring fed and doesn't have a concrete bottom, which makes Alpine Trout Lake one of the area's most unique private trout fishing ponds. More importantly, Alpine Trout Lake serves as a great ego booster for fishermen that get skunked fishing Big Bear Lake, standing as a testament to all anglers that they actually can catch fish! And why couldn't they? Anybody who can't catch a fish here must be using a beer can for a lure.

Shaded by large pines, the lake is about the size of a basketball court. It's stocked weekly with fish that aren't hand-fed, so they're always hungry. And the water is crystal clear so you can just pick the one you want to catch. Frustrated anglers aren't the only visitors, families and recreation groups spend a lot of time here. They run back and forth from catching fish in the pond to using the picnic sites to eat lunch. Once in a while it's fun to fish where you know a full stringer awaits.

Although there is no limit, no license is required and there's no fee to get through the gate, the deterrent here is that fishing will put a hole in your pocket. You pay for the fish by the pound. On the plus side, however, alcohol is allowed on the premises. So you can drink up and forget about getting skunked at Big Bear. Heck, you'll be the only one that knows because you'll leave Alpine Trout Lake with a full cooler of trout.

If you plan to make the trip, call ahead for seasonal hours. Alpine Trout Lake freezes over in the winter and is usually closed from the Monday following Thanksgiving to the first week of March. Chains may be required to get to Big Bear.

Also nearby are Big Bear Lake, Bear Creek, Jenks Lake and the Santa Ana River.

SANTA ANA **RIVER**

The cabins along the stream front make it look like private property, but it's not. Just be respectful and nobody will bother you.

Rating: 6

Species: Rainbow and Brown Trout

Stocked with 15,700 pounds of rainbow trout.

Facilities: Campgrounds, Restrooms and Picnic Areas

South Fork Santa Ana River

Need Information? Contact:
San Bernardino National Forest (909) 794-1123

Directions: From Interstate 10 in Redlands, exit Highway 38 and drive north for 28 miles to the signed bridge (for South Fork Santa Ana River) that crosses over the South Fork of the Santa Ana River. Make an immediate left into the parking area right after the bridge and follow the road that parallels the river.

Because of the size of its fish, the Santa Ana River would rate as one of the worst rivers in the Eastern Sierra. But, partly because there aren't many other rivers in the San Bernardino National Forest, it's considered one of the best. It isn't a large river, only about five feet wide in most places, but the surrounding pine trees mixed with brush and shrubs gives you a feeling you're in a place far from home.

The California Department of Fish and Game stocks more than 33,100 rainbow trout here. Most of them are small, from seven to nine inches, but nobody complains. The anglers are just happy to have a trout stream nearby.

The easiest way to access the river is via Seven Oaks Road. Where the South Fork dumps into the Santa Ana River, it's stocked downstream for seven miles. You can find fish at any point where the CA DFG can get their truck close to the river, but most are planted where the river crosses under the road.

It is also stocked exactly 3.5 miles up the road from Barton Flats Visitor Center, where Highway 38 crosses over the river, and this area receives less than half the pressure than other areas along the river. From that point, you'll find bites upstream as well as downstream for about a quarter-mile. Both are too small for lures, but if you bring along some white Power Bait, catching your limit should not be a problem.

The cabins along the stream front make it look like private property, but it's not. Just be respectful and nobody will bother you.

If you plan to make the trip, supplies are available in Redlands or Big Bear. In winter, call ahead for road conditions. Chains may be required. Campfires or stove use is only allowed in designated campgrounds and picnic areas.

Also nearby are Jenks Lake, Alpine Trout Lakes and Big Bear Lake.

JENKS **LAKE**

Shoreline access is exceptional, but those with float tubes tend to have an edge over the lounge chair fisherman, unless you're competing to finish a six-pack of beer.

Jenks Lake

Rating: 7

Species: Rainbow Trout, Sunfish and Largemouth Bass

Stocked with 11,500 pounds of rainbow trout.

Facilities: Picnic Areas, Restrooms, Wheelchair Access, and Fishing Piers

Need Information? Contact: San Bernardino National Forest (909) 794-1123

Directions: From Interstate 10 in Redlands, take Highway 38 northeast for 26 miles to Jenks Lake Road. Turn east and continue three miles to the lake.

The story of how Jenks Lake was formed is a lot more exciting than the lake itself. Back in the 1870's, Captain Lorin Shaw Jenks decided to build a logjam to divert water from the South Fork of the Santa Ana River and fill what we now call Jenks Lake. As the story goes, Jenks built the 1.5-mile long canal himself, with his own hands. Jenks used the lake to harvest rainbow trout and then sold them in San Bernardino. However, when selling trout from mountain lakes and streams became illegial in the 1890's, Jenks abandoned his operations at the lake and moved to nearby Barton Flats.

The lake has remained filled with water ever since, and with the California Department of Fish and Game stocking it every other week in spring and summer, fishing tends to be good.

The six-acre lake, located at 6,700 feet in the San Bernardino National Forest, is stocked with 22,130 trout that join a few holdovers from years past. Set in a heavily forested area surrounded by pine trees and bombarded by recreationists, the lake is almost identical to Crystal Lake in the Angeles National Forest and Fulmor Lake in the San Jacinto Mountains.

Techniques vary here, with Power Bait and small spinners having the best luck. There are also a sprinkle of bass and sunfish in the lake, but more anglers come here for the trout. Shoreline access is exceptional, but those with float tubes tend to have an edge over the lounge chair fisherman, unless you're competing to finish a six-pack of beer.

If you plan to make the trip, supplies are available in Redlands or Big Bear. Call ahead for conditions. Chains may be required. Jenks Lake is open seasonally, usually from May to November. No walk-in entry is permitted when the lake is closed. A Forest Service Adventure Pass is required to park in the San Bernardino National Forest.

Also nearby are the South Fork Santa Ana River, Santa Ana River and Big Bear Lake.

MILL **CREEK**

As soon as the truck dumps the fish and leaves, the locals run to the creek with nets – yes nets! – and scoop up all the fish.

Rating: 3

Species: Rainbow Trout

Stocked with 200 pounds of rainbow trout.

Facilities: Picnic Areas and Restrooms

Need Information? Contact: San Bernardino National Forest (909) 794-1123

Directions: From Interstate 10 in Redlands, exit Highway 38 and drive 14 miles northeast. At the junction with Forest Home Road, veer right and continue 4.5 miles to the road's end at the Falls Recreation Area. (The road becomes Valley of the Falls Drive).

Talk about a spot fit for locals, Mill Creek located 5,560 feet up in the San Bernardino National Forest, is so secret the receptionists at the local Ranger Station didn't even know it was stocked with trout. After driving to the creek and not seeing any fish or pools suitable to hold fish, I headed over to the Mill Creek Ranger Station to find out if they really do stock fish in this tiny stream. One of the wise-cracking ladies working the counter got a kick out of that one. "Honey, there's no fish in there. There's not enough

Big Falls can be seen from Mill Creek.

water." Just as I was about to leave, a park ranger came out of the back room and told me the California Department of Fish and Game does stock the creek. "You aren't going to catch any fish, though," he said. "The locals got 'em all, already."

It turns out the locals have a system during the stocking season. It's pretty simple, but it works. An old timer stands guard in town and waits for the CA DFG truck to drive through Forest Home. Once it begins climbing up Valley of the Falls Drive, the old timer gets on the phone and calls his buddies. As soon as the truck dumps the fish and leaves, they run to the creek with nets -- yes nets! -- and scoop up all the fish. Sounds illegal? Well, it is. But at secluded Mill Creek, there's no one around to catch them.

Anglers that arrive on the weekends are often frustrated when there are no fish. The locals probably get a laugh seeing people fishing for fillets already neatly packaged up in their fridges. Just in case the locals left a few for you, the CA DFG plants the fish at the end of Valley of the Falls Drive, at Falls Picnic Area. The stream is pitiful, with little to no trees for shade, and a rocky base that is a nightmare on your ankles.

The highlight of Mill Creek is Big Falls, a 500-foot waterfall that's only walking distance from the stream. It can be seen from Valley of the Falls Drive where it intersects Rock Drive, just before you reach Falls Picnic Area.

If you plan to make the trip, supplies are available in Forest Home. A Forest Service Adventure Pass is required to park in the San Bernardino National Forest. If coming in late winter, plan to arrive early. The creek is used as a snow play area and the parking area usually fills up by 10 a.m.

Also nearby are the South Fork of the Santa Ana River, the Santa Ana River, Big Bear Lake, Big Falls, Yucaipa Park Lake and Cold Creek Falls.

MILL CREEK

REGION 10

San Jacinto Mountains

CALIFORNIA

Fulmor Lake
Fuller Mill Creek
North Fork San Jacinto River
Strawberry Creek
Hemet Lake

FULMOR **LAKE**

There is a paved trail that loops around the lake and provides good access to plenty of spots for anglers to set up.

Rating: 5

Species: Rainbow Trout

Stocked with 4,500 pounds of rainbow trout.

Facilities: Picnic Areas, Wheelchair Access, Fishing Docks and Restrooms

Fulmor Lake

Need Information? Contact: San Bernardino National Forest (909) 659-2117

Directions: From Interstate 10 in Banning, exit Highway 243 (Banning/Idyllwild Road) and continue 20 miles to the lake on the left. Park in the lot on the right side of the road and walk across the highway to the lake.

Fulmor Lake gets bombarded by nature lovers, picnickers and fisherman daily. Set in a heavily forested area of the San Jacinto Mountains, it's really more of a large pond than a lake. Even if this pond weren't stocked with fish, people would still come here for its beauty. It provides an easily accessed retreat with plenty of peace and tranquillity for outdoor enthusiasts who need a break from city life.

There is a paved trail that loops around the lake and provides good access to plenty of spots for anglers to set up. For some reason the trout aren't tempted to hit lures here, but they love Power Bait. During the week after a plant, limits on Power Bait can come in less than an hour. If its size you're looking for, Fulmor Lake isn't going to cut it. Of the 9,450 fish the California Department of Fish and Game plant here, all are a half-pound or less.

As for the scenery, the tall pines and clean air in this neck of the woods is hard to beat. Especially in the winter when the pristine, snow-covered shorelines and the cold, brisk air transports you back hundreds of years before Southern California became populated.

This shallow, four-acre lake, nestled in at 5,300 feet in the San Bernardino National Forest, is also popular to float tubers and canoeists who can cover more water that the shoreline anglers. If you want to get in on the action, don't wait too long after a stock. Locals consider it their "secret spot" and if you wait too long all the rainbows will be sitting up the road in someone else's fridge.

Also, at times during the winter the lake freezes over. Don't try to walk on the ice. It's rarely thick enough to walk on. Ice fishing is definitely out of the question.

If you plan to make the trip, supplies are available in Idyllwild. A Forest Service Adventure Pass is required to park in the San Bernardino National Forest.

Also nearby are Fuller-Mill Creek, the North Fork San Jacinto River, Dark Canyon Falls, Strawberry Creek and Hemet Lake.

FULLER MILL **CREEK**

Its minimal flows depend on rains and snowmelt, but it has good-sized, well-built rock pools to sustain its fish.

Rating: 5

Species: Rainbow Trout

Stocked with 5,100 pounds of rainbow trout.

Facilities: Picnic Area and Restrooms

Need Information? Contact: San Bernardino National Forest (909) 659-2117

Directions: From Interstate 10 in Banning, exit Banning/Idyllwild Road (Highway 243) and continue south for 22 miles to Fuller Mill Creek Picnic Area on the right.

Fuller Mill Creek

Everybody who has been to Fuller Mill Creek knows it's one of the most scenic places in the San Bernardino National Forest, but what a lot of those people don't realize is it's also a great fishing hole. Fuller Mill Creek is located in a heavily forested and quiet picnic area surrounded by cedar and pine trees. It's stocked with 1,150 rainbow trout during the months of March and April.

Located 5,300 feet up in the San Jacinto Mountains, this small stream is a lot like Arroyo Seco Creek in the Angeles National Forest. Its minimal flows depend on rains and snowmelt, but it has good-sized, well-built rock pools to sustain its fish.

Access here is good, with wooden steps leading from the parking lot down to the creek where picnic tables straddle its shoreline. Fishing here is simple, requiring only Power Bait or a few salmon eggs to fill a stringer. The creek is also known for its coyotes. I saw a few near water's edge during daylight hours. Keep an eye out for 'em. They might steal your fish!

If you plan to make the trip, supplies are available in Idyllwild and Banning. A Forest Service Adventure Pass is required to park in the San Bernardino National Forest.

Also nearby are Strawberry Creek, Fulmor Lake, Hemet Lake and Dark Canyon Falls.

NORTH FORK SAN JACINTO **RIVER**

It is not one of the most popular rivers in the San Jacinto Mountains, and most of the people who visit here don't even come to fish. They come to see a spectacular series of waterfalls above the campground.

Rating: 5

Species: Rainbow Trout

Stocked with 300 pounds of rainbow trout.

Facilities: Campgrounds and Restrooms

Need Information?
Contact: San Bernardino National Forest (909) 659-2117

Directions: From Interstate 10 in Banning, exit Banning-Idyllwild Road (Highway 243) and turn south. Follow Highway 243 for approximately 22 miles to the turnoff for Dark Valley Campground on the left. Turn left, entering San

Jacinto State Park and continue eight-tenth of a mile. Veer left, following signs to the campground. Drive another 3.4 miles to the campground.

The North Fork of the San Jacinto River, located at Dark Canyon Campground in Mt. San Jacinto State park, 6,300 feet up in the San Bernardino National Forest, used to be a favorite year-round getaway for many Southern Californian recreationists. However, we can thank those same outdoor enthusiasts for the river becoming only a seasonal destination. On top of the obvious annoyances, like frozen water lines and snow covered campsites and roads, which the Forest Service must contend with in winter, they got sick of having to pull four-wheel-drive vehicles out of the snow every day. This prompted them to close the road that leads down to the river to vehicular traffic from November to May. Because the only way to get to this heavily forested area during those months is by foot, most wait until the gate is opened and drive in. Only the hardiest visit in the winter, which is a shame because the river is most beautiful when snow covers the ground.

One of the most popular rivers in the San Jacinto Mountains, most of the people who visit here don't even come to fish. They come to see a spectacular series of waterfalls above the campground. More like cascades, the falls are known as Dark Canyon Falls and can be stunning if there is a sufficient amount of water in the stream.

Once the road opens for the summer, the California Department of Fish and Game responds by stocking rainbow trout. Although it's called a river, the San Jacinto looks more like a stream and is only stocked with 660 rainbow trout from late spring through early summer. Back in 1997, the stream was stocked with 1,040 trout, but the numbers have been cut back drastically.

Anglers who fish here usually do well using Power Bait or salmon eggs. It's obvious where the fish are. You can see them in the small pools. The river is also stocked where it crosses under Highway 243. To reach this spot, drive 6.5 miles north of the Idyllwild Ranger Station to a dirt pullout on the northeast side of the road. There is a small dirt path directly behind the sign for the North Fork San Jacinto River. If coming from Banning, this spot is 17.8 miles from Interstate 10.

Highway 243, which leads to the North Fork of the San Jacinto, gets its share of snow in the winter.

If you plan to make the trip, supplies are available in Idyllwild. In winter, chains may be required. Call ahead for road conditions. A Forest Service Adventure Pass is required to park in the San Bernardino National Forest.

Also nearby are Fuller-Mill Creek, Fulmor Lake, Strawberry Creek and Hemet Lake.

NORTH FORK SAN JACINTO **RIVER**

STRAWBERRY **CREEK**

With the snow that falls off tall trees onto your head and icicles that line the bank, it makes the fishing experience a special one.

Rating: 4

Species: Rainbow Trout

Stocked with 390 pounds of rainbow trout.

Facilities: Gas, Food, Lodging, Restrooms and Campgrounds

Need Information? Contact: San Bernardino National Forest (909) 659-2117

Strawberry Creek

Directions: From Banning on Interstate 10, exit Highway 243 (Banning/Idyllwild Road) and continue 25.5 miles to the town of Idyllwild. The stream is stocked where Strawberry Creek crosses under Highway 243 just south of town.

Contrary to its name, you won't find any strawberries at Strawberry Creek. If you don't get there soon after a stock, you won't find any fish either. This tiny creek, set at 6,000 feet in the San Bernardino National Forest near the town of Idyllwild, is only stocked with 840 rainbow trout each year. Locals usually nab them before weekend anglers arrive, so you'd better get up there early.

The trout are planted in pools that restrict them from swimming up or downstream. They are virtual prisoners, waiting to be caught. During winter, the stream's banks are covered in snow. With the snow that falls off tall trees onto your head and icicles that line the bank, it makes the fishing experience a special one. Access here is good as long as you can cast around the cedar, pine and quaking aspen trees that line the shore.

So, you are going to try to catch a few? Here's what to do. Concentrate your efforts where Strawberry Creek crosses under Highway 243. If driving from Banning, it's just after Idyllwild Pines Christian Camp, and from Hemet it's just past South Circle Drive. Park as close to the bridge as you can and bring your Power Bait. The stream is also stocked at the bridge near Camp Emerson.

If you plan to make the trip, supplies are available in Idyllwild.

Also nearby are Fuller-Mill Creek, Fulmor Lake, Dark Canyon Falls, Hemet Lake and the North Fork San Jacinto River.

HEMET **LAKE**

Rating: 7

Species: Rainbow Trout, Channel Catfish, Bluegill, Crappie and Largemouth Bass

Stocked with 27,700 pounds of rainbow trout.

Need Information? Contact: Hemet Lake (909-659-2690)

Hemet Lake

Facilities: General Store, Campground, Swimming Area, Boat Launch Facilities, Boat Rentals, Restrooms, RV Hookups and a Playground

Directions: From Interstate 15 in Hemet, take Highway 74 east for 25 miles to Hemet Park located on the southwest side of the road.

First of all, Hemet Lake is nowhere near Hemet. It's actually 25 miles away. But for those who appreciate year-round trout fishing less than a half-an-hour away from the dry and urbanized desert city of Hemet, Hemet Lake is paradise. A dream come true for residents of Riverside and San Bernardino Counties sweltering in the heat, it brings to reality dreams of a high mountain lake surrounded by pines. It stays cold enough to have shorelines covered with snow after winter storms, and at 4,330 feet, it requires a few extra layers of clothes to stay warm.

At only 110-acres, Hemet Lake, like the larger Lake Cuyamaca located near Julian and Big Bear Lake, provides great year-round trout fishing. Hemet Lake is located in Gardner Valley in the San Bernardino National Forest, and for ten months of the year is stocked by the California Department of Fish and Game with 57,070 rainbow trout. It does not receive plants in December and January. Sound like a lot of fish? It used to be stocked with more than 78,000 trout each year, but over the last three years the plants have been reduced by more than 21,000 trout.

The lake stays quiet and peaceful with a 10-mph speed limit. With the exception of the dam area, the lake is shallow, giving bank anglers a good opportunity to score limits. Trollers and still boat fisherman also do well. Trollers do best working the dam area and the middle of the lake, while still boat fishermen drift Power Bait and nightcrawlers about 15 feet off the shoreline. Bait dunkers do well adjacent to the campgrounds.

Hemet Lake's best kept secret is its bass fishery. It's rapidly becoming one of the best, but least known bass lakes in Southern California. It commonly kicks out bass in excess of 10 pounds. Catfish and crappie provide the angler with another option in the summer.

If you plan to make the trip, supplies are available at the lake. A day-use fee is charged.

Also nearby are Strawberry Creek, Fulmor Lake, Fuller Mill Creek and the North Fork of the San Jacinto River.

REGION 11

Riverside County

Yucaipa Park Lake
Oak Tree Village
Whitewater Trout Farm
Lake Cahuilla
Fisherman's Retreat
Perris Lake
Reflection Lake
Anglers Lake
Diamond Valley Reservoir
Corona Lake
Lake Elsinore
Lake Skinner

YUCAIPA PARK **LAKE**

During the summer, catching catfish becomes an early morning, late evening activity. The hot, smoggy weather shuts off the bite the rest of the day.

Rating: 5

Species: Rainbow Trout, Channel Catfish, Crappie and Bluegill

Stocked with 13,200 pounds of rainbow trout and channel catfish by private vendors.

Facilities: Campground, Swimming areas, Waterslides, Picnic Areas, Snack Bar, Restrooms and Playgrounds.

Need Information? Contact: Yucaipa Park Lake (909) 790-3127

Directions: From Interstate 10 in Redlands, exit Yucaipa Blvd. Turn north and drive 2.8 miles to Oak Glen Blvd. Turn right and continue 1.8 miles to the park.

Yucaipa Park Lake

The San Bernardino County Parks and Recreation did it again. By stocking fish year-round, they succeeded in making Yucaipa Park Lake another consistent urban fishery in a dry, hot desert environment. First, they stocked it more heavily with rainbow trout (28,570) than any of the other urban fisheries run by the county parks. These trout are stocked weekly during the winter and early spring. Then, they planted channel catfish when water temperatures became too warm for the trout.

Yucaipa Park Lake, located in Yucaipa Regional Park, consists of three small lakes nestled in grassy hills. Catch rates are usually decent, with Power Bait fisherman having the best luck. After stocks the shorelines can get crowded, requiring you to arrive early for a good spot. During the summer, catching catfish becomes an early morning, late evening activity. The hot, smoggy weather shuts off the bite the rest of the day. Use night-crawlers, mackerel or chicken liver and you should have no trouble catching fish.

If you plan to make the trip, supplies are available at the lake. There are fishing and day-use fees.

Also nearby are Mill Creek, Big Bear Lake, Oak Tree Village and Fulmor Lake.Oak Tree Village

OAK TREE **VILLAGE**

Catching your limit here could put a hole in your pocket, but I promise neither you nor the kids will get skunked.

Rating: 5

Species: Rainbow Trout

Stocked monthly by private vendors.

Facilities: Restrooms, Cafe, General Store, Petting Zoo, Shopping, Carnival Rides, Gold Panning, Animal Park, Train Rides and Pony Rides

Need Information? Contact:
Oak Tree Village (909) 797-4020

Oak Tree Village

Directions: From Interstate 10 in Redlands, drive east to the city of Yucaipa and exit Yucaipa Blvd. Turn north and continue to Oak Glen Blvd. Make a left on Oak Glen and continue to Oak Tree Village on your left.

Most kids don't look forward to those weekend trips to do some shopping for arts and crafts and antiques. You know, the ones where grandma and grandpa come over and the whole family piles in the van and heads out on a two-hour drive. But Oak Tree Village has given kids a reason to look forward to those trips. No, I'm not talking about a video arcade or free food; I'm talking about fishing.

Located just minutes from Yucaipa, Oak Tree Village is a 14-acre tourist attraction with activities for the entire family to enjoy, including fishing. Centered in the famous apple growing community of Oak Glen, there are so many activities you may have trouble finding time to go fishing. For the kids, there are pony rides, an animal park, petting zoo, panning for gold, train rides and piglet races. To accommodate adults, there are monthly festivals with live entertainment from April through December, 18 shops, arts and crafts shows and a restaurant.

As I said, good luck finding time for fishing. The good thing, however, is that the fishing doesn't take long. These hungry rainbow trout are never fed. In fact, they're so hungry, when I saw a man cleaning his fish he pulled out a handful of gravel from the fish's belly. I also saw fish jumping out of the water to eat pellets of fish food kids were throwing in the water. I've never seen fish so hungry.

Oak Tree Village has three small trout ponds with fish separated by size and price. Catching your limit here could put a hole in your pocket, but I promise neither you nor the kids will get skunked. It's a great way to top off a family outing. No need to bring along fishing tackle either. It's all provided. All you need to bring is your wallet.

If you plan to make the trip, supplies are available at Oak Tree Village. There is a fishing fee and a charge for each fish caught. No fishing license is required.

Also nearby are Whitewater Trout Farm, Yucaipa Pak Lake and Fisherman's Retreat.

WHITEWATER TROUT **FARM**

Some of the trout are so hungry you don't need any bait.
They'll hit your hook.

Rating: 5

Species: Rainbow Trout

Stocked weekly.

Facilities: Picnic Area, Fish Cleaning Stations and Restrooms

Need Information? Contact: Whitewater Trout Company (760) 325-5570
or (760) 320-7875

Directions: From Interstate 10 in Banning, drive east to the Whitewater exit and turn
north, crossing over the freeway. Continue four-tenths of a mile to Whitewater Canyon
Road and turn left. Follow the road for five miles to the entrance on your left.

Imagine this: it's Friday night, you left the Los Angeles Basin a few hours ago for a
fun filled weekend in Palm Springs and your kids are getting restless because you've
been stuck in bumper to bumper traffic on Interstate 10. You've already stopped to get
them some candy to keep them occupied. It didn't help. It's time for a break, however,
you're in the middle of the desert and there's nowhere to go. Or is there? How about
fishing? Not just fishing, but "catching!" Located between Cabazon and Palm Springs,
Whitewater Trout Company guarantees it.

Whitewater's two small ponds produce some of the surest fishing in the state, yet
there is an extra catch. These hungry fish are going to cost you a bundle. Heck, if you're
headed to Palm Springs anyway, chances are you aren't worried about spending a few
extra bucks.

Whitewater Trout Farm

Whitewater is a private fish
hatchery that is responsible for
stocking the San Diego and San
Bernardino County park lakes,
as well as private lakes in
Riverside County, including
Angler's Lake, Reflection Lake
and Fisherman's Retreat. The
hatchery diverts water from the
Whitewater River in the San
Jacinto Mountains into its holding ponds that are used to grow
the fish. These holding ponds
aren't open to the public, but
the two small fishing ponds, one
is about the size of backyard

swimming pool and the other the length of an NBA basketball court, are constantly replenished with fish from one to four pounds. On other hand, it's almost like fishing in the holding ponds because the fish are so hungry.

Fishing tends to get crowded on weekends and holidays, but there are always enough fish to go around. Whitewater has also made your fishing more comfortable by sheltering you from the blazing heat with a canopy of large trees. Catching the starving fish is as easy as spotting them in the crystal clear water. Some of the trout are so hungry you don't even need any bait. They'll literally hit your hook. Most importantly, don't forget your wallet. Remember, don't catch too many fish, you still have the weekend in Palm Springs.

Fishing is always excellent at Whitewater Trout Farm.

If you plan to make the trip, supplies are available at the hatchery. Whitewater is open from Wednesday through Sunday. There is a general admission fee for those not fishing, a fishing fee for those fishing and each fish will cost you $2.88 per pound. No fishing license is required.

Also nearby are Murray Canyon Falls, Palm Springs, Whitewater Falls and Lake Cahuilla.

WHITEWATER TROUT FARMS

LAKE **CAHUILLA**

If you visit during the cooler months, it's not a bad trout lake, yielding limits to most anglers.

Rating: 5

Species: Rainbow Trout, Channel Catfish, Striped Bass, Bluegill and Carp

Stocked with 14,000 pounds of rainbow trout and channel catfish periodically.

Lake Cahuilla

Facilities: Campgrounds, Picnic Areas, Boat Launch, Showers, Fishing Piers, Restrooms, RV Hookups and a Swimming Pool

Need Information? Contact: Lake Cahuilla (760) 564-4712

Directions: From Interstate 10 in Indio, exit Highway 86. Drive south on Highway 86 for four miles to 58th Avenue and turn west. Continue five miles to the lake.

You have to feel bad for the trout stocked in the 135-acre Lake Cahuilla. Six miles from Indio, located in the foothills of the Santa Rosa Mountains it's in one of the hottest and driest regions of the state. From March through October you're having a cool day if air temperatures stay under 100 and water temperatures in this shallow lake haven't risen above 85. Any of the more than 30,000 trout stocked from November to March that don't get caught before the heat of summer, die and die fast. It's amazing that trout are even stocked in this desert oasis.

Lake Cahuilla's dam was built in 1972, allowing the farmers of the Coachella Valley to have a source of water for the dates and grapes that provide the region with its main source of income. The lake has a bottom sealed with six inches of compacted soil sediment. Its shore is spotted with the occasional palm tree so an angler will have something green to look at besides desert scrubs. Ultimately fed by water from the All-American Canal and the Colorado River, it marks the end of the Coachella Branch of the All-American Canal. Most fishermen know what this means... stripers, carp and flathead catfish.

The carp, which are the lake's most abundant fish, can get pretty big, but the flat-heads and stripers stay small. However, it's probably a good idea just to forget about the carp. If you go where the canal feeds the lake you can see tons of them, ranging from three to over thirty pounds. But good luck catching them. The only way to do it is to snag them, and don't forget, snagging fish is illegal.

If you visit during the cooler months it's not a bad trout lake, yielding limits to most anglers. The California Department of Fish and Game plants more than 20,415 trout from eight to twelve inches, and the lake purchases larger trout from private hatcheries to give anglers some added excitement.

With no gas motors allowed on the water, the lake remains quiet. Anglers with a good trolling motor have no problem catching limits, tying Panther Martins or Roostertails directly to monofilament line. The lake averages 10 feet and is only 19 feet at its deepest spot at full pool, so downriggers or leadcore aren't needed.

Lake Cahuilla marks the end of the Coachella Branch of the All-American Canal.

Recently there's been problems with cormorants. These birds have been eating a lot of the trout before anglers can catch them. Lake operators have tried shooting guns in the air in attempt to scare the birds away, but it hasn't worked. Management is currently working on a way to control them.

Once the trout begin to die off, the lake receives plants of catfish, most of which are caught when the air cools during all-night fishing sessions. Generally, these cats are in the one to three pounds.

If you plan to make the trip, supplies are available in Indio.

Also nearby is the Salton Sea.

LAKE CAHUILLA

FISHERMAN'S **RETREAT**

Fisherman's Retreat is the only private fishing hole in Southern California that is open 24 hours a day for fishing so its customers can visit any time they please.

Rating: 7

Species: Largemouth Bass, Channel Catfish, Carp, Crappie, Bluegill and Rainbow Trout

Stocked weekly by private vendors.

Facilities: Campground, Café, Bait & Tackle Store, Playgrounds, Lodging, Arcade, Recreational Activities, Fish Cleaning Stations, Swimming Pools, RV Hookups, Restrooms and a General Store

Need Information? Contact: Fisherman's Retreat (909) 795-2411

Directions: From Interstate 10 in Beaumont, exit San Timoteo and turn southwest. Continue approximately eight miles to the lake on the left.

Fisherman's Retreat sounds like a fisherman's paradise, right? Well it is and it isn't. It does provide 24 hour fishing, 365 days a year. Its lakes are stocked weekly in order to assure you at least a few fish, but it isn't the most scenic place on earth.

Fisherman's Retreat is actually made up of three small ponds located in the Moreno Valley. Two are open to the public and the third is only open to members. The ponds have been around since the early 1900's, and the lake has been run as a put-and-take fishery since 1981. The two ponds open to the public are 14 and 10 acres, and are stocked seasonally with catfish and rainbow trout.

Fisherman's Retreat is the only private fishing hole in Southern California that is open 24 hours a day for fishing so its customers can visit any time they please. Trout are stocked to 13 pounds and the largest catfish to come out of the lake was a 22-pounder.

Surprisingly, the Retreat's most hidden gem is its largemouth bass. People have no idea there are bass in the lakes. A lake record 15-pound largemouth was caught and released in the summer of 1998, however, many of the regulars talk of bigger ones being hooked and lost.

On weekends the lakes tend to get crowded, but that could just be a sign that the fish are biting. There is no fishing license required, but there is a fishing fee.

If you plan to make the trip, supplies are available at the lake. There is a fishing fee. Also nearby are Anglers Lake, Reflection Lake, Yucaipa Park Lake and Perris Lake.

PERRIS **LAKE**

At the turn of the 21st Century, catching those spotted bass has become a thing of the past, and attention has turned to the largemouths.

Rating: 8

Species: Largemouth Bass, Channel Catfish, Crappie, Bluegill, Rainbow Trout, Spotted Bass and Carp

Stocked with 26,400 pounds of rainbow trout.

Facilities: Restrooms, Boat Launches, Bait & Tackle, Boat Rentals, Marina, Gas, RV Hookups, Campgrounds, Picnic Areas, Fish Cleaning Station and Ranger Station

Fishing guide Guy Williams with a 10.73 and 7.75-pound largemouth bass.

Need Information? Contact: Fishing Guide Guy Williams (909) 427-1659, Lake Perris State Recreation Area (909) 657-0676, Lake Perris Marina (909) 657-2179, Lake Perris Camping Information (909) 940-5603, Lake Perris Information (800) 444-7275

Directions: From the 215 Freeway in Perris, drive four miles north and exit the Ramona Expressway. Turn east and continue 2.7 miles to the lake entrance.

At 2,340 acres, Perris Lake is the southernmost reservoir in California that is part of the State Water Project. In the mid-Eighties, Perris Lake's spotted bass population was one of the finest in the nation. Forty-fish days were common, and lots of lunkers were caught, too. As the latter Eighties approached, however, catch rates began to slow, and the hype about Perris's world-class spotted bass began to slip away. By the mid-Nineties, few anglers were catching any spotted bass at all.

Yet, as anglers' focus eased off the spotted bass, Perris was developing a huge population of largemouth bass. At the turn of the 21st Century, catching those spotted bass has become a thing of the past, and attention has turned to the largemouths.

The California Department of Fish and Game recently conducted a study showing Perris has an enormous population of largemouth bass in excess of 10 pounds. Enabling the fast growth of largemouths to trophy sizes, Perris has a monstrous population of shad and stocked trout for them to feed on, not to mention thousands of bluegill and crawdads. There is no shortage of forage for Perris's bass.

The bass bite heats up in early spring for those using plastics on the east end. As summer approaches, switch over to crankbaits near the dam and off the four points near the marina. Returning to the east end, use topwater lures and crankbaits in the fall. The moment the CA DFG begins to plant trout in the winter, anglers hoping to land a lunker toss trout imitation lures near the marina, off points and near the launch ramps. Others jig with Kastmasters and Hopskins off schools of shad in 60 feet of water. For shoreline anglers, the use of crawdads and nightcrawlers works well, fishing in coves and off points. In the spring of 2000, a trout fisherman landed a 17.6-pound bass, using a nightcrawler off the shoreline.

Perris is also famous for its bluegill. From May through September, anglers can catch hundreds of bluegill up to two pounds, dangling red worms, chunks of nightcrawlers or crappie nibbles, on the east end near weeds and overhanging brush, or off the points around the marina. Most average three-fourths of a pound.

My favorite fish to target at Perris is carp. These bottom feeders grow to amazing proportions, some exceeding 60 pounds. During March when the carp spawn in two feet of water, the shoreline looks like there's a bunch of seals splashing around the water. Fish with dough, bread or corn in the evenings.

Perris Lake has transformed from one of the world's top spotted bass fisheries to a great largemouth bass lake.

Don't overlook Perris's trout population. While many of the 63,450 trout planted by the CA DFG end up in the bellies of the largemouth bass, anglers catch a good number. Bank fishing near the marina, boat launches and in coves can be exceptional shortly after a plant. Trolling is also productive for anglers who use small Kastmasters, Super Dupers and Needlefish. Ideally, try to troll the points off the marina. This will allow you to have a shot at landing both bass and trout. A friend and I landed a four and six-pound bass while trolling silver Kastmasters off the points in December of 2000.

There are two problems with fishing Perris; the first is the wind and the other is boaters. From April to October, you'll have to be off the lake by 10 a.m. or risk getting tipped over by a large wake.

If you plan to make the trip, supplies are available in Perris. There is a day-use and boat launch fee.

Also nearby are Reflection Lake, Anglers Lake and Fisherman's Retreat.

PERRIS LAKE

REFLECTION **LAKE**

San Jacinto's Reflection Lake provides decent fishing, but its scenery is some of the worst in the region.

Rating: 5

Species: Rainbow Trout, Channel Catfish, Largemouth Bass, and Bluegill

Stocked periodically by private vendors with channel catfish and rainbow trout.

Facilities: Campgrounds, Restrooms, RV Hookups, General Store, Picnic Areas, Playground, and Horseshoes

Need Information? Contact: Reflection Lake (909) 654-7906

Directions: From Highway 74 in Hemet, drive west for approximately four miles to Warren Road and turn north. Continue three miles to the lake on your right.

Chances are you've never heard of Reflection Lake. Don't feel bad. Until I came across the name reading a weekly fishing report in the newspaper and decided to check it out, I hadn't heard of it either. When people talk about Reflection Lake, the first thing that comes to mind is the Reflection Lake in Lassen National Park. This Reflection Lake, located in San Jacinto, is exactly the opposite of that other Reflection Lake. Although the fishing is the pits, Lassen's Reflection Lake is one of the most beautiful in the state. On the contrary, San Jacinto's Reflection Lake provides decent fishing, but its scenery is some of the worst in the region.

The lake, only about 10 minutes from Hemet, is run as a put-and-take fishery. Reflection Lake is planted with rainbow trout in the cooler months and channel catfish as the water warms. Shaded by trees, Reflection Lake's shoreline is partly covered by private residences and motor homes, but there is plenty of space to fish. The lake is actually split into two, with one larger lake that allows boats with electric motors, canoes and float tubes, and a smaller pond-sized lake that is connected to the big lake by a narrow channel. There is a fee to fish the lake, but no fishing license is required.

The biggest thing to happen was a lake record 22-pound catfish caught in the late Eighties. One plus is that the campsites are located right on the smaller lake. During the summer months when the catfish bite picks up, you can fish all night from your campground, beating the smog and heat that blankets this area from May to September. Most of the rainbows are in the one to three-pound range and are easily fooled by Power Bait and nightcrawlers.

If the fishing doesn't sound too exciting, the peacocks are enjoyable. Upon entering the lake, you come across a peacock crossing sign that informs you of the presence of large and pretty peacocks. I was scared to death by one that I thought was a statue. A few regulars got a kick out of it when I jumped back because the high pitched cries the bird made as it awoke and scared the heck out of me.

If you plan to make the trip, supplies are available at the lake. There is a fishing fee and no fishing license is required.

Also nearby is Anglers Lake.

ANGLERS **LAKE**

Since everybody has to bank fish, most anglers choose to use night-crawlers or Power Bait for the trout, although some lures can be productive if the water isn't too murky.

Rating: 6

Species: Rainbow Trout, Channel Catfish, Largemouth Bass, and Crappie

Stocked weekly by private vendors.

Facilities: Picnic Areas, Restrooms, Bait & Tackle Shop, Snack Bar and Campgrounds

Anglers Lake owner Scott Hochstetler.

Need Information? Contact: Anglers Lake (909) 927-2614

Directions: From the 215 Freeway in Riverside, drive south to the 74 Freeway. Drive east on the 74 Freeway for six miles to Saboba Street. Turn left to Lake Street. Turn right on Lake Street and continue to Thornton Ave. Turn right and the lake will be on your right.

In 1891, runoff from Hemet Lake was diverted by canals to a tiny area that had been used as a holding facility for orange groves in Hemet. The runoff filled this area with water, forming what is now called Anglers Lake. In the mid-Forties, the lake opened as a recreational facility, and although it has changed ownership many times since, it has always been stocked with fish.

The 8.5-acre lake, similar in size and appearance to nearby Reflection Lake and Fisherman's Retreat, stocks rainbow trout during the cooler months and channel catfish as the water becomes too warm for trout. The lake is shaded by large eucalyptus trees, averages six to eight feet in depth and is 15 feet at its deepest. The remaining orange groves, still commercially harvested, are only a few feet away.

One of the most popular times to fish here is on New Years Eve. Sounds like a plan to me! Imagine sitting back in your lounge chair alongside a campfire with a group of friends, one eye on your fishing pole and the other admiring the fireworks. The lake is gated, providing local residents with a safe place to come, have a good time and fill a stringer. There are no boats or float tubes allowed. Most anglers use nightcrawlers or Power Bait for the trout, although some lures can be productive if the water isn't too murky.

The largest trout caught was a 16.8-pounder in the winter of 2000, but many fish from three to 12 pounds are caught on a daily basis. The best way to fool the cats is during the night fishing hours with traditional baits. A lake record 46-pounder was caught and kept in 1998. Because the lake was last drained and the bottom cleaned in 1976, and fish have been stocked ever since, there have to be some big ones lurking around.

The lake is open every day except Mondays for fishing. There is no fishing license required, nor is there any limit, but there is a fishing fee.

If you plan to make the trip, supplies are available at the lake. Call ahead for updated lake hours.

Also nearby are Hemet Lake, Reflection Lake and Lake Perris.

DIAMOND VALLEY **RESERVOIR**

This 4,500-acre reservoir began filling with water in March 2000, and will eventually become the largest reservoir in Southern California.

Rating: N/A

Species: Rainbow Trout, Channel Catfish, Blue Catfish, Bluegill, Carp, Largemouth Bass, Smallmouth Bass, Red Ear Sunfish and Tule Perch

Stocks: None for the public to enjoy until 2003.

Facilities: Lake doesn't open until 2003.

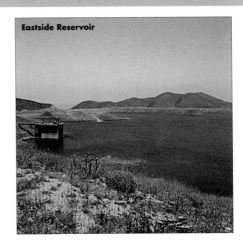
Eastside Reservoir

Need Information? Contact:
Diamond Valley Lake Recreation Project (800) 308-6767

Directions: From Interstate 15 in Ontario, drive south to Highway 79. Exit Highway 79 and drive north. Continue to the lake overlook on your right.

Although it won't open until 2003, Diamond Valley Reservoir is already raising the eyebrows of many Southland anglers. This 4,500-acre reservoir began filling with water in March 2000, and will eventually become the largest reservoir in Southern California. Formerly known as the Eastside Reservoir Project, Diamond Valley Reservoir was designed to reduce the threat of major water shortages during high summer usages and droughts. The reservoir nearly doubles Southern California's surface storage and holds a six months' supply of water in case of an earthquake or other disaster.

Located four miles southwest of Hemet in southwestern Riverside County, Diamond Valley Reservoir will be 4.5 miles long, two miles wide and 260 feet deep. It was formed by building a dam between two mountain ranges and then flooding the Diamond and Domenogoni Valleys. The $2.1 billion dollar project, funded by the Metropolitan Water District, is fed by water from the Colorado River via the San Diego Canal, and also by Northern California water from Silverwood Lake. At capacity, the lake can hold 800,000 acre-feet of water. Just to put that in perspective, one acre-foot is enough to provide water to two families for one year. The lake is expected to fill sometime in 2003, when fishermen will get their first shot at fish that have been maturing since 1998.

In order to introduce fish into the reservoir, the California Department of Fish and Game built an 80-acre pond on the dry, lakebed bottom in 1998, and began stocking large and smallmouth bass and bluegill so they could adapt to their new home. The bass have already successfully spawned three times, and now that the lake is being filled, more fish are being planted. By the lake's opening, the CA DFG hopes to plant channel and blue catfish, tule perch, rainbow trout and red ear sunfish. Planting salmon is also a possibility, but that decision won't be made until sometime in 2002.

Another plus for fishermen is that the decision has already been made not allow water-skiing. Boating and sailing, however, will be permitted. Although they won't be in place for another year, the lake will have two full-service marinas, more than 70 miles of hiking trails, a recreation complex, and it will increase the Santa Rosa Ecological Reserve by 3,700 square miles.

Here are a few intriguing facts provided by the Metropolitan Water District: the dam is the largest earth and rock-filled dam in US history (almost eight Empire State buildings, including antennas, could be laid across the lake's east dam); it would take an estimated 19,839 years to fill it with a garden hose; the tires on the dump trucks that were used to construct the dam are 12 feet high and cost $14,500 each; each of the lake's 12 pumps can release the equivalent of one 16,000 gallon swimming pool per second; the 110 million cubic yards of earth and rock used to construct both dams could build a wall seven feet high and three feet wide around the world at the equator; and the fuel bill for the equipment used to construct the west dam was estimated at $10 million dollars – before gas prices rose.

Eastside Reservoir

If you plan to make the trip, the lake will not open until sometime in 2003. Until then, the only way to view it is by going to the lake's overlook.

Also nearby are Lake Skinner, Anglers Lake, Reflection Lake and Hemet Lake.

DIAMOND VALLEY **RESERVOIR**

CORONA LAKE

Before you get your line wet it could cost you more than $50, but most anglers who come here must consider it well worth it, or all the crowds wouldn't keep coming back.

Rating: 8

Species: Rainbow Trout, Channel Catfish, Crappie, Bluegill, Carp, Bullhead, Wipers (Hybrid Stripped Bass), Blue Catfish, Sturgeon and Largemouth Bass

Stocked with 67,000 pounds of rainbow trout and 51,077 pounds of channel catfish.

David Lopez caught this 7.8-pound striper on a nightcrawler.

Facilities: Boat Launch, Boat Rentals, Picnic Areas, Restrooms, Campgrounds, Fishing Pole Rentals and General Store

Need Information? Contact: Corona Lake (909) 277-4489 or (909) 277-3321

Directions: From Corona, drive southeast on Interstate 15 and exit Indian Truck Trail Road. Turn left, driving under the interstate to Temescal Canyon Road and turn right. The lake is on the left about a half-mile down the road.

Got money? If you do, Corona Lake is a good place to go. This 58-acre lake is a small put-and-take fishery located between Corona and Lake Elsinore just off Interstate 15. It can be easily reached from anywhere in Southern California, and although it isn't surrounded by tall pine trees and blessed with clean mountain air, it beats the scenery of the nearby urban areas. This spring-fed lake has trees along most of the shoreline to protect you from the heat of the desert environment. Chances are your wife or girlfriend knows exactly where it is, because there are big signs pointing you towards the lake on the way to the Lake Elsinore Outlets, which is a dream come true to women who enjoy shopping. (My mom and grandma can tell you every store at the outlets).

Even though the fishing is usually good here, there are a few setbacks... namely crowds and cost. With estimates of more than 1,500 anglers fishing here weekly, the shoreline lacks open space, and the water is full of boats. To add insult to injury, before you get your line wet it could cost you more than $50. It costs $16 per person to fish the lake, although a fishing license isn't required. Then, most people rent a boat, which ranges from $20-$75, and basic necessities, like some worms, a mackerel and a microwave burrito, can run you another $20. So, you have to ask yourself if Corona Lake is really worth it. Most anglers who come here must consider it well worth it, or all the crowds wouldn't keep coming back.

The lake receives 118,099 pounds of fish each year. That's an enormous amount for such a small lake. The trout are trucked in from Mt. Lassen Trout Farm in Northern California, up to three times a week during the cooler months, and catfish are stocked from late spring through summer. Trout plants usually last until early May, but because the lake is so shallow (only 40 feet deep at full pool, which it rarely attains) the trout die off by mid-May. The trout average one to three pounds, however, fish up to 22 pounds are stocked and caught weekly.

Bait dunkers are the norm, with most anglers having success soaking Power Bait tipped with marshmallows or using inflated nightcrawlers. The sliding sinker method is the most effective here. Use a small sliding sinker above a swivel, then tie on a two foot leader using either two or four pound test, and attach a No. 16 or 18 treble hook to the end of the line. Advanced anglers might try using white trout teasers. They can be used with a bobber or without. Trolling can be productive as well, but with the lake being so crowded, it can be difficult.

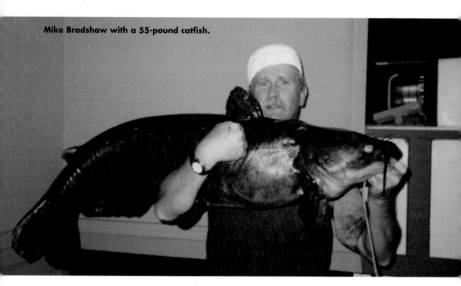

Mike Bradshaw with a 55-pound catfish.

Once the trout begin to die off, catfish season begins. All-night fishing is the hot ticket in the summer, and the way to bring in the most fish is by attaching cut mackerel to a size two or four single bait hook and then dipping it in some Hog Wild. Nightcrawlers, mealworm/marshmallow combos, shrimp and traditional stinkbaits will also catch fish. Most of the cats are caught in the coves or near the submerged trees on the east side of the lake. The most successful anglers pull their boats inside the trees, but to do this you have to use heavy line or risk losing fish.

The largest cat to come out of the lake was caught in October of 1999 and weighed more than 68 pounds. Even bigger fish have been rumored to be in the lake. Recently a 54 pounder was caught and released, and numerous fish over 20 pounds are caught weekly.

Nighttime crappie fishing is also productive in the trees, with quality fish being caught on white crappie jigs. Occasionally, an angler fishing with shrimp for catfish will hook up on a large sturgeon. The same happens to trout fishermen using Power Bait, but it only happens a few times a year.

If you plan to make the trip, supplies are available at the lake. There are fishing and boat launch fees. During the summer all-night fishing is permitted. Call the lake for exact hours.

Also nearby are Tom's Farms, Lake Elsinore and the Lake Elsinore Factory Outlets.

LAKE **ELSINORE**

Rating: 6

Species: Bluegill, Largemouth Bass, Crappie, Catfish, Rainbow Trout, Bullhead and Channel Catfish

Stocked with 5,000 pounds of rainbow trout and 5,000 pounds of channel catfish.

Facilities: Full-Service Marinas, Boat Launches, Campgrounds, Picnic Areas, Restrooms, Bait & Tackle, Snack Bars and Playgrounds

Lake Elsinore

Need Information? Contact: Lake Elsinore Marina and RV Park (909) 678-1300, Lake Information (909) 245-9308, Camping Information (909) 471-1212

Directions: From Ontario, drive south on Interstate 15 to the city of Lake Elsinore. Exit Highway 74 and drive west to the lake.

Lake Elsinore used to be a fish's nightmare. During the Eighties and early Nineties, the lake saw large die-offs of fish due to warm water and a lack of oxygen. The drop in oxygen levels was caused by high amounts of nitrogen and phosphorus entering the lake via runoff. The rise in these two elements created an over abundance of algae, and when that algae decayed it floated to the bottom and sucked-up all the oxygen needed for the fish to survive. Because it's only 25 feet at its deepest, and averages just 16 feet, the lake also warms much faster than other lakes. Low oxygen levels and warm water equaled bad news for Elsinore's fish population.

So many fish died that fishermen wrote off the lake almost two decades ago, but today, Lake Elsinore is making a comeback. Since the mid-Nineties, water quality has gradually improved, a process that the lake's biologist, Pat Killroy, said can sometimes occur naturally. However, the lake has also been given $15 million dollars for improvements, $500,000 of which will go directly to fish enhancement projects.

Until recently, the lake had no structure, but in December of 1999 after Christmas, the lake sponsored a Christmas Tree Drive and a few hundred trees were thrown into its waters to provide catfish and bass with spawning grounds. Lake operators also built catfish caves and other structures out of pvc pipe to provide more spawning areas. The next step is to remove carp from the lake and to do something about its enormous shad population. Killroy said they will most likely plant hybrid stripers to suppress the shad population.

Fishing has already improved, with crappie fairing the best. The lake has a healthy crappie population, with most of the fish weighing one to two pounds. The bass are making a slower comeback, but a stock of 3,600 fingerlings in June of 2000 should perk up the action in another year. For the first time since the early Eighties, catfish were stocked in the spring of 2000. The California Department of Fish and Game planted 5,000 cats ranging from one to three pounds, but with all the shad in the lake to feed on, they are expected to grow to trophy sizes soon.

In early spring of 2000, the lake also revitalized its rainbow trout fishery. The City of Lake Elsinore kicked off the celebration, welcoming trout back into the lake with a plant of 5,000 pounds of rainbows from Idaho. The CA DFG followed with another 5,000 pounds and have committed to continue these plants each winter as long as water quality remains healthy enough for the fish.

An overlook of Lake Elsinore.

At 3,400 acres, Lake Elsinore is the largest natural freshwater lake in Southern California. It is mainly fed by water from the San Jacinto River. With headwaters in the mountains above Hemet, San Jacinto runs through Perris and Canyon Lake before emptying into Elsinore.

As for now Lake Elsinore is not a fisherman's lake. It belongs to boaters. If you are coming to fish, try it either during the winter or early in the morning. Otherwise, you could get pushed over by a large wake!

If you plan to make the trip, there is a boat launch and day-use fee. Supplies are available at the lake.

Also nearby are Ortega Falls, Anglers Lake, Perris Lake, Reflection Lake, Corona Lake and Hemet Lake.

LAKE **SKINNER**

When the striper bite is on, it's common to see 50 boats gathered in a small area, all targeting boiling stripers, and another 25 boats trolling.

Rating: 8

Species: Rainbow Trout, Channel Catfish, Largemouth Bass, Striped Bass, Crappie and Bluegill

Stocked with 24,000 pounds of rainbow trout and 6,000 pounds of channel catfish.

Need Information? Contact: Lake Skinner (909-926-1541), Lake Skinner Marina (909-926-1505) Campground Reservations (800-234-7275)

Sarah Karam with a small striper from Skinner.

Facilities: Boat Launches, Marina, Boat Rentals, Bait Store, Campgrounds, General Store with Gas, Showers, Cafe, Restrooms and RV Hookups

Directions: From Temecula on Interstate 15, exit Rancho California Road and turn northeast. Continue eight miles to Lake Skinner County Park on the right.

Of all the Southern California lakes that are famous for their striped bass, Lake Skinner is one of the best. Because water skiers are kept off by a 10-mph speed limit, this 1,200-acre lake, located in the foothills north of Temecula, is ideal for fishermen.

Even though the lake is well known for striper fishing, it's no secret that it's overpopulated with the fish. Because it is fed by the California Aqueduct, Lake Skinner is consistently pumped with more stripers that are not needed. The problem is, even with the good striper bite here, that trout fishing suffers. The lake is also heavily planted with trout, but the stripers gobble them up before anglers get a chance to try their luck. The California Department of Fish and Game stopped planting trout in 1996, because the stripers ate most of trout before anglers had a chance at catching them. The CA DFG used to plant more than 63,000 rainbow trout each year. The lake is now stocked by Riverside County.

We fished the lake the day after it was stocked with 2,500 pounds of rainbows and got skunked, along with all the other anglers. A park ranger's explanation was that the trout were all in the stripers bellies. In recent years, the lake management has smartened up, netting off an area for trout fishing only. The netted part of the lake is small, only about the size of an Olympic swimming pool, but it receives a huge number of trout. With the stripers licking their lips from the outside, the trout fishing tends to be good. The lake now stocks about 18,000 trout trucked in from Idaho from November to April, half of which are let into the main lake and the rest are put in the netted area.

When the striper bite is on, it's common to see 50 boats gathered in a small area, all targeting boiling stripers, and another 25 boats trolling. As you might guess, most anglers do well for stripers here, but it requires getting on the lake early. The bite usually shuts off before 9 a.m. and doesn't kick back up until the early evening. Anglers trying to catch boiling stripers do best with live shad, while trollers use various trout imitation lures.

If the striper bite is slow on the east end of the lake, experienced striper fishermen head over to the buoy line adjacent to the aqueduct inflow. Lake regulations forbid tying onto the buoy line, but that doesn't stop most people. (The law usually isn't enforced.) Once tied off, some anglers cast as far as they can toward the incoming water, trying to fool stripers that wait for food to flow in through the channel. Others drop a line down to the bottom with anchovies and kick back and wait.

Lake Skinner

While fishing for stripers, anglers are often surprised by large catfish. These catfish also look to capitalize on the food being pushed in from the aqueduct. Cats up to 20 pounds are common with the lake record running 33.4 pounds. The lake plants about 6,000 catfish from one to three pounds over the summer months.

To help the lake's largemouth population Lake Matthews donated 800 pounds of bass from two to eight pounds in the summer of 2000. Each November the lake holds its annual trout derby before having the catfish derby in August.

If you plan to make the trip, get here early. There is a long line at the park kiosk early in the morning when the striper bite is on. There is a day-use and fishing fee.

Also nearby are the Diamond Valley Reservoir, Hemet Lake, Perris Lake and the Temecula Valley Wineries.

REGION 12

Palomar/Julian Area

Lake Wohlford
Doane Pond
Lake Henshaw
San Luis Rey River
Sutherland Reservoir
Lake Cuyamaca
Sweetwater River

LAKE **WOHLFORD**

Wohlford offers great access for shoreline anglers who can walk around the lake and fish the same places that the boats fish.

Rating: 7

Species: Rainbow Trout, Channel Catfish, Largemouth Bass, Crappie and Bluegill

Stocked with 26,200 pounds of rainbow trout and 6,000 pounds of channel catfish.

Facilities: Boat Rentals, Boat Launch, Picnic Areas, Restrooms, Restaurant, Campgrounds, Cabin Rentals and a Fish Cleaning Station

Need Information? Contact: Lake Wohlford Ranger Station (760) 839-4346

Directions: From Interstate 15 in San Diego, drive north to the city of Escondido. Exit Valley Parkway and turn east. Continue to Lake Wohlford Road and turn right. Follow the road to the lake.

Lake Wohlford is a popular put-and-take trout and catfish fishery, with good prospects for largemouth bass in the spring. Along with nearby Dixon Lake, Lake Wohlford is run by the City of Escondido. Trout season is definitely the lake's most popular attraction. From late December through April, the small, narrow lake is stocked with about 20,000 trout up to 12 pounds.

Trolling has never been productive here, but fishing from an anchored boat or from the shore commonly produces limits. Although fishing is good all around the lake, the best area is near the buoy lines, especially the east end where the water comes into the lake. Most people use Power Bait, but trout row is also a local favorite. Wohlford offers great access for shoreline anglers who can walk around the lake and fish the same places that the boats fish. Float tubing is also a good way to go.

In April and May, fishing the bass spawn can be fair. The bass in the lake are a smart bunch and can require some skill to catch. Even the most experienced anglers have trouble catching them. Purple, black and chocolate-brown plastic worms, as well as minnows, crawdads, and crankbaits are the best baits. The lake record is a 19.3-pound fish caught and released back in 1986.

Near the end of the bass spawn, catfish are planted. The lake plants the cats twice in June and July, and once in August. The largest cat weighed 27 pounds and was caught and released back in 1960s. Chances are it's not still around. Most of the cats are in the one to three pound range, but if you're looking for quantity, the highest catch rates are found near the east and west buoy lines.

If you plan to make the trip, supplies are available at the lake. There are fishing and boat launch fees. No boats over 20 feet or under 10 are permitted. Lake Wohlford is open daily from late December to early September. There is a 5-mph speed limit on the lake.

Also nearby are Dixon Lake, Lake Hodges and the San Diego Wild Animal Park.

DOANE **POND**

Most people, including the fishermen who loaned me his spot, fish the pond with Power Bait, but I found the best action to be on small spinners.

Rating: 6

Species: Rainbow Trout, Channel Catfish, Bluegill, Largemouth Bass, and Brown Bullhead

Stocked with 4,500 pounds of rainbow trout.

Facilities: Picnic Areas, Campgrounds and Restrooms

Need Information? Contact: Palomar Mountain State Park (760) 742-3462

Directions: From Interstate 15 in Temecula, drive south for 11 miles to Highway 76. Drive east on Highway 76 for 21.3 miles (driving past Rincon Springs) to Road S-6. Turn north and continue for 6.8 miles to Road S-7. Turn left and continue three miles to the park's entrance. Follow signs to the lake.

So, you've never heard of Doane Pond? Don't worry not many people have. But now that you have heard of Doane Pond, it would be a shame not to visit it. You ask why? Doane Pond, located in Palomar Mountain State Park, is one of only four high mountain trout lakes south of the San Bernardino Mountains.

Located at 5,500 feet on Palomar Mountain in the Cleveland National Forest, Doane Pond is also one of the few Southern California lakes that have four distinct seasons. It has a warm summer, a cool fall and in spring its meadows shake off their snow and bloom with wildflowers. After fall, Doane Pond provides the residents of San Diego County with a winter wonderland they'd more expect from Northern California and the Eastern Sierra. Following a winter storm, Doane Pond often freezes over and snow blankets the shoreline and meadows adjacent to the lake.

In spite of Doane Pond's unique weather and habitat, especially considering its

Doane Pond

southern location, visitation is surprisingly low, but you can use that to your advantage. The small, shallow, three-acre pond holds a consistent population of rainbow trout, with the California Department of Fish and Game stocking it year-round with more than 10,000 fish. With tules covering most of its shoreline, Doane Pond offers limited access, but those who arrive early and get a spot on the gravel beach on the south shoreline do well.

When I first visited the lake in March of 2000, there were only ten people fishing and none of them had caught anything. I walked back to the car, grabbed my trout rod and walked down to the lake. With no open shoreline, I asked one of the guys if I could borrow his spot for a cast. "Go ahead," he said, eyeing me dubiously. "I've been here all day and haven't caught a thing."

Although only three acres, Doane Pond can kickout staggering catch rates for anglers who fish the lake correctly.

His eyes instantly became curious when I caught a fish on my first cast. Then I proceeded to land and release 10 others on my next 13 tries. The guy was definitely confused and more than a little embarrassed. "How did you catch those?" he asked. "Easy," I replied. "The lake is so shallow you need to be able to cast out in the middle to catch fish."

Most people, including the fishermen who loaned me his spot, fish the pond with Power Bait, but I found the best action to be on small spinners. Before I left I gave him a small spinner and showed him where to cast. Bam! He caught one on his first cast, too.

The lake also has bass, bluegill and a few catfish, but none of them are as plentiful as the trout. However, in the summer of 1999, a lake record six-pound largemouth was caught, proving there are quality fish here. Catfish were planted more than a decade ago and have become self-sustaining, but most of them are on the small side. With all the tules surrounding the shoreline, the easiest way to fish the lake is with waders or a float tube.

Another attraction is the pond's large frog population. In the spring, thousands of pollywogs roam the shoreline waiting to turn into frogs. These pollywogs give kids something to do if the fishing slows. Signs say to refrain from handling the animals, but there are so many it's hard to resist playing with the cute critters.

If you plan to make the trip, there's a fee to enter Palomar Mountain State Park. Supplies are available in nearby Palomar Mountain.

Also nearby are the Palomar Observatory, Lake Cuyamaca, the San Luis Rey River, Sweetwater River, Lake Henshaw, Prisoner Creek Falls and Cedar Creek Falls.

LAKE **HENSHAW**

Bottom line, unlike other San Diego area lakes, Lake Henshaw doesn't have any trophy size fish – no more big bass, no more big crowds and no stocks of any kind.

Rating: 8

Species: Largemouth Bass, Bluegill, Crappie, Channel Catfish, Bullhead and Carp

Stocks: None

Facilities: Boat rentals, Boat Launch, Restaurant, General Store, Bait & Tackle, Cabin Rentals, Campgrounds, Swimming Pool, Showers and Restrooms

Need Information? Contact:
Lake Henshaw Resort (760) 782-3487 or (760) 782-3501

Directions: From San Diego, drive north on Interstate 15 to the city of Escondido. Continue past Escondido and exit Highway 76. Drive east on Highway 76 for approximately 30 miles to the lake.

If you walked into the Lake Henshaw General Store and looked at the pictures on the wall in the back, you'd be surprised by all the old photos of huge bass caught in the Fifties and Sixties. Then you'd notice that none of them look like they've been taken in the last 40 years. In fact, they haven't! Those pictures come from the good old days when Henshaw was owned by the Vista Irrigation District, and lots of big bass called the lake home. Days when anglers bragged about how good the fishing was here.

Here's a brief roller-coaster history of the changes the lake has gone through from then until now. Because of neglect, in the late Eighties the lake's popularity dwindled until almost nobody was fishing it. However, in 1995, Al and Gwen Socin purchased the lake and vowed to start over and turn things around. First off, they cleaned and modernized the lake's facilities. Then, to bring back the fish population, the Socins placed structure all over the lake to provide cover for the remaining fish, and also built fish spawning areas. Because the old lake records had been discarded by previous management, new ones were created.

Things were really starting to look up, but then in 1996, after they'd spent all that money on renovations, word got out that a catfish die-off occurred, and anglers again stopped coming to fish the lake. There were still tons of

Lake Henshaw in the backdrop.

fish, but people had the perception that they were gone. The Socins decided that for public relatons reasons they would stock catfish to bring the anglers back. The idea worked too well; today they have too many catfish in the lake.

Lake Henshaw

One of the lake's problems that the Socins weren't able to solve is low water levels. Because the lake relies on rain for its water supply, the lake level suffers when it doesn't rain. It currently has about four miles of shoreline, which is way shy of the 23 miles it had back in the early Forties. They pump water into the lake, but all it does is compensate for evaporation.

When you first encounter Lake Henshaw, located in a valley below Palomar Mountain, it looks like a mud puddle and you wonder if there are any fish at all. There are cows grazing along the shoreline, and it's shallow enough that you could walk across the east side of the lake if you wanted. Bottom line, unlike other San Diego area lakes, Lake Henshaw doesn't have any trophy size fish – no more big bass, no more big crowds and no stocks of any kind. As a matter of fact, Henshaw's one of only a few San Diego County lakes that rely solely on natural reproduction for its fish population.

However, the Socins have succeeded in turning the fishery around, and today fishing for smaller fish couldn't be better. Catfish fishing is excellent year-round with fish caught off the boat docks and near the dam. There is a productive crappie bite in the spring for anglers using jigs tipped with a mealworm, and fishing for bluegill and bullhead can be great during the summer months. The bass have never recovered and aren't expected to. No big deal. There are plenty of other lakes in the area where you can catch bass. Anglers come to Henshaw for numbers, not size.

If you plan to make the trip, there is a $5 day-use fee. There is a 10-mph speed limit on the lake. The lake is open daily. Bring lots of water and sun tan lotion. There is no shade around the lake.

Also nearby are Lake Cuyamaca, Doane Pond, Palomar State Park, Cedar Creek Falls and Prisoner Creek Falls.

SAN LUIS REY **RIVER**

You might want to take a quick lesson from my experience and not believe everything you hear from other fishermen. It's better to find out for yourself.

Rating: 6

Species: Rainbow Trout

Stocked with 1,400 pounds of rainbow trout.

Facilities: Picnic Areas and Restrooms

Need Information? Contact: Cleveland National Forest (760) 788-0250

San Luis Rey River

Directions: From Interstate 15 in Temecula, drive 11.2 miles south to Highway 76. Turn east and continue 30 miles to the San Luis Rey Picnic Area.

I was walking with my fishing pole in the parking lot of the San Luis Rey Picnic Area when two fellows in an old, beat-up, brown pickup truck pulled up next to me and asked me if there were any fish in the stream. I told them, "That's exactly what I'm here to find out." Before I could get any more words out, the driver announced in slurred speech that there weren't any fish in the creek. "We don't fish," he said. "But I come here all the time and I've never seen anybody catch anything." I knew something wasn't right when I looked in his car and saw two fishing poles in the back seat and an "I'd Rather Be Fishing" license plate frame on the back of the truck.

When I went down to the San Luis Rey River I found out what the two were up to. It turns out they didn't want anybody else to catch trout out of the creek, and they were trying to turn people away. There were fish in the stream and lots of them! The California Department of Fish and Game had stocked them earlier that morning. I later found out that this stream flows out of Lake Henshaw and is stocked with 3,100 rainbow trout each year, providing decent catch rates for anglers.

The stream is stocked from Lake Henshaw downstream to Prisoner Creek, a distance of about four miles. When runoff is high, the stream turns muddy and is difficult to fish, but when the water is clear, the fish are usually stacked up in pools and easy to spot. Most of the stream is shaded by large trees, keeping you cool when days get hot in the spring and summer.

You might want to take a quick lesson from my experience and not believe everything you hear from other fishermen. It's better to find out for yourself.

If you plan to make the trip, supplies are available at Lake Henshaw. A Forest Service Adventure Pass is required to park in the Cleveland National Forest.

Also nearby are Lake Henshaw, Doane Pond, Palomar State Park, Julian, Cedar Creek Falls and Lake Cuyamaca.

SUTHERLAND **RESERVOIR**

Although some anglers were bothered by the water level, others considered fishing in what was equivalent to a large, brown bathtub the best fishing ever. The fish were sitting ducks!

Rating: 8

Species: Largemouth Bass, Bluegill, Channel Catfish, Crappie, Bullhead, Red Ear Sunfish, Blue Catfish and Carp

Stocked with 3,000 pounds of catfish annually.

Facilities: A Marina, Boat Rentals, General Store, Boat Launch, Cafe, Bait & Tackle, Restrooms and Picnic Areas

Sutherland Reservoir

Need Information? Contact: Boat Reservations (619) 698-3474 Recorded Lake Information (619) 465-3474

Directions: From San Diego, drive north on Interstate 15 to the city of Escondido. In Escondido exit Highway 78 and drive east to Sutherland Dam Road. Turn north to the lake.

Pray for rain, because without it Sutherland Reservoir looks like a mud puddle. The lake, used as a reservoir for the city of Ramona, is one of the few in the San Diego area fed solely by runoff, and when rainfall is scarce lake level suffers. The worst-case scenario came true in 1990-91 during a drought when the lake fell to an appalling 2.8 percent of capacity. Although some anglers were bothered by the water level, others considered fishing in what was equivalent to a large, brown bathtub the best fishing ever. The fish were sitting ducks! Then there were still some other anglers who considered taking fish out of a bathtub too easy and unsportsmanlike.

The lake reached full-pool at 550 acres in 1996, and was four inches above the spillway in 1998. Then, water levels were threatened again in 2000 as memories of the old mud puddle began to haunt anglers once more. The lake's bass population lives and dies with the water levels. The latest survey in 1999 showed the bass population at 17,000, down from 40,000 in the mid-Nineties. Bass fishing can be popular (there's a 16.50 pound lake record), with Pig N' Jigs taking the most fish.

However, most anglers come for the catfish. As soon as the bass bite slows in late spring, the cat-

Sutherland Reservoir

fish come to life and remain on the prowl until the lake closes in the second or third week of October to prepare for waterfowl season. Each March 3,000 pounds of catfish are stocked, supplementing the already stable population in the lake. The cats get big. The lake record channel cat is only 25 pounds, but the blues in the lake easily top 50. A lake record 53-pounder was caught and released in '97.

Sutherland Reservoir

During prime catfish season, the cats congregate near the dam. Anglers tie up on the buoy line and cast as close as they can to the dam in search of larger fish. Be aware, the park rangers will let you tie off on the buoys, but if they see your boat drift inside them, they won't hesitate to throw you off the lake.

Sutherland stayed carp-free until the early Nineties when high water levels helped them to escape farm ponds and swim down into the reservoir. They didn't waste any time multiplying, either, and now they're all more than the lake. A new lake record was recently established when a carp weighting more than 30 pounds was caught on a Krocodile. There are also large crappie, red ear sunfish and bluegill over three pounds in the lake, but they aren't heavily fished.

If you plan to make the trip, supplies are available at the lake. There is a fishing and boating fee. Sutherland is open to fishing from Friday through Sunday, mid-March through mid-October.

Also nearby are Lake Cuyamaca, Lake Henshaw, the Sweetwater River, Prisoner Creek Falls, Cedar Creek Falls, Green Valley Falls, the San Diego Wild Animal Park and San Luis Rey River.

SUTHERLAND RESERVOIR

LAKE **CUYAMACA**

Lake Cuyamaca, less than an hour drive from Sea World, has been run as one of the most successful put-and-take fisheries in the state since 1968.

Rating: 10

Species: Crappies, Bullhead, Largemouth Bass, Rainbow Trout, Sturgeon, Channel Catfish, and Sunfish

Stocked with 44,000 pounds of rainbow trout every year, and channel catfish and sturgeon every other year.

Facilities:
Campgrounds, RV Hookups, Restaurant, General Store, Bait & Tackle, Lodging, Gas, Picnic Areas, Restrooms, Boat Rentals and Boat Launch

A rare shot of Lake Cuyamaca at full pool.

Need Information? Contact: Lake Cuyamaca (877) 581-9904 or (760) 765-0515

Directions: From San Diego, drive east on Highway 8 to Highway 79. Turn north on Highway 79 and continue 15 miles to the lake.

Reports were coming out of San Diego County that anglers were scoring easy limits at Lake Cuyamaca. Known as one of the best trout fishing lakes in Southern California, my friends and I decided to brave the cold winter weather and see if we could get in on the action.

We planned to camp at the lake, but after leaving my dad's 50th birthday party late

Robert Benson caught this sturgeon at Cuyamaca.

and arriving at 2:30 a.m., we opted to sleep in the car. We figured the sun would be rising in a few hours anyway. As soon as we unrolled our sleeping bags, unexpected rain, which wasn't suppose to hit for another day, came pouring down. In the next hour, more than two inches had fallen. The lake opened at 6 a.m., but fog, cold and torrential downpours kept us in the car until 8:30 a.m., when I started getting worried that the storm would shut off the bite.

Lake Cuyamaca

When the weather broke, we headed over to the park office to buy our fishing permits. The woman working the office laughed. "You guys are going to try it, huh? It's getting pretty bad out there. You know there are no refunds. A few boats went out earlier and they already came in."

As soon as we took the boat cover off and put up the canopy, the skies darkened again, the winds picked up and the temperature dropped. But we had come too far to go home early, so we went out anyway. You've probably already guessed that we were the only boat on the lake. The winds were blowing so hard we had trouble keeping a straight troll, but the fish didn't mind. All it took was a slow troll and a few small Rapalas behind the boat and the action never stopped.

After the first hour, we had eight fish on the boat and missed another ten. My friend Blake Lezak tried to keep our video camera level, another friend worked on keeping the boat straight and I just managed to handle the four rods we were running. Within a minute of letting the lines out, the trout would hit. It couldn't have been a better fishing day!

Lake Cuyamaca's dam was constructed in 1888, but the lake's fishery didn't begin to strengthen until 1962 when the dykes were built to maintain more stable water levels and ensure a quality fishery. Situated at 4,620 feet near Cuyamaca State Park in an oak and pine covered forrest, Lake Cuyamaca, less than an hour drive from Sea World, has been run as one of the most successful put-and-take fisheries in the state since 1968.

In order to keep a good trout population properly balanced for the rest of the fish in the lake, management implemented a policy stating that you must keep all of the fish you catch, expect for smallmouth bass which are strictly catch & release. I repeat there is no catch & release. If you do, you will be banned from the lake. Park Rangers and

Lake Cuyamaca is one of California's best all around fisheries.

California Department of Fish and Game wardens actually sit with binoculars on the highway looking to ticket anglers who throw fish back.

Currently, the lake is stocked with 43,000 rainbow trout from the CA DFG, and another 24,000 pounds of fish ranging from one to seven pounds stocked by private vendors. Although good year round, the trout bite is best in the winter and spring.

The key to fishing the lake is keeping a slow troll. If you drove faster than 2-mph, the fish won't bite. Lure selection is also important. Small Rapalas, Panther Martins and Cripplelures will all do the trick. But most important is where you troll. Stay about 30 yards offshore, parallel to the willow trees on the north shoreline where the water is only about three to five feet deep. Keep your lead-core and downriggers at home. The lake is only 16 feet deep at its deepest and averages 10 feet. Shore anglers also do well soaking Power Bait and night-crawlers. During spawning season, the larger trout can be caught swimming up Little Stonewall and Azaela Creeks.

Mike Long

Although there is no night fishing allowed, there is a fair catfish bite here, with cats planted as six to eight-inch fingerlings every other year to maintain a stable population. The topwater bass action is hot during spring and summer with bass averaging three pounds. A lake record came in at a tad more than 14 pounds, which proves larger fish do inhabit the lake. There are so many crappie in the lake, management donated over 2,000 adult crappie to Laguna Niguel Lake in April of 2000 in an effort to slow the population.

This 100-acre lake is one of the few in California that stocks sturgeon. They began a program in 1996 of stocking 100 of them every other year, and it has proved successful. There are currently 180 in the lake, where they will remain until they reach the legal limit. The sturgeon are often caught accidentally, but if you're going to target them, try using shrimp.

On your way up, keep an eye out for wild turkeys and deer. There is a group of more than 15 deer that can be seen daily by the lake. The kids love them!

If you plan to make the trip, supplies are available at the lake. There is a fishing fee. Free fishing clinics are offered every Saturday.

Also nearby are the historical town of Julian, Cuyamaca State Park, the Sweetwater River, Cottonwood Creek Falls, Cedar Creek Falls and Green Valley Falls.

LAKE CUYAMACA

SWEETWATER **RIVER**

There are a few pools that are big enough to cast lures into, but the easiest way to fish is with Power Bait.

Rating: 5

Species: Rainbow Trout

Stocked with 1,000 pounds of rainbow trout.

Facilities: Picnic Areas, Campgrounds, and Restrooms

Need Information? Contact: Cuyamaca State Park (760) 765-0755

Sweetwater River

Directions: From Interstate 8 in San Diego, drive east for 30 miles to Highway 79. Turn north and continue for seven miles to the stream located in Cuyamaca State Park.

Sweetwater River's biggest claim to fame is that it serves as an easy getaway from urban life in San Diego. One of only two stocked rivers in San Diego County, Sweetwater is really more the size of a creek. However, it offers good fishing after a stock, which occurs once a month from February through May with a total of about 2,650 fish.

The river's headwaters are in Upper Green Valley near Lake Cuyamaca. From there, it slowly works its way down from the upper valley through Green Valley in Cuyamaca State Park, finally flowing through the town of Descanso before emptying into Sweetwater Reservoir. The river parallels Highway 79 near Green Valley Campground where the California Department of Fish and Game stocks the trout. Located in the Cleveland National Forest, it is best accessed via Cuyamaca State Park, which is inside of the national forest. Most of the fish in Sweetwater are small and stack up in various pools. There are a few pools that are big enough to cast lures into, so the easiest way to fish is with Power Bait.

The most popular activity here is not fishing, but Green Valley Falls, a few small cascades on the river just below where it is stocked. During the winter and spring when water levels are sufficient, the cascades can be quite inspiring as water slides down the smooth, polished granite rocks. Once late spring comes, the Sweetwater River turns into a trickle and anglers patiently await another winter and the return of trout plants.

If you plan to make the trip, supplies are available at Lake Cuyamaca. There is a parking fee to enter the Green Valley Campground area. If fishing the river outside the state park, a Forest Service Adventure Pass is required to park in the Cleveland National Forest.

Also nearby are Lake Cuyamaca, Anza-Borrego State Park, Sweetwater Reservoir, Cedar Creek Falls and shopping in Julian.

REGION 13

San Diego County Urban Waters

CALIFORNIA

Dixon Lake
Lake Hodges
Lake Poway
Lake Miramar
Lake Murray
Santee Lakes
San Vicente
Lindo Lake
Lake Jennings

El Capitan Reservoir
Chollas Reservoir
Upper Otay Lake
Lower Otay Lake

DIXON **LAKE**

Some of the most popular fishing is at night, during the summer when the lake is open to fishing until midnight from Wednesday through Saturday.

Rating: 7

Species: Rainbow Trout, Channel Catfish, Bluegill, Largemouth Bass, Sunfish and Carp

Stocked with 32,800 pounds of rainbow trout and 18,000 pounds of channel catfish.

Facilities: Boat Rentals, Restrooms, Snack Bar, Bait & Tackle, Fishing Piers, Campground and Hiking Trails

Need Information? Contact: Dixon Lake (760) 839-4680

Directions: From Interstate 15 in Escondido, exit north on El Norte Parkway and drive 3.1 miles to La Honda Drive. Turn left and continue 1.3 miles to the park entrance. Turn right and drive one mile to the lake.

Dixon Lake is a small, 76-acre lake located near, and run by, the city of Escondido. The lake was named after Jim Dixon, a past superintendent of the Escondido Mutual Water Company who came up with the idea of building it. Being part of the California Aqueduct System, it receives most of its water from Northern California and the Colorado River. Most importantly for fishermen, they run it as a popular put and take fishery.

No fish are stocked by the California Department of Fish and Game, but trout and catfish are stocked weekly by private vendors, keeping fishing fair year-round. Some of the most popular fishing is at night, during the summer when the lake is open to fishing until midnight from Wednesday through Saturday. Residents of Escondido flock to the lake for a chance to catch catfish, and with more than 18,000 pounds of them planted each year, their chances are pretty good. The lake record is 27 pounds, but much bigger are known to be in the lake. The bigger ones are hard to catch as most of them stay deep in 80 feet of water in Catfish Channel. The easiest way to catch them is at night in Trout Cove along the buoy line, and in Whisker Bay.

Dixon Lake

Once catfish season dwindles in late October, the lake begins stocking rainbow trout. More than 33,000 pounds of fish to 15 pounds are stocked from November to May. Weekend trout fishing can get crowded during trout season with anglers all trying to catch a big one. The lake record is just shy of 16 pounds, with many fish over five pounds caught weekly. The easiest way to catch them is on Power Bait or by tossing lures off the fishing piers.

Dixon Lake is a popular put-and-take fishery for the residents of Escondido.

Trolling can be productive during the week when there are fewer boats on the water, but can be hard with all the boat traffic during peak fishing hours on weekends. Jack Creek Cove and Trout Cove are the best spots for trout, but the lake is so small they can be caught everywhere. As the water begins to warm in late April, the trout move deeper, and you need to troll in deep water, either with leadcore or by fishing Power Bait or nightcrawlers in 40 to 60 feet to catch 'em. There are some large bass in the lake, but anglers don't typically fish the lake for bass. Mike Long recently caught a 20.12-pound bass in April of 2001. The fish was the eighth largest ever caught in the world.

If you plan to make the trip, there is a fishing fee and a parking fee. Supplies are available at the lake. If night fishing, only battery powered lanterns are allowed on the boats. No private boats are allowed.

Also nearby are Lake Wohlford, Lake Hodges and the San Diego Wild Animal Park.

LAKE **HODGES**

A 20.4 pound largemouth was landed in May of 1985, putting Hodges on the map as one of the world's top prospects for catching a dream fish.

Rating: 9

Species: Largemouth Bass, Crappie, Bluegill, Channel Catfish, Bullhead and Carp

Stocked with 2,000 pounds of channel catfish.

Facilities: Restrooms, Boat Launch, Boat Rentals, Snack Bar, Bait & Tackle, Picnic Areas and Fishing Piers

Need Information? Contact: Lake Hodges Concessionaire (858) 272-3275, Recreational Information (619) 465-3474, San Diego Water Department (619) 668-2050

Directions: From Interstate 15 in San Diego, exit County Road S-6 (Ranch Parkway) and drive five miles southwest to the lake entrance on the left.

Chris Crawley and a pound-size cappie.

There are few lakes and reservoirs in the world that can boast about kicking out a largemouth bass in excess of 20 pounds. Lake Hodges, near Escondido, is a member of that elite group. A 20.4-pound largemouth was landed in May of 1985, putting Hodges on the map as one of the world's top prospects for catching a dream fish. While Hodges hasn't yielded any enormous bass recently, it is still a superb bass lake that must be considered one of the best.

Just the sheer numbers of bass in the lake are staggering. Based on the 2000 fishing season, the City of San Diego conducted a survey showing the lake had a population of 33,000 largemouths greater than 10 inches, and 13,602 larger than 15 inches. Based on a survey of 92.2 percent of anglers, the city estimated the bass population to be at 46,823. Wow!

Why are there so many bass in the lake? A few reasons: first, there is excellent spawning structure. The lake has many coves, tules and points, all ideal for the largemouths. More importantly, however, are the excellent food sources. Hodges has an abundant population of threadfin shad and crawdads, the perfect source of food for the bass. The only missing ingredient, which would help produce huge bass, is trout. No trout are stocked in Hodges. Because they have so many bass, Hodges was kind enough to allow the California Department of Fish and Game to remove a bunch for the initial stocking of the Eastside Reservoir in Riverside County.

Hodges is opened to fishing on Friday, Saturday and Sunday, from March through late October. With 27 miles of shoreline, action is the hottest at this 1,234-acre reservoir during March and April, the spawning period. Along with the great fishing, however, come crowds. It's not uncommon for a line of vehicles and boats to pile up at the entrance station during these months.

Crappie are also caught at Lake Hodges.

Anglers want to be the first out on the lake, so they can hurry to the best coves and have a chance at catching a lunker. By 10 a.m. all of the top big-fish producing coves have been fished pretty hard, and many fishermen have already called it a day. Typical bass baits: plastics, spinnerbaits and crawdads are the rule here.

Whereas most anglers fish for bass, a few target the lakes other fish: bluegill, crappie and channel catfish. The bite on channel catfish remains steady throughout the summer and early fall, with the City of San Diego dumping roughly 2,000 pounds of channel catfish each year. Blue catfish will be planted in fall of 2001. The bluegill population has been suppressed by the largemouths, but there are still a fair amount of them to be caught.

If you plan to make the trip, supplies are available at the lake. There is a day-use and fishing fee. Hodges is opened Friday through Sunday and on some holidays. Call ahead to check on specific dates.

Also nearby are Lake Miramar and the San Diego Wild Animal Park.

LAKE HODGES

LAKE **POWAY**

We saw an entire team make the transition from baseball to fishing. What an evening!

Rating: 6

Species: Rainbow Trout, Channel Catfish, Bluegill, Largemouth Bass and Sunfish

Stocked with 23,000 pounds of rainbow trout and 5,200 pounds of channel catfish.

Lake Poway

Facilities: Snack Bar, Bait & Tackle, Playgrounds, Restrooms, Boat Rentals, Campgrounds, Picnic Areas and a Baseball Field

Need Information? Contact: Lake Poway (858) 679-5466, Lake Poway Bait (858) 486-1234

Directions: From San Diego, drive north on Interstate 15 and exit El Norte Parkway. Drive east on El Norte Parkway for approximately three miles to La Honda Drive. Turn northwest on La Honda Drive and continue 1.5 miles to the lake entrance on your right.

How about hitting a home run and then doing a little fishing? There's no driving from one place to another involved. You simply park your car in one parking lot and then walk to each. Sounds enticing? People do it every Wednesday through Sunday at Lake Poway,

Lake Poway

about a half-hour drive from San Diego. A top-notch baseball diamond with a brick dust infield (like in the majors), a grassy outfield, two complete dugouts and a concession stand are located in Lake Poway Park. The ball field is used daily by local leagues, but the athletes who play in the evenings during the summer have the most fun because afterwards they can cruise over to the lake, get something to eat from the snack bar and go midnight catfish fishing. We saw an entire team make the transition from baseball to fishing. What an evening!

Lake Poway, a small lake just south of Escondido in the hills of Poway, is stocked year-round with fish. The most popular fishing is from November to early May when rainbow trout are stocked. The lake receives three plants of 1,200 pounds of trout each month, except for May when warming water limits plants to the first week. Whether fishing from a boat with Power Bait or tossing lures along the shoreline, the fishing always remains fair with some lunkers as big as 12 pounds caught each season.

As soon as trout fishing peters out, catfish season begins. Night fishing on Friday and Saturday is the easiest way to catch the cats, but that action doesn't usually pick up until mid-July. There isn't a large population of catfish in the lake, and they only average one to three pounds. Since just 640 pounds are stocked every other week, it takes a while for the lake to become sufficiently populated for good fishing. You have to figure only about 320 are dumped into the lake every two weeks, at least half of which are caught between plants, so it takes till later on in the summer for a population of cats to build in the lake. The best place to catch the cats is along the buoy line and west shore.

Lake Poway

There are also a few big bass in the lake, but they aren't targeted. A lake record 17.85-pound largemouth was caught in January of 1999, but the overall population suffers from extreme drawdowns. The lake has no natural runoff to fill it, and all the water comes from the Colorado River. In late spring and summer when water prices are high, the lake is brought down and then filled back up in the fall when prices drop.

Another hit at the lake is sail boating. The lake rents out sailboats, as well as rowboats, paddleboats and motorboats. There is also a walk-in campground at the base of the dam.

If you plan to make the trip, supplies are available at the lake. A fishing permit is required. Lake Poway is open to fishing from Wednesday through Sunday.

Also nearby are Lake Hodges, Sea World, the San Diego Wild Animals Park, Lake Miramar and San Vicente Reservoir.

LAKE **MIRAMAR**

Head over to the north shoreline near the tules in Carroll Cove and Bernardo Bay, anchor, and drop a line down with either pieces of nightcrawlers or redworms.

Rating: 7

Species: Rainbow Trout, Channel Catfish, Sunfish, Bluegill, Carp and Largemouth Bass

Stocked with 25,000 pounds of rainbow trout and 2,000 pounds of channel catfish.

Facilities: Boat Rentals, Restrooms, Picnic Areas, Bike and Walking Path, Snack Bar, Bait & Tackle and a Boat Launch

Brett Ross in his first bluegill.

Need Information? Contact:
California Department of Fish and Game (858) 467-4201, Recreational Information (619) 465-3474, San Diego Water Department (619) 668-2050

Directions: From San Diego, drive north on Interstate 15 and exit Mira Mesa Blvd. Turn east on Mira Mesa and continue to Scripps Ranch Blvd. Turn south on Scripps Ranch Blvd. and then turn east on Scripps Lake Drive to the entrance on your left.

Back in my college days, I frequently made the trip down to the San Diego area to visit friends at the University of California, San Diego. One time they asked me if I wanted to join them at Lake Miramar for the evening. "Fishing! You guys are going fishing," I said. "Who said anything about fishing? We're going to look for women." I was a little confused, but curious, so I went with them to see what they were up to. My expectations grew when I saw them take fishing poles out of the trunk and walk over to the bike path. They set up lounge chairs on the edge of the path, opened their tackle boxes and began to set up their poles. But they never went fishing. I don't think they even knew how to cast.

They used fishing as a way to entice the young women that walk around the lake daily, and it worked pretty well. "Excuse me, do you know what kind of bait to use here?" I heard one of them say. "Are there really fish in the lake?" My favorite was, "Can you help me put this worm on?" (I don't think anyone ever fell for that one, but it was worth a try.) Most of the women ignored them (they'd probably seen them before), but others fell for it. By the time we left, each of them had dates for that evening. They were a clever bunch of guys, but while they were practicing pick-up lines, I was surveying the lake. I came back the next morning, rented a rowboat and caught some one to two-pound bluegill with little effort. The lake is loaded with them. Getting involved in the action is best with a boat. Head over to the north shoreline near the tules in Carroll Cove and Bernardo Bay, anchor, and drop a line down with either pieces of nightcrawlers or red worms. You'll have a fish in no time. The water in the lake is extremely clear, so use light line. I got away with four-pound test.

There are also catfish in the lake, but the most prized fish are the largemouth bass. They get huge, but are heavily targeted by shore and boat anglers. Don't expect to catch a lot of bass, but if you get one, it could be a trophy size fish. The bass grow quickly because of the large shad population in the lake, and also by feeding on stocked trout. Your best shot at a big one is throwing trout-patterned plugs, right after a trout plant during late fall and winter. In spring, nightcrawlers and crawdads work well, with shad-patterned lures taking over in the early summer.

Once the water temperature cools, trout are planted by the county of San Diego. No plants are made by the California Department of Fish and Game. Most of the 17,000 fish planted are in the one to three pound range, but fish to eight pounds are stocked monthly. The best places to catch trout are on the south shore near the boat rentals and on the west end near the aeration unit. Power Bait and nightcrawlers floated off the bottom take the most fish. To keep action going in the summer, the county also stocks 2,000 pounds of channel catfish.

Lake Miramar doesn't have a lot of large mouth bass, however, kicks out some lunkers each year.

If you plan to make the trip, the lake is open to fishing and boating from Saturday through Tuesday, November through September. Supplies are available in Mira Mesa. There is a fishing fee.

Also nearby are Lake Murray, Lake Hodges, the Del Mar Fairgrounds, the San Diego Zoo and Wild Animal Park and Sea World.

LAKE MIRAMAR

LAKE **MURRAY**

Because there are expensive homes around and the residents have a fit if they can see barren shorelines from their balconies, the lake doesn't experience the same extreme drawdowns that many other city reservoirs do.

Rating: 7

Species: Rainbow Trout, Channel Catfish, Bluegill, Crappie, Carp, Red Ear Sunfish, Yellow Bullhead and Largemouth Bass

Stocked with 38,800 pounds of rainbow trout and 2,000 pounds of channel catfish.

Facilities: Boat Launch, Bait & Tackle, Snack Bar, Boat Rentals, Picnic Areas, and Restrooms

Need Information? Contact: California Department of Fish and Game (858) 467-4201, Recreational Information (619) 465-3474, San Diego Water Department (619) 668-2050

Directions: From Interstate 15 in San Diego, drive east on Interstate 8 and exit Lake Murray Blvd. Drive north on Lake Murray Blvd. and turn left on Kiowa Drive. Continue to the lake entrance on your left.

Last time I was out on Lake Murray, I saw a bunch of kids running over near the boat docks screaming that someone had a huge bass on his line. I went over to check it out and saw a guy fishing in a rental boat about 30 yards from the boat docks. His pole was bent in half, but there was no line peeling off his reel. Then, as he reeled it in, the lunker he thought he'd caught flew out of another rental boat tied onto the docks with the rest of the fleet, and skimmed across the water. It was a giant, but it wasn't a bass. It was a lifejacket.

The guy was obviously embarrassed, trying not to look over at the hecklers on the shoreline. "That's a huge one. Can you catch me a lifejacket, too," yelled one kid. "Do you think you can hook a seat cushion," yelled another. Ignoring everyone around him, he called out to the boat dock attendant who was also laughing, "Sorry, I'll bring the life-

jacket back as soon as I reel my other pole in." He should have never reeled the other pole in. On the end of his line was the biggest weed fish I've ever seen, and the kids let him have it again. "Wow! That's almost bigger than the lifejacket. Throw it out again." "I can't wait to see what you catch this time," said another kid. The guy immediately returned his rental boat and went home, but stories of his lake record lifejacket will circulate the lake for years to come.

Located just outside of downtown San Diego, due north of the city of La Mesa, Lake Murray is a popular picnic area with good fishing opportunities. During the winter, the 171-acre lake is stocked with trout from the California Department of Fish and Game and the City of San Diego. The CA DFG stocks 37,000 rainbow trout from 10-12 inches, and the city stocks another 13,000 trout from one to 10 pounds.

Fishing from the shore, by float tube or trolling can be productive from November through April, before the water becomes too warm for trout in late May. Once trout season fizzles out, anglers target the largemouth bass. After years without any big-bass hype, an 18.1-pound bass was caught in February of 1999. However, anglers still don't give the lake the same attention as El Capitan, Lower Otay and Hodges.

Lake Murray is one of the most popular recreation lakes near San Diego.

In late spring, the lake receives a plant of 2,000 pounds of catfish, giving anglers something to look forward to in the evenings through the summer months. There is also a sprinkle of bluegill, sunfish and carp, but they are seldom fished. One plus, because there are expensive homes overlooking the lake and the residents have a fit if they can see barren shorelines from their balconies, the lake doesn't experience the same extreme drawdowns that many other city reservoirs do.

If you plan to make the trip, supplies are available in La Mesa. Lake Murray is open from November through Labor Day on Wednesday, Saturday and Sunday. A fishing permit is required. There is a 5-mph speed limit on the lake.

Also nearby are the Santee Lakes, Lindo Lake, Chollas Reservoir, San Vicente and Lake Jennings.

LAKE MURRAY

SANTEE **LAKES**

Rating: 7

Species: Rainbow Trout, Channel Catfish, Bluegill and Largemouth Bass

Stocked with 12,000 pounds of trout and 35,000 pounds of channel catfish.

Santee Lakes

Facilities: Campgrounds, Restrooms, General Store, Bait & Tackle, Paddle Boat, Row Boat and Canoe Rentals, Picnic Areas and Playgrounds

Need Information? Contact: Santee Lakes Regional Park (619) 596-3141

Directions: From Interstate 5 in San Diego, drive east on Interstate 8 to the 67 Freeway. Exit the 67 Freeway, drive north and exit Prospect Street. Turn left driving back over the freeway. Turn right on Magnolia and then left on Mission Gorge. Turn right on Carlton Hills Blvd. and a left on Carlton Oaks. The lake is on your right.

Santee Lakes is close enough to the residential sections of the city of Santee for kids to ride their bikes over in the afternoon, spend a few hours fishing after school and still be home in time for dinner. The lakes, run by the Padre Dam Municipal Water District, are enclosed by fences, kept clean and are heavily patrolled by park rangers, so parents don't have to worry too much about their children.

All of the seven lakes located in Santee Lakes Regional Park hold fish, including largemouth bass, channel catfish, bluegill and trout during the winter months. With grassy shorelines and shaded picnic areas, the rectangular shaped lakes are a popular destination for family picnics on weekends.

Santee Lakes

Santee Lakes are best known for their catfish fishing. From April to December they are stocked with 1,000 pounds weekly, totaling about 35,000 pounds each year. All of the stocked cats are split between lakes No. 3 and 4. Lakes No. 1,2 and 5 are not stocked with trout or catfish, and No. 6 and 7 are stocked just four times a year with catfish. During the summer, the catfish are easy to catch if you fish with nightcrawlers, chicken liver or mackerel early in the morning or in the evening. A lot of people overlook the lakes that aren't stocked, but many of the bigger fish are caught in them. Lakes No. 6 and 7 are reserved specifically for campers.

From spring through fall, the bass bite is fair on plastic worms, spinnerbaits and Rat-L-Traps. Although you don't see any serious bass fishermen with expensive gear working the shoreline vigorously in bass boats trying to catch a trophy size fish, less serious anglers commonly catch bass to 13 pounds. The best bass lake is No. 5. To your advantage, you can rent canoes and rowboats to take you closer to the islands and in the narrow canals where some of the bigger bass lie.

Santee Lakes

Since the lakes are only five to 20 feet deep, the trout season is short because the water warms much faster than it does in deeper lakes. From January to March, lakes No. 3 and 4 are planted with trout. Most of them are about a pound, but a few trout over 10 pounds are caught each season. You guessed it, use Power Bait, fly & bubble combos and small spinners. Best of all, no license is required, just a day-use fishing permit.

If you plan to make the trip, supplies are available at the lake. There is a day-use parking fee.

Also nearby are Lindo Lake, Chollas Reservoir, San Vicente Reservoir and Sea World.

SANTEE LAKES

SAN VICENTE **RESERVOIR**

Most recently, SanVicente became nationally known in March of 2000 when the lake kicked out a state record 101-pound blue catfish, and the largest freshwater fish in California state history was caught.

Rating: 10

Species: Channel Catfish, Blue Catfish, White Catfish, Largemouth Bass, Bluegill, Green Sunfish, Red Ear Sunfish, Brown Bullhead, Black Bullhead, Carp, Rainbow Trout and Crappie

Stocked with 12,000 pounds of rainbow trout.

Facilities: Boat Rentals, Boat Launch, Concession Stand, Picnic Areas and Restrooms

Need Information? Contact: Anglers Edge Bait & Tackle (619) 938-0020, San Diego Fishing Hotline (619) 465-3474, California Department of Fish & Game (858) 467-4201

Michael Crawley caught this bluegill on a red worm.

Directions: From Interstate 5 in San Diego, drive east on Interstate 8 to Highway 67. Drive north on Highway 67 to Vigilante Road and turn east. Continue to Moreno and turn left to the entrance.

San Vicente is known for its trophy size fish. Not just trophy size bass, but bluegill, rainbow trout and catfish. This is a big lake as well as a big fish lake, with 1,069 acres, 14 miles of shoreline and a maximum depth of 190 feet. The only setback is, unlike most other San Diego area lakes it must be shared with water-skiers. The lake is opened to water-skiing and fishing on Thursdays and Fridays year-round, and opened only to fishing on Saturdays and Sundays from mid-October to mid-May.

Most recently, San Vicente became nationally known in March of 2000 when the lake kicked out the largest freshwater fish in California state history, a state record 101-pound blue catfish. Biologists said the fish was planted as a two-pounder in 1985. Lots of big cats are

John Alford smiles after catching a rainbow trout and a handful of blugill.

also caught monthly at the lake. Most of them are hooked in deep water near the island on shiners or large chunks of mackerel.

With lots of shad, crawdads and trout to feed on, bass grow big quickly here. The lake record currently is an 18.12-pound fish that was caught back in 1981. Bass fishing is best from March to May, using white or chartreuse spinnerbaits on spawning beds, or on plastics in Grassy Bay and Kimball Arm. In the evening, try using something that resembles a minnow. Once summer approaches, work the points off the island and drop-offs around the lake, jigging worms and using plastics.

Bluegill are almost too easy to catch. From June to September the bite is insane with 100 fish days per person common. Use red worms, mealworms or pieces of night-crawlers in the backs of coves and on sandy beaches during spawning periods from mid-May to mid-June. The best spot is in Grassy Bay. During post-spawn, from July to September, the bigger ones are caught off points and drop-offs, but action can be found all over the lake. To catch more fish, downsize your tackle using four to six pound test with a No. 8 hook and a small splitshot.

Bluegill are abundant in San Vicente Reservoir.

The lake's biggest secret is its large holdover rainbow trout. There are tons of rainbows from five to 15 pounds, but nobody seems to know (or care). The lake is stocked with 12,000 pounds during the trout season, but people quit fishing for them as spring approaches and the stocks cease. Then the trout move into deeper water and stay in the deep channel from the island to the boat docks. The easiest way to catch them is when all the other anglers are targeting bass and catfish. Go 30-50 feet off the end of the boat docks or along the buoy line near the dam and use a sliding sinker rig with a snap swivel, wrap a nightcrawler around a treble hook and drop it down. This works best if you use a fish finder to mark the fish. If you don't have a fish finder, you might have better luck trolling the same area with Needlefish or Rapalas. Often, bass fishermen using shad hook into large rainbows as well.

If you plan to make the trip, supplies are available in Lakeside. There is a fishing and boat launch fee. It gets hot and dry in the summer and there is no shade around the lake, so plan accordingly.

Also nearby are Lake Jennings, Santee Lakes, Lindo Lake and El Capitan Lake.

LINDO **LAKE**

Rating: 4

Species: Channel Catfish, Bluegill, Rainbow Trout, Carp and Largemouth Bass

Stocked with 1,500 pounds of rainbow trout.

Facilities: Restrooms, Picnic Areas, Playgrounds, Tennis Courts and a Baseball Diamond

Lindo Lake

Need Information? Contact: California Department of Fish & Game (858) 467-4201, San Diego County (858) 565-3600

Directions: From Interstate 5 in San Diego, drive east on Interstate 8 to Highway 67 in El Cajon and turn north. Continue for 3.75 miles to the Winter Gardens Blvd. Exit and turn right. Turn left on Woodside. You'll see the lake on the left in a half-mile.

Quack. Quack. Quack. Quack. Do you like ducks and geese? If you do, you'll fall in love with small Lindo Lake, located in a county park in the town of Lakeside. It's the kind of place parents go for an evening walk with their kids, bring along a loaf of bread, feed the ducks and geese, let the kids have their fun and then head home in time for dessert.

Most of the ducks and geese are friendly, but you never know when one is going to get a little aggressive and snatch a piece of bread right out of your hand. I think some of the ducks can read! We saw about 50 of them resting next to a sign that said, "$20,000 fine to those who harass the wildlife."

Not everybody comes to feed the ducks. During the winter and spring, Lindo Lake is stocked with rainbow trout by the California Department of Fish and Game. From late November through early March, 3,235 trout from eight to 12 inches are planted. Although the water is cloudy, those who use Power Bait tend to do well.

Lindo Lake is actually split up into two lakes divided by a dirt road. The one on the west is a bit larger, but the one to the east has a ton of tules making it a great hangout for bluegill and small bass during the summer. There are a few catfish in the lake, but they are planted irregularly, every couple of years when they have a special event at the lake. Most anglers don't realize that there are catfish in the lake at all and are surprised when they catch one. Not being heavily fished, some of the cats have a long time to grow and get pretty hefty.

If you plan to make the trip, supplies are available in Lakeside.

Also nearby are the Santee Lakes, San Vicente Reservoir, El Capitan Reservoir, and Lake Jennings.

LAKE **JENNINGS**

The last time I visited, park rangers told me stories of 80-100 pound blues spotted by divers sent down to repair the dam.

Rating: 8

Species: Rainbow Trout, Channel Catfish, Blue Catfish, Largemouth Bass, Bluegill, Red Ear Sunfish, Crappie, Carp and Smallmouth Bass

Stocked with 12,000 pounds of rainbow trout and 6,000 pounds of channel catfish.

Facilities: Restrooms, Snack Bar, Playgrounds, Fishing Docks, Picnic Areas, RV Hookups, Campgrounds and Bait & Tackle

Need Information? Contact: Lake Jennings (619) 443-2510, Campground Information (619) 565-3600

Directions: From Interstate 5 in San Diego, drive east on Interstate 8 to Lake Jennings Park Road. Exit north and continue approximately one-mile to the lake on your right.

For San Diego area anglers who don't like to deal with the cold, wintry weather at the region's most popular trout lake, Lake Cuyamaca, Lake Jennings provides a closer and warmer option. True, it is not high in the mountains surrounded by pine trees and fresh air like Lake Cuyamaca, nor is it anywhere near as beautiful. On the other hand, Lake Jennings is planted with larger fish and considered by many to be the best urban trout lake in the region.

Located near the city of El Cajon, Lake Jennings is run by the Helix Water District and receives its water from Northern California and the Colorado River. The 184-acre lake, with a maximum depth of 140 feet, supplies water to La Mesa, Lakeside, El Cajon and Spring Valley, and also sells water to other San Diego areas. Because it relies on pumped water rather than being fed by runoff, it is drawn down in the summer when water prices are high and filled up in the winter when prices decrease.

Lake Jennings

The lake is stocked with the biggest fish in the San Diego area, receiving 10 monthly plants of 1,200 pounds of rainbow trout over the course of the season. The trout average two to three pounds with some weighing in as much as 15. As an added bonus, five 15 pounders were stocked in the lake in spring of 2000 and only two have been caught.

For shore anglers, using blue, rainbow or orange Power Bait, as well as inflated night-crawlers work well. Trollers should use silver spoons, copper Phoebes and Roostertails, three to 20 feet below the surface. The lake also has holdover rainbows that can be caught in the summer, working leadcore line or downriggers in 30 to 50 feet of water.

Midnight catfish fishing is the main attraction in summer. The lake is stocked with 6,000 pounds of catfish from June through August, and the best time to catch them is at night in Hermit, Century and Half Moon Coves. When the water warms into the seventies, the big, blue cats move close to shore, giving you a chance to catch a huge fish. The lake record blue is 60 pounds, and the largest channel weighed in at 33 pounds.

The last time I visited, park rangers told me stories of 80-100 pound blues spotted by divers sent down to repair the dam. The divers were so scared they refused to go back down without cages. The lake plans to take underwater video equipment down to photograph the monsters.

Lake Jennings

Until recently, the bass population has struggled because of a lack of structure. In the late Nineties, 300 plastic cages were put in the lake to provide the bass with cover and spawning areas. With a large shad population and stocked trout to feed on, bass should have no problem growing to trophy sizes. (A 16.5 pounder has already been caught.) During the spawn, inflated nightcrawlers, minnow imitation lures and tube baits worked on spawning nests are your best bets. During post spawn, jig black or brown colored worms for the best action.

Concern has been expressed about the introduction of stripers into the lake. These stripers sneak into lakes through the Colorado River and from the Northern California aqueduct, both of which feed Jennings. Although none have been seen to date, introduction of this species could be detrimental to the lake's fish population.

If you plan to make the trip, supplies are available at the lake. A day-use and fishing fee is charged. Lake Jennings is open to fishing on Friday, Saturday and Sunday. Private boats up to 22 feet are permitted, but there is a 10-mph speed limit.

Also nearby are the Santee Lakes, Lake Murray, Chollas Reservoir, El Capitan Reservoir, Loveland Reservoir and Lindo Lake.

EL CAPITAN **RESERVOIR**

In 1990, the California Department of Fish and Game used El Capitan as a guinea pig, placing size limits on bass and crappie.

Rating: 10

Species: Largemouth Bass, Channel Catfish, Crappie, Bluegill, Blue Catfish and Red Ear Sunfish

Stocks: None

Facilities: Boat Launch, Restrooms, Boat Rentals, Concessionaire and Picnic Areas

Need Information? Contact: El Capitan Reservoir (619) 668-3287, Recreational Information (619) 465-3474, San Diego Water Department (619) 668-2050

Directions: From the junction of Interstates 8 and 5, drive 22 miles east on Interstate 8 to Lake Jennings Road. Turn north and drive two miles to the city of Lakeside. Turn right on El Monte Park Road and continue nine miles to the lake.

What a difference a few special fishing regulations can mean to a lake. In 1990, the California Department of Fish and Game used El Capitan as a guinea pig, placing size limits on bass and crappie. No bass less than 15 inches and no crappie under 10 could be taken from the lake.

The concept was simple: with these new size limits, one-half to one-third of the caught fish would have to be released, allowing the fish to successfully complete at least one more spawn. Because of the regulations, when fish longer than 15 inches are taken from the lake, there are always fish to take their place. Added to this, the voluntary catch & release rate is greater than 80 percent here. For this reason, El Capitan has proved to be one of the most consistent crappie and largemouth bass producing lakes in California.

Fishing is good at El Cap all but two weeks of the year in mid-August. The bite shuts off

then because it gets so hot that the fish get sluggish. The biggest problem the fish at El Cap have to deal with is fluctuating water levels; however, if they get one good rain year in three, the fish aren't affected much. Based on a survey of 95.6 percent of the anglers, the City of San Diego estimates that in El Cap there are 27,524 bass longer than 12 inches, and 12,277 longer than 15 inches. These numbers are based on the 2000 fishing season.

Although there are very few crawdads for the bass to feed on, threadfin shad, silver sides and golden shiners are abundant in El Cap, allowing the bass to grow to respectable sizes. The lake record tipped the scales at more than 15 pounds. Most bass anglers are regulars at the 1,572-acre El Cap and usually target the lake's north end, as well as various rock piles.

In recent years, fishing for both black and white crappie has been excellent. The crappie population boomed from 5,447 in 2000 to more than 25,000 in 2001; however, anglers harvested 12,000 of those crappie as of mid-May of 2001. The crappie population explosion is a direct result of high water levels from the El Nino season in 1998. Most of the crappie are caught on mealworms in April and early May.

El Capitan

El Capitan is vital to the overall blue catfish population in all the San Diego City Lakes. In order to reproduce, blues require a fast flowing river or stream to enter a lake. El Cap is the only one of the nine city lakes where this occurs. The San Diego River enters El Cap on the north end, giving the blues an important spawning area. Then, broodstocks are taken from El Cap, in order to stock blues into other lakes in the region.

The spawn typically occurs near the submerged trees at the back of the lake, from July through September. Because there isn't a good source of aquatic plants, catfish grow slowly in the lake; however, cats in the three-to-six pound class are abundant. If El Cap had plant life it would allow crawdads and small organisms to thrive. But since there is no plant life, the cats instead have to target smaller fish for food while they are young.

Bluegill and red ear sunfish haven't faired well in El Cap. Red ear were last planted in 1980 and '81, but are rarely caught. Both species need high water levels to spawn in the summer; they also require lots of aquatic plants both for food and protection from predators, neither of which is found at El Cap.

If you plan to make the trip, supplies are available at the lake. There is a fishing fee. El Capitan is opened Friday, Saturday, Sunday and Monday, and also on certain holidays. Call ahead for exact dates.

Also nearby are Lake Jennings, Lake Murray and San Vicente Reservoir.

CHOLLAS **RESERVOIR**

Located about two miles from San Diego State, the reservoir doesn't get a lot of visitors.

Rating: 4

Species: Rainbow Trout, Channel Catfish, Carp and Bluegill

Stocked with 4,500 pounds of rainbow trout.

Facilities: Playgrounds, Bike Path, Fishing Piers, Horseshoe Pits, Picnic Areas and Restrooms

Chollas Reservoir

Need Information? Contact: Chollas Lake Park (619) 527-7683

Directions: From Interstate 805 in San Diego, drive east on Highway 94 to College Ave. Turn north on College Ave. and drive two-tenths of a mile to College Grove Blvd. Turn left and continue seven-tenths of a mile to the reservoir on your right.

For the last few years, most anglers from Southern California who wanted to fish Chollas Reservoir (in San Diego) have been unable to. Why? Because they couldn't find it! The funny thing is, everyone gets lost in the same place. (It happened to me, too.)

The last time I went there, I saw a car with fishing poles in the back and two guys in the front seat frantically looking over maps. I pulled up next to them and said, "You guys looking for Chollas Reservoir? Follow me." They looked at me like, "How did this guy know?" When we got to the lake, I asked them if they'd tried following the directions published by the California Department of Fish and Game. Sure enough they had. The CA DFG tells you to turn left on Ryan Road just after exiting the freeway. Well, guess what? There is no Ryan Road.

Chollas Reservoir

Now that you have the right directions, you can make the trip, but I'm not so sure you want to. The reservoir isn't one of San Diego's finer fisheries. It's meant more to provide an opportunity for residents living in urban San Diego to get out and do a little fishing without having to drive too far.

Located about two miles from San Diego State, the reservoir doesn't get a lot of visitors. However, it is visited by the CA DFG during the late fall and winter when they stock rainbow trout. The truck usually comes seven times, beginning in late November and ending the last week of March when the water becomes too warm for the trout. More than 9,545 rainbow trout are planted in the small reservoir with a circumference of eight-tenths of a mile. Inflated nightcrawlers and Power Bait are your best chances at catching the trout.

Fishing piers provide better access to anglers at Chollas Reservoir.

With a dirt path around the lake, and large trees above to keep you shaded from the sun, the reservoir is a lot like Reseda Park Lake in the San Fernando Valley and Ranch Simi Park Lake in Simi Valley, just not as clean. Although catfish aren't stocked regularly, they are planted periodically for derbies and other special events that provide anglers with something to do during the summer.

If you plan to make the trip, snacks and duck food are available at the park office.

Also nearby are the Santee Lakes, Lindo Lake, Lake Murray and San Diego State.

UPPER OTAY **LAKE**

It was opened to the public for catch and release fishing in 1996, with the provison that you use artificial lures with barbless hooks.

Rating: 7

Species: Largemouth Bass, Channel Catfish, Bluegill, Crappie and Rainbow Trout

Stocked with 1,600 pounds of rainbow trout.

Facilities: Restrooms

Need Information? California Department of Fish and Game (858) 467-4201, Recreational Information (619) 465-3474, San Diego Water Department (619) 668-2050

Directions: From Interstate 805 in San Diego, drive south to Chula Vista and turn east on Telegraph Canyon Road. Drive five miles, then bear right on Otay Lakes Road and continue two miles to Wueste Road. Drive approximately one mile past Wueste Road to a dirt pullout on your left next to a locked gate. Park and walk about 200 yards past the gate to the lake.

There are tons of fishermen that have never heard of Upper Otay Lake, but ironically they have probably caught many bass that were born in the lake. Upper Otay Lake is used as a broodstock fishery for Florida strain largemouth bass. When the 20-acre lake first opened as a broodstock fishery in 1959, it was closed to fishermen. It was later opened to the public for catch & release fishing in 1996, with the proviso that you use artificial lures with barbless hooks.

Upper Otay Lake

Just to give you an idea of a few of the lakes Upper Otay has stocked, bass were taken to originally stock Casitas, Castaic, Clear Lake in Northern California, and big bass lakes in Texas and Arizona. As a matter of fact, the giant 20-pounder that was caught out of Casitas in the Eighties was taken from Upper Otay. Biologists identified it by a tag it still had on its fin. Most recently, 2,500 bass were taken to Silverwood Lake in an attempt to bring back a battered population that was devastated by drawdowns when work was being done on the dam.

Upper Otay is used as a broodstock lake for bass.

Currently, there is a population of 3,000 bass still in the lake, with many as large as 14 pounds. Most anglers fish with float tubes, but the lake is small enough that shoreline fishing is just as good. Casting spinners and small Rapalas can be a lot of fun from a float tube in the middle of the lake.

To give fly-fishermen a chance to do some angling, the lake is planted with 1,600 pounds of rainbow trout each January before the opener. Many of the trout are snatched by birds before they are caught, and those trout that aren't eaten or caught eventually die-off by late spring because of warm water. So, if it's trout fishing you're coming for, get here before the end of April or it could be a long day.

If you plan to make the trip, a fishing permit must be purchased at the Lower Otay concession stand. Upper Otay is open to fishing on Wednesday, Saturday and Sunday from mid-January through September. No boats are allowed.

Also nearby are Lower Otay, Barrett Lake, Twin Lakes Resort, the Mexican Border, Sea World and the San Diego Zoo.

LOWER OTAY **LAKE**

**Bass in the teens are commonly caught here, but methods
differ due to fluctuating water levels.**

Rating: 9

Species: Channel Catfish, White
Catfish, Blue Catfish, Bluegill,
Crappie, Largemouth Bass and
Carp

Stocks: None

Facilities: Boat Launch, Boat
Rentals, Snack Bar, Restrooms and
Bait & Tackle

Lower Otay Reservoir.

Need Information? Contact: California Department of Fish and Game (858) 467-
4201, Recreational Information (619) 465-3474, San Diego Water Department (619)
668-2050, Boat Rentals (619) 390-0222

Directions: From Interstate 805 in San Diego, drive south to Chula Vista and exit
Telegraph Road. Turn east, continue five miles to Otay Lakes Road and bear right. Drive
two miles to Wueste Road and turn south, continuing four miles to the boat ramp.

Every bass fisherman has heard the story of the historic day when Jack Neu used crawdads to fool five bass that combined weighed a lake record 53.12 pounds, not to mention
another 30 fish that were checked in tipping the scales at over eight pounds each that day.
After hearing about this, many anglers drive to Lower Otay Lake in San Diego County and
expect to have the same success. Although Lower Otay is packed with large bass, don't let
Neu's record deceive you. This kind of occurrence doesn't happen that often at Lower Otay
or anywhere else. As a matter of fact, it may never happen again.

Lower Otay is a 1,110-acre reservoir located just east of Chula Vista near the
Mexican border, and is used as a training facility by US Olympic Athletes. Although
heavily fished, and still one of the more popular bass lakes in California, Lower Otay
doesn't kick out the large amounts of giant bass it used to. The reason more lunkers
haven't been caught in recent years is related to the water levels. Throughout the Eighties
and prior to 1994, when lunkers were common at Otay, the water was low, below the
tules, leaving bass vulnerable. However, since 1995, water levels have remained above
the tule line giving bass a place to hide. When the bass do come out to spawn, there is
only a two to three week window when you can catch them. At all other times they are
20-30 feet back in the weeds in spots anglers only wish they could reach.

With great shoreline access for shore anglers, and the use of private boats and float
tubes allowed, Lower Otay gets heavily fished. Bass in the teens are commonly caught
here, but methods differ due to fluctuating water levels. Because this lake is loaded with
structure, including fallen trees, underwater rock piles and tules, depending on the sea-

Lower Otay is home to some of the largest blue catfish in California.

son and water levels, you can use many different kinds of bait, including crawdads, minnows, crankbaits, shad, jigs and spinnerbaits. The most consistent action is found in Otay and Harvey Arms, but your best bet is to check in with the office to see what has been working before you head out on the water. You can also ask the reservoir keeper who is knowledgeable about fishing the lake.

Lower Otay used to be home of the state record 85.9-pound blue catfish caught in 1997, but that was recently slashed by a 101-pounder pulled out of San Vicente. However, while electro-shocking in September of 1998, biologists pulled out a fish that was three inches longer and two and a half inches fatter than the record caught out of San Vicente. They estimated the fish was more than 110 pounds, but were unable to weigh it because their scale only went up to 100 pounds.

Lower Otay's large blues are a product of a stock of blues back in 1984, but there aren't tons of huge blues left in the lake. Most of that stock has been caught, and the ones that are left are getting old. Since blues can't reproduce in Otay because they need free flowing water such as found in El Capitan, more will be stocked in 2001 to maintain a stable population. During the winter, experienced anglers catch blues in deeper water, near the buoy line. As spring approaches, the blues are seen all over the lake chasing bluegill, and are often accidentally caught by bass anglers retrieving crankbaits.

Once summer approaches, concentrate your efforts in the back of Harvey Arm. There is a healthy population of channel catfish up to 20 pounds, but they aren't targeted as much as the prized blues. The lake is also home to a large crappie and bluegill population. Back in 1991, the state record 3.5-pound bluegill was caught here.

The Olympic Training Center is located behind the boat launch. Olympic hopefuls can often be seen running around the lake or taking rowing practice on the water.

If you plan to make the trip, supplies are available at the lake. There is a boat launch and fishing fee. Lower Otay is open Wednesday, Saturday and Sunday from mid-January through mid-October.

Also nearby are Upper Otay, Sweetwater Reservoir, Barrett Lake, the Mexican Border and Sea World.

REGION 14

San Diego County (East)

Loveland Reservoir
Barrett Lake
Twin Lakes
Lake Morena

LOVELAND **RESERVOIR**

Loveland and Century Lake in Malibu Creek State Park
are the only two bass lakes in Southern California
where hike-in fishing is the only way to go.

Rating: 6

Species: Largemouth Bass, Carp,
Channel Catfish, Bluegill, Bullhead,
Green Sunfish and Red Ear Sunfish

Stocks: None

Facilities: Vault Toilets

Need Information? Contact:
Sweetwater Authority (619) 420-1413
or (619) 422-8395 ex. 2222

Directions: From San Diego, drive east on Interstate 8 to Tavern Road. Turn south on Tavern (it becomes Japutal Road). Continue 3.8 miles and on your right you'll see a dirt parking lot signed for Loveland Reservoir.

Hike-in bass fishing is unusual anywhere in Southern and Central California. Almost every lake with bass, whether they be smallmouth, largemouth or striped, is easily accessible with boat launches and roads leading to the shoreline. Loveland Reservoir, located in San Diego County about a half-hour east of Sea World, is an exception.

Used as a water storage facility for the cities of Bonita, Chula Vista and National City, water is released from the lake into Sweetwater River and ends up in Sweetwater Reservoir where it is treated and put into the drinking water supply. The lake was first opened to fishing by the Sweetwater Authority in January of 1997 and has remained open for day-use since then.

Loveland Reservoir

The 454-acre lake was constructed in 1945. However, only one-third of the lake's shoreline (a five-mile stretch) has ever been open to shoreline fishing. No stocks have been made. The fish enter the lake by being pushed over Palo Verde Lake Dam in Alpine when water levels are high.

Loveland and Century Lake in Malibu Creek State Park are the only two bass lakes in Southern California where hike-in fishing is the only way to go. However, there is a big difference between Loveland and Century Lake. Century is overcrowded and the fishing is the pits, whereas Loveland is remote, quiet, uncrowded and offers fairly good fishing. Most anglers feel privileged to have access to Loveland.

Loveland Reservoir is one of a few hike in bass fisheries in Southern California.

The hike to Loveland is only about one-fourth of a mile, but it's not a good place to bring little kids because once you reach the lake its steep banks require a little skill to reach parts of the shoreline. Action is best in the spring because as summer approaches severe drawdowns put a damper on the fishing. On a more positive note, lake management tries to hold off on drawdowns until after the fish have spawned.

In May and June, fishing shad raps, Rapalas and Zara Spooks work well on the bass, although shiners, crawdads and waterdogs are productive all year. A 16-pound bass was caught in 1998, but most tend to be in the one to four-pound class. Catfish to 30 pounds are caught on cut mackerel and chicken liver, while bluegill and red ear sunfish are commonly caught on nightcrawlers and mealworms.

If you plan to make the trip, supplies are available in Alpine. There are no services at the lake. No boats or any type or floatation devices are permitted.

Also nearby are the Sweetwater River, Barrett Lake, Lower and Upper Otay, Lake Morena and Lake Cuyamaca.

BARRETT **LAKE**

So, Barrett has once again become a healthy fishery, but more importantly, as the last lake in San Diego County to hold the northern largemouth bass, lake operators are trying to preserve the strain.

Rating: 8

Species: Smallmouth Bass, Largemouth Bass, Bullhead, Bluegill and Crappie

Stocks: None

Facilities: None

Need Information? Contact: California Department of Fish and Game (858) 467-4201, Recreational Information (619) 465-3474, San Diego Water Department (619) 668-2050

Len Taylor caught this bass at Barrett.

Directions: From Interstate 5 in San Diego, drive east on Interstate 8 to Japatul Road and turn south. Continue past Loveland Reservoir to Lyons Valley Road and turn left. Continue to the gate.

People have a lot of misconceptions about Barrett Lake. When it first opened to fishing in 1994 after being closed for 25 years, the lake was compared to the world-class bass lakes in Mexico where you could catch fish on every cast, no matter what lure you used. However, since the end of the 1996 season, Barrett Lake has changed entirely.

Prior to the close of the 1996 season, Barrett's bass population was infected with a parasite of the liver. Although the infected bass were still able to eat, the parasite that infected them, called the little white grub (also known as the little yellow grub), restricted the fish from metabolizing any food. The bass constantly had a feeling of being famished and they attacked anything that came their way that looked like food. Catch rates at Barrett were staggering, with anglers catching fish on nearly every cast. However, that group of infected fish has since died off, paving the way for younger, healthier fish to grow.

To help these new fish grow faster, minnows and shad were stocked in 1998, and the bass have responded well. So, Barrett has once again become a healthy fishery, but more importantly, as the last lake in San Diego County to hold the northern largemouth bass, lake operators are trying to preserve the strain. This is why the lake is strictly catch & release and only artificial lures with barbless hooks are permitted. An array of baits, including crankbaits, plastics and spinnerbaits work well.

Recently, there was a scare that some Florida strain bass that came in from Lake Morena were going to take over the lake, but the northerns have remained strong. In spring of 2000, three plants totaling 140 adult smallmouth bass were introduced into the lake to spice up the fishing. There are also bluegill, crappie and bullhead, but only 54 of these fish were caught in 1999 because they are difficult to catch with artificial lures and barbless hooks.

Barrett Lake is run differently than all other California lakes. The only way you are allowed to fish it is by reserving a slot through Ticketmaster. The reservation includes a boat rental, which is important because there is no private boat launch or private boats allowed on the lake. You are not able to freely come and go as you please either. The road leading to the 811-acre lake is private and cars must be escorted in and out.

Located near the Mexican border, a half-hour drive east of San Diego between Lake Morena and Lower Otay, Barrett Lake still offers great fishing (2,711 anglers caught 27,810 bass in 1999), but it's not like it used to be. Anglers have to work harder for the fish now.

Michael Taylor and a two-pound bass caught and released at Barrett Lake.

If you plan to make the trip, there are no supplies available at the lake, not even water. Plan accordingly. Make sure you arrive at the gate at the specified time. If you aren't on time, the convoy will leave without you. It happened to me. Lake Barrett is open from April through September on Wednesday, Saturday and Sunday. However, sometimes in August and September the lake is only open on the weekends. Call ahead to verify operating hours.

Also nearby are Lake Morena, Loveland Reservoir, Upper and Lower Otay, Twin Lakes Resort, Kitchen Creek Falls and Cottonwood Creek Falls.

TWIN **LAKES**

The easiest way to catch any of the species is with worms.
They just can't resist a juicy nightcrawler.

Rating: 4

Species: Largemouth Bass,
Crappie, Bluegill and Channel
Catfish

Stocks: None

Facilities: Campgrounds,
Restaurant, Restrooms, Cabins,
Picnic Areas, RV Hookups,
Swimming, Horseshoes,
Volleyball Courts and a
Clubhouse

Twin Lakes Resort

Need Information? Contact: Twin Lake Resort (619) 478-5505

Directions: From Interstate 5 in San Diego, drive east on Highway 94 just past the city
of Potrero to Potrero Valley Road and turn north. Twin Lakes Resort is on your right.

If you live in San Diego and want to go on a trip to some far away place but don't
feel like taking a long drive, how about going to Twin Lakes Resort? It's only 45 minutes
from downtown San Diego, yet it feels like you're hundreds of miles away in the country
with civilization nowhere in sight.

Most people come to this clean, quiet place, located only minutes from the Mexican
city of Tecate, to relax and escape city life for a few days. A small, private, 70-acre
mountain retreat with cabins, campgrounds and RV sites, Twin Lakes also offers many
San Diegans a quick weekend getaway.

Almost nobody comes specifically for the fishing, but there are two small, spring-fed
lakes that have largemouth bass, bluegill, crappie and channel catfish. These lakes are
surrounded by large trees and picnic areas and provide good access for anglers. None
of the fish are trophy size, but they are easy to catch. The easiest way to catch any of the
species is with worms. They just can't resist a juicy nightcrawler.

If you plan to make the trip, supplies are available at the resort. Twin Lakes are only
open to visitors of the resort.

Also nearby are Barrett Lake, Lake Morena, the Mexican border and the San Diego
Railroad Museum.

LAKE **MORENA**

Because of poor water quality, low oxygen levels and less forage, small die offs of fish have occurred, and more can be expected

Rating: 6

Species: Rainbow Trout, Largemouth Bass, Crappie, Bluegill and Channel Catfish

Stocked with 5,600 pounds of rainbow trout.

Facilities: Picnic Areas, Restrooms, Boat Launch, Campground, Showers, Ranger Station, Lodging, Hiking Trails and Boat Rentals

Lake Morena

Need Information? Contact: San Diego County Parks and Recreation (858) 694-3049, Reservations (858) 565-3600

Directions: From San Diego, drive approximately 50 miles east on Interstate 8 and exit Road S1. Turn south, drive about 3.5 miles and turn west on Oak Road. Continue 1.7 miles to Lake Morena Drive and turn north. Drive 1.3 miles to the lake.

In a fisherman's utopia, all reservoirs would remain full year-round. Although that might occur in an ideal fishing society, we can't forget the purpose of a reservoir. Local water districts build nearly all reservoirs to retain water for domestic uses, which include irrigation and the creation of hydroelectric power. Unfortunately for fishing philosophers, they are not built strictly for recreational purposes.

Some reservoirs in Southern California are kept virtually full throughout the year, while others get sucked down to a mud puddle. Built by the City of San Diego, Lake Morena's fishing suffers from drawdowns, and while most anglers don't like the low

Lake Morena

water levels, we can't forget the purpose of the reservoir. In above average rain years, the city tries its best to keep Morena as full as possible. In poor rains years, on the other hand, it has no choice but to drain the lake down.

The worst-case scenario has unfortunately come true the last few years, and drought-like conditions have forced the city to draw the lake down to extreme levels. While the County of San Diego operates the lake's recreational facilities on average the city draws Morena down from 1,120 acres in December to 675 acres by July. That's a loss of one vertical inch per day.

These low water levels have been detrimental to the lake's bass population. Because of poor water quality, low oxygen levels and less forage, small die offs of fish have occurred, and more can be expected. Morena needs another El Nino year to turn the corner and once again become a productive fishery. With less acreage, the fish have been squeezed into a smaller area and forced to compete for a reduced food supply, which in turn means smaller fish.

Realizing the fish are concentrated into a smaller area, a few fishermen have looked at the drawdowns as a good thing; the fish are easier to catch. Morena has great structure for bass, including rock, brush piles and fallen trees; if you're going to fish here, concentrate on areas with underlying structure.

Lake Morena's fishery has suffered from extreme draw downs.

While Morena's bass have been hurt by a lack of rain, trout fishing remains good in the winter and spring. Run as a put-and-take fishery, the California Department of Fish and Game plants 14,550 rainbow trout, keeping prospects good for trollers and shore fishermen at this 1,540-acre reservoir (when full), located at 3,040 feet, just a few miles from the Mexican border.

If you plan to make the trip, supplies are available in Morena Village. There is a day-use and boat launch fee.

Also nearby are Kitchen Creek Falls, Cottonwood Creek Falls, Twin Lakes and Barrett Lake.

REGION 15

Imperial Valley

CALIFORNIA

Finney Lake
Ramer Lake
Wiest Lake
Alamo River
All-American Canal

FINNEY **LAKE**

Rating: 5

Species: Largemouth Bass, Channel Catfish, Carp, Bluegill and Crappie

Stocks: None

Facilities: Portable Toilets, Boat Launch and Primitive Campsites

Finney Lake

Need Information? Contact:
Imperial Wildlife Area (California Department of Fish and Game) (760) 359-0577

Directions: From Interstate 10 in Indio exit Highway 111 and drive south for approximately 65 miles to Rutherford Road. Turn left and drive to Perimeter Road. Turn left and the lake will be on your left.

Almost nobody except the waterfowl hunters know about little Finny Lake, and they'd like to keep it that way. These hunters shoot birds in late fall and winter and then come back as the angling heats up in the spring and summer. When I say, "heats up," I'm not really talking about the fishing. Daily temperatures range from 100 to 120 from late April through October, about the same time fishing turns on.

Finney Lake, located below sea level in the Imperial Valley Wildlife Area, is kept so low-key that most of the locals don't even mess with fishing it. Many of the lake's visiting anglers are out-of-towners that come here because of the lack of pressure the lake receives. The lake is a lot like its neighbor Ramer Lake. It's shallow and murky, but a lot less structured. There are also more trees along the shoreline of Finny, providing shade from the blazing sun.

This desolate, little lake gets little to no pressure, and those who do fish here use that to their advantage, keeping its secrets and tips to themselves. One fellow I talked to told me he hadn't caught a fish all day, but when I walked by his car I saw a cooler filled with crappie and catfish.

For catfishermen, there are primitive campsites located all around the lake, so you can fish the lake through the twilight hours. Bass fishermen do well with nightcrawlers and spinnerbaits early in the morning and just before sundown. The easiest way to fish the lake is with a boat, but you'll have to leave the gas-powered ones at home, because only electric motors are permitted. The most popular way to fish is with float-tubes or waders.

If you plan to make the trip, supplies are available in Niland and Calipatria. Call the CA DFG during hunting season, because at certain times the lake is closed to fishing.

Also nearby are the Salton Sea, the Wister Unit, Ramer Lake, Sunbeam Lake and Wiest Lake.

RAMER **LAKE**

Rating: 6

Species: Channel Catfish, Carp, Crappie, Bluegill and Largemouth Bass

Stocks: None

Facilities: Portable Toilets and a Boat Launch

Ramer Lake

Need Information?

Contact: Imperial Wildlife Area (California Department of Fish and Game) (760) 359-0577

Directions: From Interstate 10 in Indio, turn south on Highway 111 and continue approximately 63 miles through the town of Calipatria to Titsworth Road. Turn left and the lake will be on your right.

For those who know what they're doing, Ramer Lake can be heaven; for those who don't, it can feel like hell. Ramer Lake is a small, shallow lake located below sea level in the dry and hot Imperial Valley, and it's damned difficult to fish.

As part of the Imperial Valley Wildlife Area, the lake is used by waterfowl hunters in the winter, so to attract birds the California Department of Fish and Game keeps the water level stable, and the formula also benefits the fish. Most of the lake is less than six feet deep, with thousands of trees and bushes sticking out of the water. The problem for most fishermen is not that there are not enough fish in the lake, but that there is so much structure, shore angling can be nearly impossible. One way to fish is with a boat, but no gas-powered motors are allowed, so either you bring an electric trolling motor, use a rowboat or a float tube.

The most successful guy I saw was wearing full-body waders and carried an extra long rod so he could present his jig exactly where he wanted, to prevent from getting it snagged. He came out looking like a mud ball, but he also had a full stringer of pound-sized crappie.

No stocks are made, but there are tons of catfish, largemouth bass, crappie and bluegill in the lake. There aren't many trophy size fish in the lake. Most anglers that fish the lake are locals, and they'll tell you how difficult the fish are to catch. Even if you hook one, there's no guarantee you're going to get it in because the fish try to entangle your line in the many trees and break you off. It's hard to say what to use to trick the fish because hot baits change weekly.

If you plan to make the trip, supplies are available in Niland and Calipatria. Call the CA DFG before coming because during waterfowl season the lake is sometimes closed to angling.

Also nearby are the Salton Sea, the Wister Unit, Finney Lake and Wiest Lake.

WIEST **LAKE**

From late November through February, the lake receives about 1,000 fish a week. And during trout season, it's easy to catch 'em.

Rating: 3

Species: Rainbow Trout, Channel Catfish, Largemouth Bass, Carp, Bluegill and Crappie

Stocked with 6,000 pounds of rainbow trout.

Facilities: Boat Launch, Picnic Areas, Restrooms, Campgrounds, and Swimming Area

Need Information? Contact: Wiestt Lake (760) 344-3712

Directions: From Interstate 10 in Indio, drive south on Highway 111 for 65 miles to Rutherford Road (about 5.5 miles south of Calipatria). Turn left and drive approximately two miles east to the lake.

The Imperial Valley is known for blazing hot, unbearable temperatures, but did you know that one lake in the valley is also known for its wintertime trout fishing? Wiest Lake and Sunbeam Lake are the only two lakes in Imperial County that are planted with trout. It sounds amazing that trout are planted at all, considering temperatures can hit 110 daily from April to October. However, once winter comes and the water cools, the California Department of Fish and Game rushes to the 55-acre lake and plants more than 12,000 trout.

Wiest Lake

From late November through February, the lake receives about 1,000 fish a week. And during trout season, it's easy to catch 'em. Trolling Needlefish or bank fishing with Power Bait works well. However, as soon as the heat returns, this place becomes a blazing inferno, the trout die off and fishing reverts to an early morning/late evening affair. Since fishing is allowed nightly till 10, anglers can beat the heat (at least the sun because it stays hot through the night) from spring through fall and hook up with catfish to 18 pounds.

Bass fishing, on the other hand, can be a bit more difficult. There's a lot of boat traffic on the lake and the bass are active on plastics, nightcrawlers and Rat-L-Traps in the early morning and just before dusk. Most of the bass are in the one to two pound range, but fish to eight pounds have been caught.

The lake's most abundant fish is probably carp. Most lakes will do anything to stay carp free, but Wiest Lake doesn't mind having them. Park operators have implemented a catch & release only policy on them because they say the carp eat all the weeds in the lake. I'm not sure if they're aware that they eat bass, bluegill and crappie eggs, too.

Located below sea level Wiest Lake offers good trout fishing in the winter.

Frogging is also a popular attraction at night. The lake's shoreline is covered by cattails with big bullfrogs hiding in them. However, if I were just going frogging, I'd probably head over to the Alamo River that runs adjacent to the lake. The conditions are better there. It's much muddier and there are more weeds.

If you plan to make the trip, there is a $2 day-use fee for vehicles and a $0.50 fee for walk-ins. Supplies are available in nearby Brawley and Calipatria.

Also nearby are the Salton Sea, the Wister Unit, Ramer and Finney Lake and Sunbeam Lake.

WIEST LAKE

ALAMO **RIVER**

Despite the quality fishing the river does offer, many anglers choose not to fish here because they can't get any information about how or where to fish.

Rating: 6

Species: Largemouth Bass, Channel Catfish, Flathead Catfish, Bluegill, Crappie, Carp and Tilapia

Stocks: None

Facilities: None

Alamo River

Need Information? Contact: Imperial Irrigation District (760) 339-9418, El Centro Chamber of Commerce (760) 344-3160, Calexico Chamber of Commerce (760) 357-1166

Directions: From San Diego, drive east on Interstate 8 and turn north on Highway 111. On Highway 111 continue to Old Highway 80 and turn east. After Old Highway 80 becomes Highway 115, continue to where the road crosses the river. Access is also available near the cities of Brawley, Calexico, El Centro and at the river's inlet to the Salton Sea.

Trying to find information about fishing the Alamo River may be one of the toughest tasks a fisherman will ever have to do. Yes, even harder than throwing a penny onto a glass plate, trying to win a giant stuffed animal at a carnival. Almost nobody can tell you how to fish the river.

I first contacted the Chamber of Commerce in all the cities the river passes through or near. The only information they were able to provide was where the river was. The Bureau of Land Management said it was out of their district and the Department of Fish and Game couldn't tell me anything. The Imperial Irrigation District knew all about the river, but nothing about fishing it.

My only hope was to drive down to the river, look for fishermen and ask a few questions. I didn't find many anglers, but the few that I did run into were very knowledgeable. "Nobody cares about this river," said one farmer who owned farmland nearby. He was fishing with a friend. "Hank and I come here every weekend and we never see anybody else. We don't get many visitors. We like it that way. More fish for us." Of all the anglers I chatted with that weekend, none lived more than 20 minutes away and most weren't willing to give away any secrets. But one thing I noticed about all of them was their stringers of fish.

Despite the quality fishing the river does offer, many anglers choose not to fish here because they can't get any information about how or where to fish. There are no tackle shops in the area that can point you in the right direction. You have to learn how to fish the river on your own. For anglers who take the time to learn the river, catch rates are often rewarding.

The river's murky, dirt colored water is well inhabited with largemouth bass, channel and flathead catfish, carp, bluegill and tilapia. Techniques differ, but the most consistent producers are live bait, including shiners, nightcrawlers and goldfish. However, beef and chicken liver and mackerel are also popular. A sliding sinker rig works well, but when anglers find a place where the river slows, some choose to fly-line their bait.

Whatever you do, don't get the river confused with the Alamo River that flows through San Antonio, Texas. A remote river with no services, California's Alamo River begins in Mexico and flows under the All-American northward though a pipeline to its eventual outlet at the Salton Sea. Although the river picks up some water from agricultural fields in Mexico, most of its waters are the result of storm and irrigation runoff from farms in the Imperial Valley.

Alamo River

Many anglers choose not to eat the fish from the Alamo because of all the pesticides and chemicals that are in the water. Something else to consider before making the trek is the heat. Temperatures range well into the 100's on a daily basis from April through October.

If you plan to make the trip, supplies are available in Brawley, Calexico and El Centro.

Also nearby are the Salton Sea, Wister Unit, Finney Lake, Ramer Lake, Sunbeam Lake, Wiest Lake and the All-American Canal.

ALL-AMERICAN **CANAL**

For the best action, find an area where the water slows. These can be found where the river turns or at one of the pumping plants.

Rating: 8

Species: Striped Bass, Largemouth Bass, Bluegill, Carp, Channel Catfish, Tilapia and Flathead Catfish

Stocks: None

Facilities: None

Need Information? Contact: Imperial Valley Irrigation District (760) 339-9418, Calexico Wal Mart (760) 768-5013, Yuma Chamber of Commerce (520) 782-2567, Calexico Chamber of Commerce (760) 357-1166, United States Border Patrol, Calexico Sector (760) 357-2441

Directions: From Interstate 5 in San Diego, take Interstate 8 east to Highway 111. Turn south on Highway 111 and drive through Calexico. In Calexico turn right on Cole Road. Turn left on Scaroni Road to the canal. The canal can be accessed from many sites in Calexico and Yuma. The Calexico and Yuma Chamber of Commerce have a map of all the sites.

The All-American Canal is one of the most productive of the little known and seldom fished waters in the United States. Despite the fact that it's a great place to catch fish, all indications point to the fact that it will continue to remain seldom fished. The reason: fear. "People are afraid to fish the canal?" you ask. Afraid of what? If the fishing is so good, why won't anglers come here? Are there problems with snakes, killer bees and coyotes? Nope. Those varmints are all around, but don't pose a major threat.

Picture this: you are sitting alone in an old, rusty lounge chair with a beer in one hand and a turkey sandwich in the other. Your pole is pegged into the dirt alongside the chair, resting in a rod holder, and your car is right behind you. It's dark where you're sitting on the north side of the canal. But house lights and car lights can be seen on the other side.

You are in the desert at one of the southern most points of the United States, where its border with Mexico extends into California. Thousands of stars can be seen overhead, and with the exception of the wind and the howls of a few coyotes, it's absolutely quiet.

At least it was absolutely quiet until you heard something move in the bushes down by the canal. You think it's just a bird and then you see two four-wheel drive vehicles speeding towards you with their sirens on and lights flashing. Two spotlights on the vehicles are turned on and you finally make out what is written on their sides: "United States Border Patrol" "What are they doing here?" you ask. Well, that bird you thought was in the bushes wasn't really a bird. It was a group of illegal aliens who just crossed the international border on a raft, and you couldn't see them because of the darkness. In this neck of the woods there are no roads that cross the border, which is formed by the

All-American Canal, a popular, but dangerous spot where Mexican citizens in search of a better life try to illegally enter the United States.

This sort of thing happens all day and all night at the canal. Most of the time fishermen aren't bothered by the émigrés, but the sirens, flashing lights, darkness and a general sense of insecurity scare off most anglers before they even begin to think about fishing here.

My first time at the canal, after I left the border-city of Calexico and veered onto one of the dirt roads leading to the water, I was stopped by a border patrol vehicle and warned to be careful while fishing the river. "We don't usually have problems, but sometimes trouble finds fishermen," said the officer, who had four illegal aliens in the back of his car. "We've had people's cars stolen and others robbed." The officer said the safest way to fish the canal is during the day, but if you must fish at night go with a large group of people and chances are you won't be bothered. The problem with fishing the canal during the day is that the fish only seem to bite at night. Daytime fishing is the pits in the barren, hot, dry desert climate.

The All American Canal, fed by the Imperial Dam in Arizona, flows down through Yuma, Ariz., and forms the Mexican/American border for much of its way before ending near Calexico. The canal is 82 miles long, cost $25 million to build and provides water to nine cities and to more than 500,000 acres of agricultural farmland in the Imperial Valley. Built in the 1930's by the Bureau of Reclamation to create hydroelectric power and for irrigation purposes, it has held water and fish since 1940. The 150-200 foot wide canal is supplied with water from the Colorado River, which also constantly feeds stripers, catfish, carp and other fish into its fast flowing currents.

Although fishing tends to be good year-round, the best season is from late spring through the fall when the water is warm. For less experienced anglers, the canal can be difficult to fish because of its fast flows and swift currents. For the best action, find an area where the water slows. These can be found where the river turns or at one of the pumping plants. However, if you need to fish the swift currents, use a heavy weight and line. I recommend 12 to 16 pound test. Most of the fish in the canal are hefty and if you fish with nightcrawlers, anchovies, stink bait or liver your chances of catching one are pretty good.

What makes fishing the All American Canal really worth it is that you never know what you're going to catch. Stripers to 30 pounds, catfish to 50, carp to 40 and good-sized largemouth bass, tilapia and bluegill are caught regularly. Although there aren't many anglers who are willing to overlook the fact that the canal is a popular crossing point for émigrés, those who do are very much rewarded with exceptional fishing.

If you plan to make the trip, supplies are available in Calexico and Yuma. There are no facilities along the canal, so plan accordingly. It gets hot and dry here from April through October. Bring ID along; chances are you will be checked by the US Border Patrol.

Also nearby are the Alamo River, Sunbeam Lake, the Colorado River, Salton Sea, Finney Lake and Wiest Lake.

ALL-AMERICAN CANAL

REGION 16

Salton Sea

Salton Sea
Wister Unit Ponds

SALTON **SEA**

Despite all the heat, dryness and isolation, the sea, less than a three-hour drive from San Diego and the LA Basin, offers some of the best fishing in the world.

Rating: 10

Species: Corvina, Talapia, Sargo, Croaker, Channel Catfish and Striped Bass

Stocks: None

Facilities: Lodging, Food, Gas, Mini Marts, Boat Launches, Picnic Areas, RV Hookups, Bait & Tackle, Campgrounds, Playgrounds and a Visitor Center

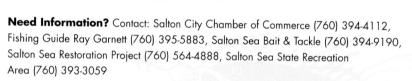

Salton Sea

Need Information? Contact: Salton City Chamber of Commerce (760) 394-4112, Fishing Guide Ray Garnett (760) 395-5883, Salton Sea Bait & Tackle (760) 394-9190, Salton Sea Restoration Project (760) 564-4888, Salton Sea State Recreation Area (760) 393-3059

Directions: From Interstate 10 near Indio, take the Highway 111 exit and turn south. Follow it to the sea.

It was nearly midnight. I was anxious, excited and curious. I had heard the stories, gone through weeks of planning, made countless phone calls, read tons of brochures and was finally on my way. On my way to see one of the most unique places in the world.

I pulled into Ray and Carol's Motel and Lodge, shined my headlights into the office window and out came Ray. No shirt, socks, shoes – just a pair of old shorts, glasses and a half asleep, sluggish body.

Fishing guide Ray Garnett

"Are you Ray?" I asked. "I talked to your wife on the phone earlier today. She told me to wake you up whenever I got in."

There were no welcomes, no hospitality, nothing. All I got was a cold vibe.

"I thought there were only going to be two of you," he said, seeing four of us in my 1997 Suburban. "I don't know if I can let you stay here. This is against fire codes."

Fire Codes. What! The room was huge, it had two double beds, a bathroom, dresser, a table and chairs and enough space to put six extra guys on the floor with sleeping bags.

I got Ray to budge, but not before he upped the price by $25 dollars and demanded to be paid in cash... immediately. Did I mention that before even knowing who I was he told me I would never be allowed to stay at his hotel again? I later went on the internet and found that the price he charged me was $35 more than the off-season rate I was suppose to be charged.

I was confused. You'd think the guy would need the business. After all, the local economy wasn't booming down here. Located on the west shore of the Salton Sea, it was the only open motel or hotel in Salton City, and we were one of only two groups staying at the hotel.

The rest of the city was empty, literally.

I experienced only pockets of sleep that night, partly because I was eager to see if the rest of the region was as welcoming as Ray, and also because I was excited to finally get my first glimpse of the world famous Salton Sea.

Blake Lezak and author, Chris Shaffer hold up a limit of corvina caught from the Salton Sea.

As soon as the first beams of sun crept over the Chocolate Mountains, I got my first view of the Salton Sea. It was bigger than I thought. Much bigger! "The sea," as the locals refer to it, is 40 miles long, as wide as 17 miles, with 120 miles of shoreline.

As for Salton City, I got a tingling feeling in my bones when I saw it. "Where is the city?" I asked myself. "Where are all the people? This looks like a ghost town."

Roads were built to accommodate miles of housing blocks, but there were no homes. And where was the Burger King or McDonalds? What about a grocery store? Gas station? Mini Mall? This was a city right? I quickly learned that the meaning of "cities" is different here.

There are no cities as we know them. To us, cities are filled with people. The Salton City (population 4,000) is nearly barren of humans. Its most common occupants are dirt, dust, a few tumbleweeds, some chaparral and a few motor homes.

It appears that developers planned on rapid development in the region, but that growth never occurred. That was probably because of the extreme heat and isolation. Temperatures are known to reach 110 on a daily basis from late spring through the fall, and the air can be as dry as crackers. Your tongue gets so dry it feels like sandpaper.

The region is the most bizarre I've ever been to, but that's what makes it so special and inspiring to visit. There is nothing to compare it to because there is no other place like it on earth. At 276 feet below sea level, the bottom of the Salton Sea is only six feet lower than Badwater, in Death Valley National Park, the lowest point in the western hemisphere. It is also the largest lake in California and the second largest body of water west of the Rockies, second to the Great Salt Lake.

The sea, more than 10 times saltier than the Pacific Ocean, is one of the saltiest in the world. In addition to runoff from winter storms, the New, Alamo and Whitewater Rivers feed the lake, but with no outlet and lots of shallow water its salinity levels always stay high. The only way water leaves the sea is through evaporation. With water temperatures commonly above 90 degrees on the surface in the summer, and an average depth of 30 feet, the sea can lose over six vertical feet of water during the summer months.

The Salton Sea was formerly known as the Salton Sink, a dry desert area in the Imperial Valley. It began to rapidly fill with water in 1905 when a flood on the Colorado River broke through a poorly built levy south of Yuma, Arizona, sending nearly all of the water from the river into the basin. Water continued to flow until 1907 when the Army Corps of Engineers built a line of protective levees by using boxcars to dump boulders into the breach from the Southern Pacific Railroad tracks.

With as little as a quarter-inch of rainfall each year, the Salton Sea is one of the driest places in the United States. However, even more uncomfortable to visitors than the dryness is the smell of the sea. It can best be described as a sulfur smell, and it is almost unbearable. For some vacationers it's a good enough reason to plan a trip elsewhere.

Vacationers that are used to spending their time away from home at the Marriott need to revaluate their plans. There are almost no services in the immediate area surrounding the sea. There are no fast food restaurants, department stores, beauty parlors, grocery stores or full service gas stations. Visitors from Beverly Hills better take a class on pumping gas before heading into the region, because there are no full service lanes, either. There are a few scattered, hole-in-the-wall gas stations with one pump. They also double as the region's pharmacy and grocery store. Unfortunately, most of them don't accept credit or ATM cards. It's time to load up on cash.

The people are a different breed, too, but that's what adds to the sea's personality. When you ask someone how he or she is doing, you aren't going to get your accustomed "Pretty good," or "I'm all right." They'll tell you exactly how they are doing. If their cat is sick, you're going to hear about it! It's called being friendly. Something we're not used to.

Most of the locals live in trailer parks and spend their days sitting on lounge chairs, wearing shorts, a tee shirt and a pair of sandals, with a beer in one hand and a piece of broiled corvina in the other. In other words, time is only kept on a clock here.

Although different, they are some of the nicest people you'll ever run across. Rags or riches, they treat everybody the same. They all seem to be hardy, over-tanned and aged, a sign that the sun has already taken its toll.

What sets the Salton Sea apart from other lakes are its recreational opportunities. It offers thousands of acres open to boating, swimming, jet skiing, fishing, bird watching, canoeing and kayaking.

Despite all the heat, dryness and isolation, the sea, less than a three-hour drive from San Diego and the Los Angeles Basin, offers some of the best fishing in the world. Yes, the world! It is not uncommon to catch more than 100 fish in a half-day outing. But surprisingly, this lake isn't heavily fished. Even the hardiest fishermen are kept away from the lake by the heat, smell and most importantly by its appearance.

Recent studies have proved that there are more than 200 million fish in the lake, 100 million of which are talapia. Although the lake is packed with millions of fish, there are also thousands of dead fish, which can be seen on the shoreline or in deep water. It's not unusual for 10,000 dead fish to be scattered along the shorelines, a site most vacationers choose not to preserve in their photographic mementos. The dead fish are in hundreds of pieces and seem to follow you wherever you go. It's mind boggling how a sea with no outlet can be so productive, but the fish multiply in staggering numbers. It's safe to say the sea is the most productive fishery in the state. The key to catching fish is finding brown water. It's sounds funny, but the brown water holds a majority of the fish. Brown water contains more oxygen than green water so the fish congregate there.

Sunsets can be breathtaking at the Salton Sea.

The lake's trophy fish is corvina, closely related to white sea bass. They were introduced to the sea in the 1950's when the California Department of Fish and Game planted 250 corvina taken from the Gulf of California. The corvina's estimated population is well over a million, and with the abundance of food available, the fish grow rapidly. These schooling fish feed on croakers and sargo, two smaller fish that inhabit the sea. The largest corvina was caught in 1988, tipping the scales at 37 pounds, but fish in excess of 20 pounds are caught on a regular basis. Corvina average from two to 12 pounds and have teeth, so make sure you bring gloves and a big net. You shouldn't handle them with bare hands.

The easiest way to catch corvina is on mudsuckers, but finding them is hard. Most of the tackle shops sell out the day a shipment comes in. Shore anglers cast spoons, use nightcrawlers and live croaker. Those with the luxury of a boat, catch easy limits trolling

Chris Shaffer poses with a three-pound corvina.

Thin Fin Silver Shad lures from 1.5 to 2.5-mph on a medium sized rod with eight to 12-pound test.

Tilapia is the Salton Sea's most plentiful fish. They weren't planted in the lake and it's unknown how they actually got here, but the most logical way is via the New and Alamo Rivers. Farmers stocked them into canals that feed the rivers to get rid of unwanted weeds. Tilapia reproduce every 30 days during the warmer months and can be caught with little to no effort. Tossing out nightcrawlers, spoons or jigging with crappie jigs, you'll catch as many as you desire. There is no limit.

The best time to fish the lake is at night during a full moon in summer. When a full moon occurs, pile worms come out to mate and the fish respond by going into feeding mode. Many fisherman fish the lake at night just to beat the heat, but temperatures can still topple 100.

Many other fish, including halibut, were introduced into the sea after the early 1900's, but the only other fish in significant numbers are sargo and croaker. Both are schooling fish and both are small, ranging from a half-pound to three pounds. These fish are fun to catch on light line and can be caught on pieces of nightcrawlers and half-inch silver spoons.

Ray Garnett is the lake's only guide. He's been fishing the lake for more than 15 years and knows the fish patterns better than anyone.

Now you have all the information you need. Try not to plan your trip from late March to mid-April. During that period, high winds can stir up 10 to 12 foot seas. Plan on having fun. Compared to other lakes in Southern California the sea doesn't get bombarded with visitors. You may have it all to yourself.

A quick tip. If you're going to use your tackle, make sure you change your line and clean out your reels immediately after your trip because the salt will ruin them.

If you plan to make the trip supplies are available in Salton City, Niland, Calipatria and Mecca. There is a day-use fee at many of the recreation areas.

Also nearby are the Wister Unit, New River, Alamo River, Wiest Lake, Finney Lake and Ramer Lake.

WISTER UNIT **PONDS**

To be successful, plan to arrive between late February and March. If you come any later, you'll be sorry. The dry heat and unbearable mosquitoes can chase away even the hardiest of anglers.

Rating: 6

Species: Largemouth Bass, Channel Catfish, Bluegill, Crappie and Carp

Stocks: None

Facilities: Vault Toilets

Need Information? Contact: California Department of Fish and Game (760) 359-0577

Directions: From Calipatria on the east shore of the Salton Sea, drive north on Highway 111 for approximately 13 miles to the turnoff for the Wister Unit. Turn right and follow the road to the ponds.

Brett Ross caught his first bass at Wister Unit.

For those of you who thought the Salton Sea region had nothing to offer besides salt water, heat and desolation, think again. The Wister Unit, located less than a mile from the Salton Sea's east shore, offers great bass fishing. It also provides a decent shot at catching some bluegill, catfish, crappie and carp.

The unit is part of the Imperial Valley State Wildlife Area, but the California Department of Fish and Game runs the area as a wildlife management unit and a fishery. It's comprised of six small ponds lined with cattails that limit access to those without waders or a float tube. The shallow, acre-sized ponds were built as permanent reservoirs for storing water and to provide irrigation needed for waterfowl habitat.

These ponds are loaded with good-sized largemouth bass that are eager to bite if you come during the right time of the year. Closed to fishing from October through January (with no real winter), the season to catch them doesn't last long before summer temperatures soar daily into the 110-degree range, putting a damper on the bite. To be successful, plan to arrive between late February and March. If you come any later, you'll be sorry. The dry heat and unbearable mosquitoes can chase away even the hardiest of anglers.

Because of the seclusion from major cities, outsiders seldom fish the ponds, but the locals that come here usually go home happy. The most abundant fish are carp, but bass provide the most consistent action. Using yellow or white spinnerbaits and nightcrawlers will yield bass up to seven pounds.

To help keep a consistent fishery, catch & release style fishing is urged here.

If you plan to make the trip, supplies are available in Niland. There is a $2.50 fee to enter the reserve, but if you have a fishing license the fee is waived.

Also nearby are the Salton Sea, Finney and Ramer Lakes and Wiest Lake.

REGION 17

Colorado River

Colorado River
Lake Havasu

COLORADO **RIVER**

Top fishing spots include anywhere near Laughlin and Bullhead City, specifically the Riverside Casino, Nevada State Park, Bullhead City Community Park and Davis Camp.

Rating: 6

Species: Channel Catfish, Flathead Catfish, Bluegill, Striped Bass, Largemouth Bass, Rainbow Trout and Bluegill

Stocked with 20,000 pounds of rainbow trout.

Facilities: Lodging, Casinos, Boat Launches, Restaurants, Gas, Campgrounds, Picnic Areas, Restrooms, Boat Tours and Watercraft Rentals

Need Information? Contact: Arizona Game & Fish (602) 942-3000, Laughlin Chamber of Commerce (800) 227-5245, Bullhead City Chamber of Commerce (800) 987-7457, Bullhead City Kmart (520) 763-7878, Bullhead City Walmart (520) 758-7222, Laughlin River Tours (800) 228-9825, USS Riverside River Tours (800) 227-3849, All Wet Sports (800) 763-9939, Fishing Guide Bob Lee (520) 855-3406, Fishing Guide Ron Liesen (520) 855-2700

Directions: From Ontario, drive north on Interstate 15 over the Cajon Pass to the city of Barstow. In Barstow, exit Highway 40 east to just before the Arizona border in Needles. From Needles, exit River Road and drive north for one mile. Turn east into the marina. For access in Nevada, continue on River Road for 21 miles to Laughlin. To get to Bullhead City from Laughlin, take the Laughlin-Bullhead City Bridge across the Colorado River. Access to Laughlin is also available by driving north on Highway 95 from Needles to Highway 163. Turn east on Highway 163 and continue to the river.

This section of the Colorado River runs from Davis Dam, below Lake Mojave, to the northern most end of Lake Havasu. Although there are plenty of fish around, boating, water-skiing and gambling are the biggest attractions, making it a fisherman's nightmare. The river can look more like a two lane highway with boats competing to see who can drive the fastest, look the coolest, drink the most beer and scream the loudest.

Although there is a decent bite on stocked trout during the winter, the best time to fish is in the spring when the stripers spawn up the river towards Davis Dam. Peak striper fishing occurs in April and May, with the best results coming to those who throw trout and shad imitation lures, as well as large plugs, just below the dam. The striper bite perks up just after trout plants, as well.

The California Department of Fish and Game used to stock the river near Needles with 7,000 pounds of rainbow trout, but that program was halted in 1995 because of striper predation. The Arizona and Nevada Game and Fish Departments have both chosen not to stock, as well, but the US Fish and Wildlife Service does. The US FWS has a federal fish hatchery located near Willow Beach, below the Hoover Dam. They stock 24,000 rainbow trout from October to March. To try to put more fish into fishermen's fridges instead of stripers' mouths, they have stopped stocking the small eight to 10-inch trout and have begun raising and stocking fish from 12-14 inches. The larger fish have helped, but the stripers still pick off a bunch of fish after they are stocked.

According to hatchery officials, the stocks have continued only because the local economy benefits from them. The casinos want to keep visitors coming during the winter and early spring when the weather keeps water and jet-skiers away. This way, people visiting Laughlin can fish all day and gamble at night.

The fish are stocked from the base of Davis Dam for about three miles downstream. The river is no longer stocked near Needles, or anywhere else along the California border, for that matter. It is only stocked along the Nevada and Arizona borders. Top fishing spots include anywhere near Laughlin and Bullhead City, specifically the Riverside Casino, Nevada State Park, Bullhead City Community Park and Davis Camp. Stripers

Colorado River

and largemouth bass can also be caught from the Highway 40 bridge down to Lake Havasu, but the water is fast moving and difficult to fish. Just above Havasu there are a series of backwater channels and ponds connected to the river that offer decent bass fishing. These shallow areas are also good spots to target catfish.

If you plan to make the trip, supplies are available in Laughlin and Bullhead City. In the summer, temperatures range from 105-120 daily, so bring along lots of liquids and lotion. To fish the Colorado River you need to purchase a Colorado River Stamp and, if fishing for stripers, you'll need a Striper Enhancement Stamp.

Also nearby are Lake Havasu, Las Vegas, Lake Mojave, the Hoover Dam and Laughlin.

LAKE **HAVASU**

*If you must visit Lake Havasu on weekends and holidays to do
your fishing, do yourself a favor, get on the water early
and get off early, before the crazies ruin your day.*

Fishing guide Bob Lee

Rating: 9

Species: Rainbow Trout, Channel Catfish,
Flathead Catfish, Blue Catfish, Smallmouth
Bass, Largemouth Bass, Red Ear Sunfish,
Striped Bass, Bluegill, Carp and Crappie

Stocks: None

Facilities: Full-Service Marinas, Boat Launches,
Boat Rentals, Picnic Areas, Bait & Tackle, RV
Hookups, Fishing Piers, Campgrounds, Food,
Gas, Lodging, Restrooms, and Shopping

Need Information? Contact: Fishing Guide
Bob Lee (520) 855-3406, Fishing Guide Ron Liesen (520) 855-2700, Lake Havasu
Marina (520) 855-2159, Lake Havasu Landing and Marina (800) 307-3610, Site 6
(520) 453-8686, Lake Havasu State Park, Windsor Beach (520) 855-2784, Cat-tail
Cover State Park (520) 855-1223, Sandpoint Marina (520) 855-3413, Lake Havasu
City Chamber of Commerce (520) 855-4115, Lake Havasu Tourism Bureau (800) 242-
8278 or (520) 453-3444

Directions: From the Los Angeles area drive north on Interstate 15 to Barstow. Exit
Highway 40 east and continue 40 across the Arizona border and over the Colorado
River to Highway 95. Turn south on Highway 95 and continue to Lake Havasu City.
  Lake Havasu is well known by nearly every college student in the country as the most
popular spring break hang-
out west of the Rockies, and
it produces wild memories
for young adults who choose
to party here. During this
time, near Copper Canyon,
London Bridge and the Sand
Bar, the lake gets so crowded you can walk from boat
to boat without having to
touch water for nearly a
quarter-mile. In recent years,
local authorities have decided to crack down on these
nationally known parties,

Stripers are plentiful in Lake Havasu.

sending out sheriffs to the popular boat jam areas to break up problems before they begin. This change in law enforcement partly came about because a few years ago a man was stabbed in the middle of one of the boat jams, and emergency crews couldn't get through all the boats to reach him. Luckily, that man survived, but the incident opened authorities' eyes to the dangers that could occur on crowded weekends.

Besides spring break, Lake Havasu gets busy on New Years, Fourth of July, Memorial Day, Labor Day and on most weekends. However, on normal weekdays, Lake Havasu is just like most other lakes that are favorite spots to fishermen and water-skiers. The 45-mile long stretch of water is an easy drive from anywhere in Southern California, Arizona and Southern Nevada.

Catching stripers like this one is common at Lake Havasu.

Produced by damming the Colorado River, Lake Havasu forms the border between California and Arizona, although almost all the access is on the Arizona side. Its most prized fish, stripers, are pretty easy to catch, partly because the majority of them are small. Although Lake Havasu was created when the Parker Dam was completed in 1938, stripers were not introduced into the 19,300-acre reservoir until 1959, when a group of them was transported from the Atlantic Ocean. Additional plants followed in 1960 and '61. The population grew to large sizes until the early Seventies, when the number of stripers leveled off and the fish size started to get noticeably smaller.

The reason for the loss of these larger fish was due to a combination of factors. First of all, anglers got smarter. From the Seventies to present day, seminars have been held regularly to teach anglers about stripers' feeding patterns and how to capitalize on those patterns to catch more fish. Other reasons include better tackle, new technology, over-fishing and a newfound knowledge of how to use fish finders.

Havasu's freshwater fisheries enhancement project has allowed bluegill to flourish.

Back in the Seventies, a lake record 50-pound striper was caught, but fish approaching that size are a rare occurrence today. That's not to say there aren't any large fish left in the lake, because every so often someone will catch a huge one. But in the Seventies they caught lunkers daily. Today, the lake's large population of stripers is mostly in the one to three-pound class.

During the summer, there are two ways to catch stripers. The easiest way is to anchor anywhere around the lake where there are points and dropoffs. Then baitfish with anchovies using a light rod with six to 10-pound test. Chumming with anchovies is also a popular way to entice the fish to move in. For those who know how to find striper boils, cast Rat-L-Traps and white shad-looking lures into the boils. Once boat traffic hits the lake at about 9:30 a.m., the boils disappear. During the fall, jigging three-fourth ounce spoons off the bottom is your best bet.

In the winter, stripers are found in 15 to 20 feet of water, and you'll need to use a slower presentation to catch 'em. Also in the winter, trolling anywhere you meter fish can also be productive. Most anglers troll Rapalas, Rat-L-Traps and Red Thin-Fin Shad. During the spring, most of the stripers move up the river to spawn, eventually getting all the way to Davis Dam.

However, the absolute best way to catch stripers is to call fishing guide Bob Lee before heading out to the water. Bob has been guiding on the lake since the mid-Seventies and will be happy to tell you where the fish are. Sometimes he'll even let you meet him at the marina and lead you to a hot spot. Where else can you find a guide who will do that? It's obvious he's not just there for the money.

As for the rainbow trout, they were last stocked in late Seventies, but most of them were nabbed by stripers before anglers could catch them. Once in a while an angler will catch one that drifted down the river, but that's pretty rare. From late April through October, fishing for catfish and carp can be hot.

For the bigger flathead and blue catfish, fish near Parker Dam. Many anglers fish near the dam at night, using heavy tackle with a full mackerel, and attach a light onto their line to attract fish. Surprisingly, they catch many fish in the 20-40 pound range, but most of the bigger fish are caught in the river below the dam. If you want to catch a larger quantity of smaller fish, work the north end of the lake after sundown. You can do it from your boat, a houseboat, off the lighted boat launch ramps or fishing docks. One practical advantage of the Arizona side of the lake is that you can camp almost anywhere and have easy access to fish.

If you really want to catch a lot of fish, I'll give you a tip. Go to the grocery store and buy a loaf of bread. Then head out to a lighted area at night and take about five slices, cut into 50 or so smaller pieces, and toss them onto the water. Wait about 10 to 20 minutes, set up your poles and begin fishing. Here's how it works: baitfish are attracted to light so they've already moved into shallow water, bringing with them carp, stripers and catfish that feed on them. The bass and bluegill already live in the shallow water, so throwing out the bread is like chumming and the fish go into a feeding frenzy. Soon you'll see fish splashing on the surface, stealing pieces of the bread.

Now it's time to catch 'em. The best way is to buy a second rod stamp so you can fish with two poles. Then use bread on one pole and corn on another. If you have friends along and want to fish more poles, use nightcrawlers, dough or some type of catfish bait. You'll catch all sorts of fish this way. However, it only works at night when there's no boat traffic. Two friends and I fished one night from 10 p.m. to 4 a.m. and caught three carp to 25 pounds, a four-pound largemouth bass, 15 catfish to 10 pounds and two pound-sized bluegill. That's not to mention missing another 10 fish.

It's important to pay attention to whether or not the fish are feeding off the bottom. If they aren't, you'll need to use a bobber to keep your bait afloat. The easiest way to find out where they're feeding is to watch and see where the carp are eating the bread from. If they are eating it off the top you'll need a bobber, but if they are waiting for it to sink and eating it off the bottom forget the bobber.

Stephen Wiessner searches for fish with an underwater video camera.

If you really want to go wild and crazy, you're allowed to spearfish for carp in Havasu, but check regulations just in case they've changed. Largemouth bass fishing has taken a hit over the last decade because of too much pressure and water fluctuation. The problem is a lack of structure for the fish to spawn and too many tournaments. Each week-end, as many as three tournaments can take place, never giving the bass time to rest.

In 1992, local anglers teamed up with the Bureau of Land Management, California and Arizona Departments of Fish and Game, Anglers United, US Fish and Wildlife Service, the Metropolitan Water District and the Bureau of Reclamation to launch the largest ever freshwater fisheries improvement project in the United States. The 10-year, $28.5-million project aims at providing safety for smaller fish and the protection of spawning grounds. The lake doesn't have much structure, and the little structure that is available usually ends up above the water line after drawdowns. By placing structure

Blake Lezak and Stephen Wiessner show off fish caught during the twilight hours at Havasu.

and fish habitat in 42 coves, the program intends to increase and improve angler access and bring back fish populations that were beginning to dwindle. The lake, with 400 miles of shoreline, has already seen an increase in fish size and populations.

Before heading to Havasu, you need to take into account that from May through September it is hot and dry. Daily temperatures range from 100 to 115, and the lake offers no escape from the heat. There's no shade – it's all rocks, hills, sand and water. Each year over 1.5-million people visit Lake Havasu City, mostly on weekends and holidays, so try to plan your trip around these days. The boat ramps become zoos, and half the boat operators have no idea what they're doing. A lot of inexperienced operators have no clue how to launch their boats and maneuver in such tight spaces. On these days, fishing from 10 a.m. to 6 p.m. is worthless. The lake looks like a highway, with speedboats racing to see who is the fastest, coolest and loudest. If you must visit Lake Havasu on weekends and holidays to do your fishing, do yourself a favor, get on the water early and get off early, before the crazies ruin your day.

If you plan to make the trip, supplies are available in Lake Havasu City. During day-light savings time there is a one-hour difference between Pacific Standard and Mountain Time. Make your plans accordingly. The lake can be fished with a California or Arizona fishing license, but a Colorado River enhancement stamp is required. If fishing for stripers you'll need a striped bass stamp as well.

Also nearby are the Colorado River, Parker Dam, Davis Dam, London Bridge and Laughlin.

About The Author

Writing the Definitive Guide to Fishing in Southern California has been a labor of love for avid outdoorsman, Chris Shaffer. Shaffer has spent the last five years of his life exploring, investigating and most importantly fishing the lakes, rivers and streams of Southern California. A native of Southern California, Shaffer started his fishing career at the tender age of four. To say the least, he has been hooked ever since. A graduate of Cal State Northridge, Shaffer also is a contributing writer to the Los Angeles Times. He is currently working on four follow up books including: The Definitive Guide to Fishing in Central California, The Definitive Guide to Fishing in Northern California, The Definitive Guide to Waterfalls in Southern & Central California and The Definitive guide to Waterfalls in Northern California. To purchase additional copies or other titles by Shaffer please go to www.fishingcalifornia.net

Index

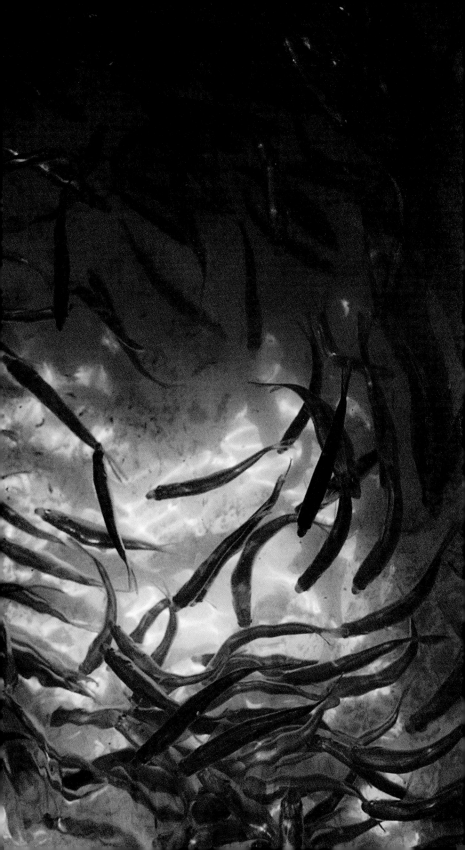